Once in a generation an idea so bold, so new bursts forth it shatters our neat categories and changes the way we view an unsolvable problem. David's book is a galvanizing probe into an uncommon but very effective way of treating drug addictions.

Here is Berner at his best—wise, funny, outrageous, rabbinical, maddeningly offensive, smoldering, and profane—yet tender, compassionate, and loving.

A *watershed book*—a must read for any health care professional.

LEE PULOS, PH.D., ABPP CLINICAL PSYCHOLOGIST

David Berner has blessed us with a roller-coaster memoir—a blood and guts drama revealing how a therapeutic community offered abstention from addiction. It is laced with humor, irony, and profanity. Berner writes the way he speaks—with rambling brilliance, at times uproarious, sometimes marvelously warm or lethal.

And in the process Berner reveals the charlatanry of Vancouver's supervised injection site: a pitiless revolving door enabling addiction.

This is Berner the Bard at his best.

JUSTICE WALLACE GILBY CRAIG

Be warned: Don't begin this tome as late sleepy-bye reading before a hot conference at nine the next morning. You will arrive a red-eyed, fur-tongued readaholic. Start for the style and storytelling, stay for the wisdom and insight. Profane, profound, impatient, painful, but ultimately a love story for the drug-users and drink-addicted ex-cons that only a fool about humanity would take risks for, the book is as unsparing about the complex Berner himself as it is about X-Kalay, the group he founded in his early twenties so raw and fresh that "we were making it up as we went along." His experience-shaped bombsight in the addiction trenches—what's a little mixed metaphor among friends?—unerringly targets the blundering and costly nostrums of the *fashionistas* in the media, academe, conventional counselling, and frightened politics. This is no fawning blurb: I've always cast a cynical eye on any book described as "a real page-turner." Berner's written one.

**TREVOR LAUTENS,
COLUMNIST FOR *BUSINESS IN VANCOUVER***

All the Way Home is a startlingly candid memoir of a maverick in the world of addiction treatment. David Berner, well known for his unorthodox yet highly effective methods, grabs his readers' attention with a style so crisp and punchy, it pops. His well honed wordsmithing and thoughtful insights are the mark of a master therapist who has been awake and listening intently. Berner navigates the contours and complexities of the addicted mind with home truths precisely drawn.

JESSICA MALKIN, M.A., M.S.W.

All The Way Home

Building Recovery That Works

Dear Jeff,
To a fellow Seeker,
Love,

[signature]

DAVID BERNER

Library and Archives Canada Cataloguing in Publication

Berner, David, 1942–
All the way home : building recovery that works / David Berner.

ISBN 978-0-9918220-1-0

1. Substance abuse--Patients--Rehabilitation--Canada.
2. Substance abuse--Patients--Services for--Canada. I. Title.

RC564.67.C2B47 2013 362.29'180971 C2012-908414-X

Editing by Carole Audet
Cover design by Barbi Braude
Content design by Fiona Raven

These are my memories; I am the teller of my own story. Certain
episodes are imaginative recreation. To protect the privacy of
others, some names have been changed and characters conflated.

If you would like to publish sections of this book,
please contact the publisher for permission.

Published by
David Berner

www.davidberner.com

This book is dedicated to Geoff Cue.

Geoff has been my friend, mentor, father, and brother.

Without his quiet and steadfast guidance and insistence, the first therapeutic community program in Canada for alcoholics, drug addicts, and ex-convicts would not have even begun, let alone thrived the way it has.

Without Geoff, I would not have discovered what I can do and what I was meant to do in this life.

contents

foreword

In 1967 I met a man who would shortly make the world a better place. His name was David Berner. He was a volunteer with the Company of Young Canadians—the CYC. I was just finishing up my eight weeks of CYC training at a place called Val David, Quebec. Volunteers and staff from several different projects showed up to tell us about the work they were doing. David Berner was one of them.

He explained that he was the volunteer on a project in Vancouver called the *Indian Post Release Centre*. He worked alone. He said that the Indian Post Release Centre had originated with a group of inmates in the British Columbia Penitentiary. He described the project as a halfway house for ex-convicts. But then he went on to say that the halfway house still wasn't much more than a good idea in a few people's heads. There was no actual building yet and many of the inmates who had come up with the idea for the Centre were still behind bars.

A short time later I ended up working on a CYC project in British Columbia. When I stepped off the plane in

Vancouver, David Berner was waiting to pick me up. During my first few weeks in Vancouver he showed me around the city, talked to me about some of his ideas for the future of the yet-to-be-seen Indian Post Release Centre and invited me to accompany him on one of his many visits to the BC Penitentiary.

I was never officially involved with the Indian Post Release Centre project. But David saw to it that I stayed involved anyway. He saw to it that a lot of outsiders stayed involved. He had a way about him that was difficult to ignore and impossible to refuse. That's how it happened that I was invited to participate in the Centre's first group therapy marathon session. I had no idea what to expect when I showed up for it but I learned pretty quick. There were a bunch of other outsiders in attendance who had to learn fast as well. We had all been invited to participate in the marathon because there were only a handful of ex-cons living in the halfway house at the time.

The marathon session was held in a small room in the second rented house that the Indian Post Release Centre ever called home. It started around eight o'clock in the evening and wound down twenty-four hours later. The marathon was a gruesome ordeal. There was a lot of baggage in that room and it all came out in an environment that was hot seat gestalt therapy to the core. The marathon bristled with heated words and overflowed with more than just a few tears. Offending people and then fuming over being offended yourself, oh yeah, and then laughing hysterically about it afterwards, were the rules of the day and we were all into that crazy game like wild animals. We never left that small room. We even ate our meals there. I specifically remember this because of something that happened that involved a plate of food. At some point one of the original residents of the Indian Post Release Centre—a big, scarred-up guy who turned beat red when he got mad—jumped out of his chair, threw his plate of food against the wall and screamed, "Halfway to what? Halfway to something I don't want to go back to anymore?"

In my mind, that incident marked the beginning of the end of the Indian Post Release Centre. Within a year, a new philosophy for the halfway house had begun to emerge and the place itself had a new name—the X-Kalay Foundation, the "Unknown Path" Foundation. What was the unknown path? We were. Our dreams were reality. Step out in their direction.

Very shortly X-Kalay had thrown open its doors to anyone who wanted to walk through them. Men, women, children and even entire families were welcome. The place wasn't just for ex-cons anymore and it wasn't halfway to something else either. People could stay in X-Kalay for as long as they wished, for their entire lives if they chose to. People didn't just attend X-Kalay as a condition of their parole plan. They were resident members of the foundation. X-Kalay was their community and it became their way of life.

God those were heady days! There was something very real going on at X-Kalay and it was quite extraordinary. Many of the people who became resident members of the foundation had been written off by other helping professionals as hopeless drug addicts, mental health misfits, lousy parents and unrepentant career criminals. Yet here they were, clean, straight and sober. They were changing and growing. They were taking responsibility for their own lives. These new, strong people were idealistic, passionate and engaged. They had big dreams and two rules: no violence or threats of violence and no drugs or alcohol. But as the number of resident members grew larger and larger and the number of crime- and drug-free days mounted up, as the foundation itself opened and ran businesses and became more and more self-reliant in the process, well then that was when the X-Kalay detractors came out in full force.

I watched all this happening from the outside and frankly I can understand why the foundation had a contentious reputation and a lot of enemies. Twenty-four hour marathon sessions every now and then, two-hour Games every day, Psychodramas, Stews, haircuts—both literal and figurative haircuts— making your own bed, waiting for the first time in your life and even an organization that was being run by the people who lived there were all cutting edge ideas for their time. People didn't understand what was going on and what they didn't understand they turned against.

And then there was David Berner himself. The man had loud presence. He didn't suffer fools easily and wouldn't waste any time letting you know if he thought you were one of them. He was charismatic, opinionated, controversial, outspoken, sometimes full of himself, often pushy and always larger than life. Some critics accused him of turning X-Kalay into a cult and anointing himself as its undisputed leader. I don't know if the man ever responded directly to these allegations. His attention was directed elsewhere. His work challenged the holy tenets of the addictions treatment and penal reform gurus of the day and these folks were really pissed off at him. They were giants in their fields and they came at him with both guns blazing. But David was well-named. He brought those Goliaths to their knees with a slingshot called X-Kalay.

When I left the CYC, I got a job in British Columbia as a probation officer. I worked out of a number of field offices before finally ending up developing parole plans for inmates incarcerated in the Haney Correctional Centre in Maple Ridge. Out of all of these job placements I sent referral after referral to X-Kalay. I never regretted making any of them. Why should I? I witnessed miracles. I saw people change and grow and get strong and enjoy being in the company of the person who was standing in their shoes. Not everybody changed mind you, and not everybody changed for good. But enough did and for long enough for it to count.

My job in the Haney Correctional Centre was the last one that I held in British Columbia before moving to northern Manitoba. By that time there was an X-Kalay program in Manitoba as well and the program in BC was winding down. I was saddened when I heard that X-Kalay had relocated to Manitoba for good and that the doors of the foundation in BC were closing for the last time.

And then David Berner was gone too. He resigned from X-Kalay and disappeared from my life. I would not hear from him again for over thirty years. But the work that he had done didn't disappear with him. The X-Kalay program in Manitoba thrived and grew. The foundation went through a couple of name changes and today it is called down the Behavioural Health Foundation. It is located in St. Norbert Manitoba. It enrolls the children of its resident members in its own school, conducts its own upgrading programs for the members themselves and employs its own army of therapists, social workers, psychologists, court workers and public speakers. Much of the wildness has been stripped away from those early controversial therapeutic programs of X-Kalay. Yet the Behavioural Health Foundation still has its detractors. Maybe this is because the heart of those stripped down programs remains the same. People are still the unknown path and it is still worth it to step out in the direction of their dreams. After more than forty years, the Behavioural Health Foundation continues to save hundreds of lives every year.

A few years ago, Jean Doucha, the Executive Director of the Behavioural Health Foundation, re-established contact with David Berner. She invited him to visit Winnipeg and make a presentation about X-Kalay to the staff and resident members of the foundation. I talked to Jean a week or so after David's visit and asked her how it had gone. She was still elated about it. No, elated isn't the right word. She was ecstatic. The words tumbled out of her as she described what had happened, how moving and meaningful it had been. She told me how eloquent David was and how the resident members—who didn't know what the CYC was or what the Indian Post Release Centre had been or what X-Kalay meant before David's visit, and who had never met the man who was telling them about these things—she told me how people came up to him after he had spoken with tears in their eyes and shook his hand and thanked him for what he had done. David had tears in his eyes too and so did Jean.

I don't know if he made this up or got it from some

reference book somewhere, but David used to be fond of saying that we should always walk off the stage when we're a star. I think he got that right or at least half-right anyway. Sometimes we should do a curtain call too so we can judge for ourselves how well our performance was received. It must have been a moment of sheer wonder for David to witness the results of something that he had a hand in creating so many years ago. You can't buy this kind of moment and you can't sell it. You can't even give it away. You can only earn it and once it is yours it is yours forever.

It was sometime near the end of 2009 when—out of the blue—David contacted me by phone. He told me he had written a book about the early days of X-Kalay and asked me if I would read a draft of *All The Way Home*. I was swept away by the book. I laughed out loud at some things and wept over others. It was like I was back there again, back at the beginning and my heart swelled up with pride as I remembered those brave early days of X-Kalay.

All The Way Home is a true story. It is a nuts and bolts true story, a very real true story and the time has come to tell it. People need to read this book because they need to understand how truly noble the idea of X-Kalay was and how authentically heroic the people were who first wrestled that marvelous idea into reality.

I was only a witness to the sometimes unbelievable events that surrounded the birth and early years of X-Kalay. But I am thankful that I was given the opportunity to watch them unfold. As for David Berner himself, well we have met once over coffee since that day he contacted me, we talk on the phone every now and then and we exchange emails on occasion. It's not what you'd call a close personal friendship. But I'm awful proud to know David. This world is a better place because he's in it.

Dale Seddon
December 2, 2012

acknowledgements

Bob Ransford was the first to insist that I write this story. Tony Mayer has loved the story from day one. Dale Seddon, who had been witness to much of what happened in the first years of the founding of X-Kalay, was going to tell the tale himself, until he learned that I had already completed the first of many drafts. From then on, Dale has been the biggest cheering section for the book. Now, he has blessed us with the foreword. Jean Doucha, the Executive Director of the Behavioural Health Foundation, has been an enthusiast from the beginning. Luis Molina, writing all the way from Geneva, corrected me on some key dates and people, including his own important contributions. Tom Berger read an early draft and encouraged his publisher to have a look. Mo Yan Min has been a loving and supportive friend. My son, Sean, is a great and steady companion. To all of these people, and to the extraordinary souls whose stories are told herein, many thanks.

If I am not for me, who will be?
If for me alone, what am I?
If not now, when?

The sage, Hillel, says in
The Talmud

1 I read the news today, oh boy

Richard was a killer.

What did I know?

I was twenty-four and I had places to go, people to see.

The slate-gray skies were a perfect match for the cold stones of the penitentiary. Today, chic town homes gaze out from this site over the great width of the Fraser River. But on that morning, January 5, 1967, the British Columbia Penitentiary still dominated the landscape. It is Alcatraz North—punishing, impenetrable, a caution on the hill. Get your poor self on the right side of the street or claim a crib here, Boy!

The Indian Friendship Group in the penitentiary had decreed that I should begin our new adventure by picking up a man who was about to be released after serving his full sentence. His name was Richard Sims. Richard and I would rent a house and head up the Yellow Brick Road to Rehab Heaven, wouldn't we? Then we could fly to the moon, compose a symphony or two and discover a cure for the common cold. Lovely.

The first snag in this little vaudeville was that the prison authorities didn't want me to meet Richard Sims at the penitentiary. They had nothing against either of us personally, not yet. But they did have their protocols. The house rules dictated that they had to return the man being released from their care to the place where he had originally been arrested, which in Richard's case was Prince George, in northern B.C. They were going to drive Sims to a bus depot in New Westminster, a few minutes away from the Pen. I argued that the moment the bus stopped anywhere in Vancouver, Sims would get off the bus and into my car. Check it out. I was twenty-four and on my first day on the job I was arguing with the hairy arm of a federal government department. What fun. What folly.

What was the point? The point, of course, was that bureaucracy has a mind and a style all its own. The good people at Corrections Canada were afraid that if they allowed me to pick up Richard at the front door, some unsuspecting soul might interpret this kindness as a sign that they were officially sanctioning our outrageous idea of having Indian ex-convicts living together in a sort of halfway house.

Thus began a long series of arguments I would have with the Penitentiary and Parole services over the coming years. In this case, they relented and agreed to release Sims directly from the Pen.

The front gate rose above me and I pulled my green and white Nash Rambler station wagon into a holding area where all persons and vehicles going in or out were subject to inspection. The gate fell back behind me. Unless you are going on further to deliver vegetables, you are now trapped between two gates that look remarkably like every huge iron gate in every castle in every Robin Hood movie you've ever seen.

A guard emerged from his little sentry box and glared at me.

"What are you doing here, son?"

"I'm here to meet an inmate who's being released today."

"Who's that?"

"His name is Richard Sims."

"You are meeting Richard Sims here today?"

"It must be all the stone work. There's a kind of echo in here."

Perhaps I haven't mentioned yet, I was a high-handed little shit.

The guard met my gaze with more scrutiny and disbelief.

"And may I ask you *why* you are meeting Sims?"

"Not that it's any of your business, but we're going to start a halfway house, a place for Native inmates coming out of the Pen."

Suddenly, the guard was gasping for air. His laughter caromed off the walls; no doubt they heard him in metal shops several hundred feet across the yard. This was the funniest thing he'd ever heard. Eventually, he found his breath again. "Do you *know* Richard Sims? Have you met him?"

"I think he was in the last meeting I attended with the group in the library. I'm not sure."

'Do you know what his nickname is? Do you even know what he's doing time for?'"

"No. Actually, I don't care. I mean I don't want to know what he's done time for."

3

"That's your prerogative, son. But let me tell you just the same…"

"It doesn't really matter to me, because, you see…"

"Mr. Richard Sims is called Crazy Horse in here."

"Crazy Horse?"

"And he's doing time for murder, for carving up a guy with a big Bowie knife, know what I'm saying?"

. . .

Richard was not big and he was only scary if you sat and looked intensely right into his eyes for a few minutes, which was, generally, not a good idea. His face was creased with markers that hadn't just come with age, and he walked with a strange gait, rolling from the hips, like the back end of a bear. He was—what, twenty-six, twenty-eight? I had no idea. I wondered if his bargain basement clothes had been sitting in storage for him these past three years. Perhaps they were kind donations from the Sally Ann. He didn't look at me. In the coming weeks and months I would notice that he rarely looked directly at anyone. *Don't look at me. I'm just an Indian from the north. I am unworthy of your notice, sir. I am nothing.* This averted gaze was his passport to invisibility. Richard got into the car, and no sooner had we headed down the hill away from the penitentiary, he insisted that we drive to Newton to see someone, the mother of his "partner" in the Pen. I didn't know what partner meant or where Newton was. Partner, I was to learn not long after, meant lover. If this guy had a boyfriend in the joint, who was going to argue with him? Newton was a part of Surrey, today a city larger than Vancouver, but in 1967, it was still a village, and not quaint or adorable—an ugly little village.

"I'm not going to Newton," I told him matter-of-factly. Time was of the essence. We had real work to do, a project, a goal. I had to stay on track. "We're going to Vancouver to see if we can rent a house." Richard cast a furtive, menacing glance in my direction and didn't say another word until we got into town. Oh, perfect. Granite silence from the Bowie knife killer. Just the ticket for our first thirty minutes together. Bonding never went so well. There was a brief moment when I thought he might just kill me. Maybe he considered it. I dismissed the idea as the product of my over-vivid imagination—way too many movies! Oh, my god. What have I got myself into here? Never mind. Stop kvetching. Stay on track.

A house on Nanaimo Street had a For Rent sign. Let's try that. A middle-aged, Eastern European woman answered our knock on the door. What did she see? Two men. One was a Jew with long hair and a moustache. The other an Indian, with a carved up face, scars on his scars, looking the other way, like he didn't want to be recognized—or remembered.

"We'd like to rent your house?"

"Vat for?"

"A kind of halfway house for Native Indian men coming out of the B.C. Penitentiary." Brilliant. Tell the truth and shame the devil.

"I'm zorry. Ze houz is rented." She slams the door shut. She locks it. Click, clack. She double locks it.

Next!

· · ·

We stopped at Helen's Grill at 25th and Main. Richard ordered a strawberry milkshake, ran to the back alley and threw up. Then he went to the counter and tried to buy lighter fluid. He thought he was at the PX in the penitentiary, where he could get chocolate bars and razor blades and writing paper. Imagine you've been inside prison walls for some years. The day you come out, you are deranged. You have no idea about anything. Your life inside is The Bells. Bong, bong, get up. Bong, bong, have your shit. Bong, bong, come to breakfast. You're lucky you can walk without crashing into dogs and fences. Recently, I was visiting a recovery center and an ex-con told me, "Dave, I don't know how to go into a grocery store!" We put people into lockups for long periods of time. We remove from them all possible traces of responsibility for even the simplest acts. Then, grinning with self-congratulation, we release them into the community and expect success. We report to parliamentary committees and trumpet our successes. We may be crazier than the inmates.

Richard and I retired to the Balmoral Hotel on Skid Road for a beer. *Great idea, David.* I knew nothing. I understood less, and my thinking process was barely functional. My comprehension of alcoholism or addictions was non-existent. I learned everything the hard way—en route. Moments after our beers arrived, a fight broke out at the table to my left. Richard, sitting on my right, rose as if in an auto-trance. He crossed in front of me. I grabbed his wrist and demanded to know what he was doing.

"I'm going to get into that fight."

"Are you insane? You just got out of the Pen! For god sakes, sit the fuck down!"

Crazy Horse, the Bowie knife killer, sat down and stared at me. I'd been in the guy's company for less than two hours and twice already I had the distinct sensation that he was going to do me serious bodily harm.

Somehow we survived our first day of close intimate cooperation. When night fell, I scurried to my apartment and Richard found some temporary accommodations with a friend of a friend of a friend. For the next several weeks I began rounding up other Native Indians who had been a part of the group in the Pen. One guy was living with his mother. Several were in flophouses on Skid Road. We met a few times trying to find some shape to this project. Everybody had an opinion, but nobody, myself included, had a playable hand. We were all being way too polite, and the more we talked so carefully about this dream, the more it drifted into the familiar Vancouver winter fog. Maybe that was the problem right there—too much talk, not enough action. One night, the inevitable showdown emerged. There were about eight of us sitting around an office on West Broadway. Suddenly, my impatience erupted. I really couldn't take this non-committal bullshit a moment longer. I took out my wallet and threw $50 on the table. Richard followed suit. Tony Lavallee took a deep breath, smiled nervously and added $30 from his own pocket.

"We're in and you're out," I announced to the less adventurous in the room.

The others were suitably outraged, but Tony and Richard and I didn't care. We had jumped off the diving board and into the water. Put up or shut up. You gotta pay to play. Nobody gets on the bus without a ticket. Pick your cliché.

Tony Lavallee was, at least on the surface, the antithesis of Richard Sims. Tony was fat and jolly and he was always laughing or smiling, except when he was trying to con you out of your clothes or your car or your basic belief system, at which time he took on an air of reverential seriousness. Elmer Gantry meets Sitting Bull. If he wanted you to believe in something he was espousing, he became at once a terribly serious little boy who had just won the science prize. A week earlier, Tony and I had been part of a small melodrama that played out like a modern day re-enactment of Androcles and the Lion.

Tony had called me in deep panic mode.

"David, they're going to yank my parole!"

"For what? Who's telling you this?"

"My parole officer."

"You broke the law? You did something?"

"No, no."

"So, what's the problem?"

"I moved."

"This is a federal offence, moving?"

"See, the thing is you're supposed to tell your parole officer where you're living and all that shit and if you move you have to tell him that too."

"So tell him you moved."

Savor the irony of this situation. In the 1960s, 1970s, and 1980s, parole officers could be found in people's homes or in coffee shops or pool halls with their clients. They knew the guy's wife and kids and which particular A.A. meeting the guy was going to and which ones he was skipping. This was an honorable and worthy profession and I met many wonderful men and women, rich in character and personal experience, who brought their own unique brands of practical wisdom to the job. Today, parole officers are so consumed by paper work that they rarely get to actually sit across from their charges and look them in the eye. Cover your ass. Cover it fast and cover it often. In the laissez-faire social order in which they now function, officers more often than not turn the other way while parolees create utter havoc around them. What indignity would a parolee have to perpetrate today before he was yanked from the street? When would his parole supervisor get wind of it? Who would want such indignity disguised as a paycheck?

"Yah, but I moved and it was all in a hurry, you know, problem with the landlord, and I found a better place, and basically, in the rush, I forgot to tell the asshole."

"When was this?"

"Last week."

"So?"

"So, he revoked me. And now I'm like legally at large or some fucking thing and there's probably a warrant out for my arrest. A buddy gave me a heads up. He saw my parole officer and the guy told him and he told me. This prick's going to send me back to prison and I haven't done anything, except I forgot to give him my new address."

"Tony, can you absolutely, positively swear on a thousand bibles that you are totally squeaky clean? That you haven't done a single thing that's out of line? Can you do that?"

"Yes, I can. Yes."

"Because I'm going to put my neck out for you and if you're shitting me, we're both in big trouble."

"You know what I did? I moved and I forgot to tell the fucker, that's it."

"OK here's what we're going to do. Meet me in twenty minutes at the parole office on Haro Street."

"David, I can't go to the parole office. They'll revoke me and ship me back. Don't you get it?"

"You're going to the parole office and you're meeting me there and we're going to clean up a simple misunderstanding and nobody's revoking anybody, OK?"

"How do you know? How do you know they won't nail me right there?"

"I have a little deal with them. They want this project of ours to go ahead, and they're not going to let this kind of minor league bullshit get in the way."

"You have a deal with them?"

So I exaggerated a little. It wasn't exactly a deal. More like a hint of a suggestion of the possibility of maybe an understanding. Sort of, almost. A few days earlier, I had met with the local parole service and described the dream of the halfway house project we wanted to build. The parole officers asked me some tough questions. "What would you do if a guy under your supervision broke his parole? Would you turn him in?"

"Nobody is under my supervision. I'm a helper, not a cop. I have no official status of any kind."

"Fair enough, but what would you do?"

"Depends on the circumstances."

"Like?"

"Like say the guy did something real terrible or threatening, I might very well report him myself. On the other hand," echoing Tevye the Milkman, "if the infraction or violation seemed petty or irrelevant, I might help the guy escape or hide from an authority that's overstepping itself. We're trying to do things in a new way, find ways of getting people to stay out of prison and that might take some fancy footwork on occasion."

The parole people seemed to buy that response at the time and now I was gambling that they would somehow honor the spirit of our conversation. Tony was finally persuaded to meet me at the parole office.

"Look, I guarantee you this is a story that will end well. If it doesn't, if something goes wrong—and it won't—I will run with you. I will put you on a bus to Mexico or Banff or somewhere. I give you my word."

The first person we ran into in the second floor hallway of the parole service was Kyle Stevenson, the head of the local office. I did something that to me felt perfectly natural, but that I later found out constituted a small revolution.

"Hi, Kyle. This is Tony Lavallee. Tony, Kyle Stevenson. He's the head man here."

They shook hands.

Let me say that again.

They shook hands. Apparently, this sort of social discourse was unheard of at the time. It simply wasn't done. Parolees and regional heads of the Canadian National Parole Service were not given to a whole lot of physical contact, like, say, hand shaking.

Tony turned on that thousand-megawatt smile of his and Kyle, a gracious and soft-spoken, decent fellow heartily greeted Tony Lavallee, parolee. The three-way conversation that followed became a four-way conversation as the parole officer in charge of Tony's case joined us. This particular bureaucrat, we were to learn over the coming years, was a man married entirely to his own personal career ambitions. In time he would become a member of a parliamentary committee on drug use and the head of the Drug Commission in British Columbia. What he knew or truly understood about his area of expertise you could stuff in a thimble and have room for a barn dance. Nevertheless, on this day in 1967, little misunderstandings were sent off into the ether, assurances were offered and accepted, and more hands were shaken. It's kind of hard to throw a guy in jail after you've shaken hands with him. Tony and I walked out of the parole office building. I think his smile stayed for several days. I had made a promise to one of the guys on our team and I had been able to keep it. Tony and I took the first important step in a bond that would grow stronger over the next year through difficult and exciting times.

So now, here we were a week later sitting around a table with eight Aboriginal ex-cons. I had thrown $50 of my own money on the table and Richard Sims had followed suit. Tony Lavallee tossed in his $30 like he was anteing up for a good round of poker. He didn't really have $30 to spare, but he believed that if I said I was going to do something, well hot damn!

I found a bungalow along a row of identical bungalows just off Point Grey Road. It took a lie to rent the place. I passed myself off to the landlord as a university professor; I told him I might rent an extra bedroom to a graduate student or two, if that's all right. Tony, Richard, and I, the three guys with the big investments, moved into the little house at 2974 West 5th Avenue. Thus began our brave experiment in democracy and rehabilitation. There were no rules; there was no plan.

2 across the stone divide

What secret scriptures ushered me to the penitentiary that morning?

Nothing in the previous two years could have suggested for a moment that any of these events might unfold the way they did. Since arriving from Winnipeg, I had settled comfortably into the Lifestyle of the Lost. I drank. I smoked pot. I lived in Teotitlán del Valle, a mountain village in the province of Oaxaca in Mexico for three months. I drew pictures and wrote poems and the first three chapters of a novel, which began with these immortal words, "Me Vendraga. Yes, Vendraga. I say I am Vendraga, Keeper of The Clues." I taught myself the basics of playing the alto sax. One day I might perfect "Stars Fell on Alabama." I was often ecstatic and equally often miserable. I drove late night shifts for Yellow Cab and rarely went to sleep before three in the morning. My life was cash and crash.

In Winnipeg, I was a Jew. In Vancouver, *British* Columbia, I was an exotic. People settling into my taxi often asked me what I was.

"Sorry?"

"What are you?"

I had a hundred different answers, depending on the time of day, what I had tossed down for lunch or how busy I was. Sometimes I would play dumb and just ask what they meant. More often I would be Chinese, Indian, Métis, Greek, Italian, Jewish, of course, or Macedonian. The passengers would accept whatever I told them. "Oh, Interesting." Sometimes I was, "Just a man. What're you?" On occasion, I sold liquor to underage drinkers for a usurious fee. Twice I pimped a Seymour Street hooker. This was not only stupid—it was dangerous. Just what I needed was the girl's real boss finding me messing in his territory.

Middle–aged women and men regularly propositioned me. Sometimes, I politely declined. Sometimes, I offered a witty, "Fuck off." Sometimes, I bought in. A quick visit to the apartment, or engine and lights off on a side street completed the deal.

During the day, I hung out at a famous literary bookstore. My daylight and off-work hours were devoted to writing and music and friends. My working hours were all about money. Pennies, sure enough, but money, money, money nevertheless.

Omens and new directions always fall unbidden from the most unlikely skies. My old friend, Bob Hunter, encouraged me to try something new, and it wasn't dope or skydiving. Hunter and I had grown up together in Winnipeg. We went camping and canoeing together, we drank an awful lot of beer and we argued and laughed into the night about everything, large and small. We were unashamed literature freaks, obsessed with the great writers of the era—Durrell, Henry

Miller, Beckett, Joyce. Before he was twenty, Hunter was an accomplished reporter for the Winnipeg Tribune newspaper and he was already writing books. A few years later, Hunter and his friends would sail their boat into the waters of Amchitka, Alaska and challenge an American nuclear test. Thus, Greenpeace was born. Today, Greenpeace is a movement, an icon, a corporation, and a chunk of contemporary social history. In those days, it was just Hunter and some of his buddies going off the deep end. Now, in the sweet summer of 1966, Bob Hunter was writing for the *Vancouver Sun*, and handing out free and providential advice.

"You know, Berner, you should check out the Company of Young Canadians."

"Company of Young Comedians?"

"Canadians. It's sort of like the Canada Council. They pay people to do all kinds of crazy things. You should talk to them."

The Company of Young Canadians was not at all like the Canada Council. In fact, it was the brainchild of the Prime Minister, Lester B. Pearson. Pearson modeled it after the American Vista Program, which was really a domestic version of the Peace Corps. Take young, urban educated men and women and send them into communities at home that were struggling with poverty, crime, fatherless children, addictions, and all the other social ills that define disenfranchisement.

I was twenty-three years old. In the coming years, people would ask how I came to be a therapist and I'd always say, "Yellow Cab." After a year of driving night shift, I came in out of the rain and became a radio dispatcher for the cab company. That was better than driving, but it was hardly a solution for the itch that plagued me. I was bright and energetic, but unfocused. Finishing second year university in Winnipeg at the age of eighteen, I dashed off to northern Manitoba to teach high school math and science. I took an ocean liner from New York to Gibraltar and spent the next year discovering Europe and art and food. Back in Winnipeg, I tried third year university twice, bombing beautifully both times, deeply committed to beer, cigarettes, sex, literature, and lethargy. Vancouver was my Mecca. So here I was in 1966 in my own personal Shangri-La. I was lonely and compulsively social. I rarely went to bed before 4:00 a.m. or rose before noon. I drove drunk or stoned, sat in cafes and bars arguing obscure philosophies until the joint closed because I couldn't bear the thought of going back to my house or apartment alone. I was afraid of almost everything and therefore intent on building a reputation as a risk taker. Travel, geographic cures, sleeping with the next available lonely soul—what did any of that really cost? I had no clear goals and I urgently needed to grab onto something I could get excited about and run with. Hunter's advice to check out this new agency kept echoing back to me.

One morning a few weeks later, I walked in to the offices of The Company of Young Canadians, B.C. Region.

I met a man named Geoff Cue. I had never met anyone like him. For years, I called him The Big Boy Scout. He was just about the squarest guy in the world. Pleasant, strong, even-tempered, fair-minded. To me, this was some exotic creature. I grew up in an orthodox Jewish family in the north end of Winnipeg, surrounded by Jews, Poles, and Ukrainians. Everybody yelled. Speech was a manual exercise. "You talk, my hands are cold." Everybody was passionate, opinionated, volatile, critical, and acerbic. Boy, did I belong! I cannot speak about the immigrant experience for the Welsh or Burmese. But I can tell you this. Yiddish—the very language of Jews in the Diaspora—is fraught with pouring emotion. What became "therapy" in the fifties, sixties, and seventies, was the lingua franca in our house, and, I suspect, in similar houses of Jews from Russia, Latvia, Germany, Poland, and the Ukraine now residing and being drawn into the mainstream in Winnipeg, Toronto, Montreal, and New York. Conversations about the simplest matters could be highly charged with accusations, recriminations, entreaties, and apologies. These and more were the coinage of the realm. My aunt, Toby, who certainly loved my mother, her sister, dearly, once in anger said, "I'll split her head with an axe." This came from a woman who was known throughout the large extended family as the soul of human kindness. Being nurtured and challenged and frustrated in this hothouse of passions bordering occasionally on madness, how could I not become a therapist or a subversive or a bit of both? You need school for these vocations?

Now, here in Vancouver, British Columbia in the offices of something calling itself the Company of Young Canadians was this frighteningly *reasonable* man. What the hell is that?

"Look, you seem like a really nice guy, but I don't think you really know what you're talking about. I mean it seems that you're just getting started here with this office and you don't quite have your work lined up." This is Mr. Know-It-All, Mr. Say-What's-On-Your-Mind-Why-Hold-Back challenging a man fifteen years my senior.

"Yes. That's right," Geoff said. "I just took on this assignment after years at the Y and at Neighborhood Houses, and, well, yes, that's true, we don't have our projects up and running yet."

"Well, I think you're great, I really like talking to you and I want to talk to you again. But the thing is I'm going to Mexico in a few days."

"Mexico?"

"I'm going to stay with some friends from Berkeley in a little village in the mountains south of Oaxaco. I'll probably smoke a lot of pot. So here's the thing. If I get back, which you never know, and if I have any brain cells left, which is even more unlikely, well, if I'm still in my right mind, I'll come see you again, OK?"

"That would be great."

We talked for a good long time and parted with vague promises to one another.

Forty years later, Geoff Cue, my dearest and most valued friend, would laugh and tell me that the last person he ever expected to see again was me. None of us could have guessed that the Company of Young Canadians would spawn Canada's first and longest running residential treatment center for addicts, alcoholics, ex-cons, and others.

My friends in Mexico were a young couple with three little boys. I grew up in my grandparent's home. My mother was a single parent and I was an only child. You'll understand that I've spent much of my adult life collecting surrogate parents. Fred and Evelyn, Ted and Rosalie, Alex and Elaine. Dozens more. All lovely, decent souls. None capable of filling whatever void I thought they should. Even when I had my own family, I envied other families. In Mexico, the boys played and we grown-ups drew and painted and smoked dope and danced and smoked dope. Then, I don't know if mentioned this, like, if we had nothing else that was urgent, well, we smoked some more dope.

Three months later, I walked back into Geoff Cue's office. I told him all about the Zapotec village where I had stayed, and Geoff told me all about taking his wife and infant daughter to the Pacific Island kingdom of Tonga. Wait just a minute, folks. There's more to this character than I realized. Then he handed me a stack of documents. "Look. Here are four projects, that is, four groups who want to start something and they need someone to work with them. Take these files home, have a look and tell me what you think."

What he didn't tell me until many years later was that the fourth project request, the one decidedly at the bottom of the pile was at the bottom for a very good reason. Geoff explained, "Aboriginal men in a federal prison? That's what we used to call the Graveyard of Social Work. No one would ever willingly choose this kind of assignment."

I was back the next day. "These first three don't interest me at all. Blah, blah, blah. I've had enough talk for a lifetime. But this one, these guys in the Pen, now that is real. Wow. That just might *be* something."

The project request was simple but daunting. We are natives in prison. We want to build a sort of halfway house. We'd like to get out of prison and, better yet, *stay* out.

The stakes were high. The recidivism rate in Canada in 1967 for Native inmates was a shocking 97 percent. (Almost fifty years later, the odds have not much improved. What does that say about the deep thinking found in public policy?) If you were an Indian and you were coming out of one of the Queen's best "hotels," there was an overwhelming chance that you would soon be back. The sad, dry joke that Native inmates made to their departing friends, "We'll keep your bunk warm for you, buddy," was based on the sad, dry truth.

Geoff didn't let on for a second that I had chosen to stroll enthusiastically into a minefield. "Well, sure, David. Why don't I arrange for us to go out there and meet some of these fellows?"

Two weeks later, Geoff and I were led past the high tiers of cells in the Pen to a meeting room.

. . .

"What are you laughing at?"

Charlie Wass was the President of the Indian Friendship Group that met every Sunday in the library of the British Columbia Penitentiary. This was my first encounter with the group who wanted a little help getting their prize project off the ground. Charlie was very big and very concentrated on his small kip of power. On this particular afternoon in the fall of 1966, two months before I was to meet Richard Sims at the front gate, there were about forty inmate members in attendance, as well as a dozen "square john" visitors. There were a priest, a gaggle of social workers, some folks from the Downtown Native Friendship Society, and assorted helpers and well-wishers. And there was Charlie, who was quickly tiring of this silly white boy who couldn't stop giggling.

"What are you laughing at?" he asked again, with that throaty rumble of his.

Charlie Wass was like a lot of dangerous men. If you didn't see him under red lights, tanked up on booze and armed and ready to rock 'n roll, if you caught him in a state of enforced sobriety and under heavy armed guard, he appeared the most reasonable of fellows. Strong and movie star handsome, Charlie spoke with a punishing, controlling softness. He had no need to shout or demonstrate. He was all power of personality. It took me a moment to realize that I was being addressed.

"Well, to tell you the truth I was actually laughing at you," I offered in all my full-blown innocence and stupidity.

Tableau. Everybody freezes, everybody except the guards who instinctively caress the triggers of their riot guns.

"You are laughing at me? Just at me or all of us?"

This was my first visit to a prison. When I was a boy, a friend moved to Stonewall, Manitoba. I would take the Greyhound bus to spend the occasional weekend and the driver would wave to the turret guards in the Stony Mountain Penitentiary. The guards would wave back with their sub-machine guns. I lived much of my young life in the movies. Three double bills a week for many years. Tuesdays and Fridays with my mother, Saturday afternoons with my school chums. There was one very odd similarity between this particular moment and all those James Cagney films: they were both in black and white.

It was mid-afternoon, which for me meant low blood sugar. In public school I had dozed every afternoon, never learning anything about history or geography. In the Air

Force, my predictable after-lunch tittering had so annoyed the classroom sergeants that I was forced to spend an entire month of lectures standing beside my desk—giggling, of course. Now, having just returned from months in an Indian village in Mexico, with hair still curled down to my shoulders, my leather sandals and Zapatista moustache, I was laughing uncontrollably at convicts. These were silent, glaring Aboriginal men doing Federal time for who knows what crimes. I was simply too young and too dumb in the ways of the world to be scared.

"Well, what are you talking about, gentlemen, really? I mean, think about it." I pressed on in the central belief that as long as I was speaking, I was in control of the situation. "You're going on about this halfway house idea and all. And that's great. But you keep harping on all these grand notions like self-government and self-financing and, oh Lord, self-determination, whatever the heck that is. And, I mean, what do you really know about such things? Look, I don't mean to rain on your parade, fellows, but quite frankly if you knew what all these things were, you wouldn't be here in this prison."

My freewheeling monologue was met with cold stares. "What are you exactly, a social worker or something?"

"No, no. I'm not anything really. I'm a cab driver. I told the Company of Young Canadians—that's the group that Geoff here is running—that I was kind of interested in your project. They, uh, want volunteers. I told them…"

"So Mr. Volunteer, maybe you could tell us stupid Indians what you would do." Charlie spooned out his irony with a perfectly straight delivery. "We go in, we go out; we go in, we go out. Stupid Indians, that's us. That's all we are, stupid Indians. There are more of us in this joint than there are white inmates in all the penitentiaries all across the country."

"Yes. That's terrible."

"Yes. That's terrible, isn't it? And we have told all these good people about this plan every Sunday for the last two years. And still we are sitting here talking into the air about nothing."

"Yes."

"Yes. So now you can tell us what we should do because we are just stupid Indians and we can't seem to get anything right. But you are a white man and you seem to know many things, even for such a young person. So now we are listening to you. We will learn from you."

"No. I don't know a damn thing," I said. "That's the whole point. I'm a very simple guy. So talk to me about bacon and eggs or shoes and socks or something I can understand."

"Bacon and eggs?"

"See, you're talking about self-determination, Charlie, and that's a wonderful thing but it's very abstract and we could talk till the cows come home and never agree on what the hell that means. Whereas, this halfway house idea, see, that's real, that's something I can grasp, I mean that's something we could all work on, we could make that happen. I mean I can see that. But, here's the thing. Think about this meeting. Think about what's going to happen after this meeting is over."

More stares and glares. Forty Native inmates, a dozen white do-gooders and I'm holding court like I know what I'm talking about or have been given some authority to speak on these matters. "See, I'm going to get up from this table in my fashionable store bought clothes and I'm going to get into my four-door Ford Galaxie 500 and I'm going to drive to my apartment, which isn't much to speak of, really, but I've paid the rent in advance for the next three months. Then I'm going to grind some coffee beans which I bought at a beautiful little store on Robson Street called Murchie's and brew some fresh coffee and then I'm going to light a tailor-made cigarette and sit down and think about this crazy conversation we've been having."

"And what?" Charlie grunted.

"And, well, that's very different from what you and these other guys are going to do." I tried to keep low-key. "Because you're going to get up in these government-issue jeans and those brown wool jackets with the number stitched on the tit and you're going to march single file back to your tier and to your little squirrel cage and maybe you'll spill some tobacco on those jeans trying to roll a cigarette for yourself." The silence drove me on. "So self-government and all that stuff, you're probably not going to learn about that in this rat hole; so maybe what we ought to do is just think about how we can find a place and how we can start and who'll live there and what'll everybody do all day, you know what I mean?"

Three weeks later, I was invited back to the penitentiary. This time, I was the only guest. This meeting was much more a work session. It was time to move into action. How could we get this halfway house idea off the ground, who would start, what would my role be, how would the members on the outside report back to the group inside? What would we call the thing? Charlie and the boys settled on The Indian Post-Release Centre Society.

I got the car on to the Trans-Canada Highway heading back into town, and after a few minutes pulled over onto the shoulder. I was sobbing uncontrollably. The penitentiary was evil. I knew that these men had broken the law and, in doing so, had no doubt severely hurt people. But this, this was the House of Pain. I was twenty-four and a dreamer and I secretly vowed to tear down the walls with acts of goodness.

Madness.

Youth.

A few weeks later, I met Richard at the front gate and the party was on.

3 will Howie or James ever get laid?

So there we were in February 1967, Tony Lavallee—the fat jolly parolee who forgot to tell his parole officer that he had moved—and Richard Sims—Crazy Horse, the Bowie Knife killer—and I living together in harmony, in pastel peachy domestic bliss. We were sharing a two-bedroom bungalow on a quiet, leafy street on the west side of Vancouver. Hey, we had taken step one and found a house. This was easy. Better yet, we were near the beach. What could be better? A local church group donated the beds and dishes and furniture. Now, if someone could just tell us what we were supposed to be doing.

It was 1967, but there were no wars or floods or debates in houses of government. Not for us. The next April, when Martin Luther King was shot, when Bobby Kennedy made the dreadful announcement on a small platform in a park, when James Brown threw a huge concert in Boston the next night to keep the peace, we barely noticed. We were focused. We were looking inward. Lost, determined, hopeful, dazed.

Neither Tony nor Richard made any pretence about finding work. The old saw used to be, "Just get a job and keep your nose clean. That's how you'll stay out of jail." Valiant thought—and completely out of touch with reality.

The truth is that for most men and women, regardless of their crimes, unless they have a strong and clear supportive structure waiting for them, they are too stunned by their prison experience to do much of anything for a while. They are not unlike soldiers returning from the wars. Even if they are blessed with a family and a home and friends who are not criminals—all unlikely and rarely the norm—the period of adjustment is inevitable and often fraught with a thousand and one little stumbling blocks. One wrong turn, one misinterpreted sideways glance on the street, one moment of bad service in a café and the accumulated tensions can explode. Almost every ex-con I was to work with over the coming years expressed the same feeling in his first weeks on the street. "Why is everyone looking at me?" No one was looking, not at all, but the overriding sense of being a freak, or being a recognizable outsider, someone who didn't belong, who didn't *qualify,* was unavoidable. For some, the world is neatly divided. For the Permanently Scarred—the addicts, alcoholics, and ex-convicts—there is the tiny and unassailable group called The Anointed. And then there are all the rest of us suckers. For The Anointed, all the treasures that life can offer pour mysteriously from the heavens. Jobs are not sought; they are tendered on platters. Opportunities of power, sex, and wealth stream down the mountainside like golden lava. And what gifts are set aside for the rest of us? We are left perennially banging on the door, kicking furiously at the gods who have locked us out once again. Even if the door, on occasion, opens, we enter the marbled Halls of Opportunity angry and out-of-sorts because we have been kept waiting. The short-handed begin every day with this wail, "Is there any justice in the whole miserable world?"

It was a feeling I could identify with on a gut level. My own sense of pervading illegitimacy was always percolating just below the surface, ready to pop up full-blown at the slightest hint of judgment or disapproval. My mother had legally changed her name from her maiden name, Segal, to my absent father's name. But she insisted on always signing her name with parentheses around the title, Mrs. as in, (Mrs.) Helen Deborah Berner. She might be married. She might not. She might be a widow. Who is to know? She told me often enough, teasing it turned out, about my twin brother, Daniel, who, of course, did not exist. She spoke regularly about my father as if this were a person we both knew well and saw every day. When on occasion she would oh so casually mention "your father," I became so agitated I thought I would explode. I couldn't say the word "father" until I was an adult. I was an outsider at an early age—a fatherless son in a deeply traditional and conservative family, a Jew in a gentile world. It wasn't until almost forty years later that I realized with some clarity that I was seen by most of the people in my large extended family as a "mumser," a bastard child, a not entirely welcome guest who had the gall to appear without a father. To this day, I will run into second or third cousins who still look at me with judgment and embarrassment. Have they nothing else to do but cling to old gossip and family lore? Later, I would add to the felt, but unexamined, sense of alienation by being an intellectual and a considerably left of center political animal. Marginalization can be much subtler than skin color or employment status.

This sense of being an outsider can be a double-edged sword. Yes, a feeling of being in the presence of Kryptonite, a buckling of the knees in the company of too much so-called normality is always a possibility. Under different skies, one embraces this mild oddness, wearing it with pride, like a distinctive cloak. The word Hebrew means "the other side." While not a particularly observant Jew, I must be a veritable Hebrew, for I am a contrarian, very much a soul from the other side. If the world tells me that things work such and such a way, I am bound to disagree and find an alternative. Want to get something done? Just tell me, "No, David, you can't." I have used the internal engine of anger to drive so many of my private and public accomplishments. Perhaps I shouldn't be surprised to look back and see how flexible and conditional my attentions were. And, while I am no longer a drinker or a drug user, I shouldn't be surprised by my instinctive understanding of the alcoholics and addicts with whom I've worked over the years.

We found a few warm bodies, begged and borrowed some bunk beds and jammed people in as best we could. Two more ex-cons, Freddie and Willie were typical of some of the early house members. Both of these phantoms were tall, skinny, and silent. What I learned about them in the short time I knew them was less than minimal. They were both from somewhere up island, which is the local way in British Columbia of describing someone who came from any of the tiny logging or fishing communities on Vancouver Island.

Freddie and Willie (you would never say one name without the other) seemed to know each other from another movie and, when they weren't giggling like school children, they could be very helpful about little things around the house. Truly, they were like characters in an old black and white silent two-reel comedy. They darted about the house and the yard, laughing at a joke only they understood. They didn't walk or run so much as flit, like butterflies or juncos, and they were just as knowable. Although we lived together in two different houses over a period of almost a year, I'm not sure I ever exchanged seven words with them.

One night I took Richard, the Bowie knife killer, to Geoff Cue's house for dinner. Geoff's children were too young to note anything other than the excitement of having guests at the dining room table. Geoff and his wife, Dorene, were exactly what I would have expected of them—warm and gracious hosts.

Richard, a Carrier Indian from a reservation in Fort Fraser in northern British Columbia, must have felt he was on some as-yet-to-be discovered planet, or maybe he'd just landed in Tibet. He did his best to eat with the right fork or spoon and carry his end of the chatter, but his discomfort at this utterly foreign experience was palpable.

At the end of the first month, we threw a little Open House. We had nothing much to report, but we invited some community leaders to join us in the front room for some goodies and conversation. Geoff's wife, Dorene, gave us a wonderful recipe for baked beans (don't forget the molasses!), and we played The Beatles' "A Day in the Life" for background music. "I read the news today, oh boy…" We joked that the song was just something that we had cooked up over the last few days, and two wise church leaders complimented us on our musicianship. Seriously.

The highlight of the evening was a short, surprising speech from Richard. "David took me to Kits Beach." Everybody stared at this declaration and waited for more. "We went to Kitsilano Beach last week." That was it. You had to sit there and absorb the meaning of this little gem. "Well, I wouldn't go there. By myself, I mean." The assembled somehow got the message that perhaps there was more to social reintegration than getting a job and visiting your parole officer once a month. For Richard Sims, who had just served three years straight in a maximum-security prison, strolling down to Kitsilano Beach in Vancouver was not going to happen without a guide and when it did happen, it was a memorable occasion and some kind of personal accomplishment.

. . .

One morning I was awakened by a dreadful noise in the kitchen. I put on a bathrobe over my naked body. The room was lit by a full moon shining through the window in the breakfast nook. Make that the smashed window in the breakfast nook. Tony and Richard were facing each other, crouched forward, frozen in battle. Tony had five steak knives in his hands. Crazy Horse, the Bowie knife killer, had one very large, very lethal chef's knife. Both men were drunk. They had been sitting in the nook sharing a bottle of cheap wine. The conversation turned, as it seemed fated to, to the one girl they had both been pursuing. Words were said. Tony drove a glass into Richard's face. In swinging hard back at Tony, Richard's bent elbow went through the window. Tony grabbed at the counter for some armament, but Richard had taken on the role of house cook and he knew, of course, where the choice knife and best weapon could be found. Over the coming months, as I came to know Richard better, I found myself believing that the location of that large butcher's blade was of central and strategic importance to him. He put it where he could find it, quickly—just in case. We are what we think; we do what we dream.

I stepped between the two men and ordered Tony from the house. My heart was pounding and I thought if I could talk to Richard alone I might defuse this moment. After all, I knew him better than anyone, didn't I? Tony protested valiantly and then left us alone in the kitchen. Richard rocked drunkenly in front of me. He waved the knife at my exposed chest.

"You fucking white man. I'm going to carve you to pieces, many, many pieces!"

The pounding in my chest stopped. I was elevated to a place of preternatural calm. I am standing on mysterious white shores. The light has no beginning or end. It's over. I am dead. I will die. Maybe the knife coming through the skin of my belly will hurt. My insides will hurt. I don't know. I hope this is over quickly. I am dead.

"You hear me, you white man fuck? Millions of pieces! That's what I'm going to do to you."

From where did the following come? To this day, I have no idea. There wasn't the tiniest impulse to be clever. I opened my mouth, and very quietly, almost in a hush, came these words.

"OK, Richard, OK I hear the words you are using. I hear the words, Richard, but also I hear you saying something else, something different, I guess." My mother had told me, "Listen to what people are *not* saying. Listen to the opposite to hear the truth."

"What the fuck you saying? You bastard! I'll kill you…"

"Yah, I know, Richard, you'll kill me, I know." All that I really knew was that drunk, Richard was entirely another person. And this other person was here before me in the moonlight and he had a butcher knife in his hand. "But what I am hearing is that you are scared…"

"Fuck you!"

"You are very frightened now, being outside that prison after all these years. I hear you saying that you are frightened. You wish someone would help you. Please help me. This is what I hear. You are saying, 'Please help me.'"

The eternity that passed may have been in reality a few seconds. There is no good reason for me to have outlived this moment. Richard stared, open-mouthed, and waved the knife. Slowly, his right arm slid to his side. He simply opened his hand, and the knife fell to the floor. He stepped closer, and collapsed, sobbing into my arms.

"Help me. Please, help me."

. . .

The next afternoon I was walking down Cornwall Street opposite Kits Beach. I was trying to make sense of what had just happened in the early morning hours. How did I say the words that may have saved my life? Why was I spared?

Does this seem too melodramatic, too self-serving? I am not a Christian, so I cannot speak of being "saved" or being "born again." I have no faith in lightning conversions. But you'll forgive me if I tell you that I did think this: "I have a calling. This is a strange and delicate responsibility. This is a gift that I utterly don't understand. However, think a moment. I must honor this mystery and do something useful with it. I am twenty-four years old and I have been horsing around for far too long, doing not much of anything really. Now is the time to get serious and do some real work. For the first time in my life, I will not stop until we have built something worthwhile, until something of real substance is standing before us."

. . .

I was no knife man, but I had already built up my own small history of violence. I slapped my cousin Beverley across the face when I was six and she was five. What was her transgression? Why did she deserve such an assault? Why, she had had the effrontery to win my Zaida's kindness and approval in a way that I had never managed. My grandfather had kissed her on the cheek. He never kissed me on the cheek. I lived in the same house, slept in the bedroom next to his. Why her? Why not me? My jealousy demanded that that very same blessed cheek be slapped.

Around the same period, Maxie Weinstein, a boy whose family owned the corner deli, had laughed at me for skipping rope and playing with the girls. I pushed him backwards and he fell on his own arm. I attended his birthday party later that week at the store, a birthday he celebrated with an arm in a cast. When we were about ten, my cousin Donnie teased me and teased me on the front lawn until I pushed him down. When he fell, his open palm was exposed. I jammed the heel of my leather shoe sharp into that flesh and sent the big bully home crying to his mother.

About a year before I met Richard Sims, I was maneuvering my Yellow Taxi through rush hour traffic on West Pender Street. A man in a private car began darting in and out, clearly in some personal contest with me. When a light stopped us, I deliberately nudged his car from behind. He got out of his car, stood by my window, looked up at the taxi dome light and said, "Car 88, eh? OK." As he headed smugly back to his car, I leaped out, pushed him against the hood and hit him three times very quickly and hard in the face. In a split second, I had entered the red zone, and as quickly, I came to. "Oh, for god sakes, I am so sorry man. I don't know what I am doing. Sorry, sorry..."

Maybe I had more in common with these men than I realized.

. . .

There were no rules; there was no plan. With beds stacked in every available corner and the most judicious management of one bathroom, we quickly filled the little bungalow with more lost souls, young Indian men sent from the white man's prisons to become model urban citizens. Their welfare checks helped pay the bills. Friends, churches, and local community groups donated dishes, mattresses, linen, and even food. We had no official sanctions, and thus, no funding of any kind. We were an experiment. We were making it up as we went along. It didn't even occur to me until about the fourth month that we needed a form or shape to make this thing work. We lurched from one crisis to the next, one melodrama to another.

. . .

A boy from Kingcom Inlet, playing about one afternoon, jumped off the garage roof and hurt his ankle. His name was Alvin Wallace. I dropped him at the emergency entrance to St. Paul's Hospital. "Tell them your name and what happened, and I'll pick you up in about an hour." What was I doing that morning that was so important? I look back at this incident from the vantage point of some forty years and ask myself why it wasn't obvious at the time that I come into the hospital with him.

An hour later, I found Alvin hobbling up Burrard Street. They had told Alvin he had to go to the Indian Clinic. This was Vancouver in 1967. We drove back to the emergency ward. The encounter at the nurses' station soon included several doctors and interns.

"This young man was told he has to go to something called the Indian Clinic to see if he's broken his leg."

"Yes, that's right. And who are you?"

"Where exactly is this famous Indian Clinic?"

"It's in the Immigration Building."

"Let me see if I understand this correctly. The only place where this young man, who is a citizen of this country, a lifetime resident of this sovereign province, a First Citizen, by the way, can get medical attention is at a clinic in the Immigration Building. Is that right?"

"Who are you, sir? What business is this of yours?"

"And the Immigration Building, if my cab driver memory serves me correctly, is down on the docks at the foot of this street, right?"

"That is right."

"OK. All right. OK."

"All right, sir?"

"So my question to you is this: Where is the Jewish Clinic?"

"Excuse me."

"I asked where the Jewish Clinic might be located?" With each new question, my voice rose. "And the Ukrainian Clinic, where is that? The Scottish Clinic? The Irish? German?"

"Young man, please calm down."

Within five minutes, nineteen-year-old ex-con Alvin Wallace from Kingcom Inlet had three fully qualified Canadian physicians examining him. They took X-rays and determined that the young man had only sprained his ankle. He should stay off that leg as much as possible for the next little while and, please, we recommend no more jumping from the garage.

· · ·

One night, Richard didn't come home.

The next morning I found out that he had been in the city jail overnight for Drunk and Disorderly. I ran into Tony's bedroom. It was about eleven in the morning and, of course, Tony was still sleeping. I reached under the mattress, grabbed the springs and flipped Tony out of bed. Before he could recover, I slammed him against the wall and started hollering at him.

"Why didn't you tell me that Richard was in jail, you asshole?"

Not long after, Tony laughed at this incident. "You know until that morning where you charged into my bedroom and went nuts on me, I didn't really take you seriously. I thought you were just our little social worker. That's what we all called you, our little social worker. But that's when I knew you really cared."

This was actually the second confrontation that Tony and I had survived with each other.

Only a few weeks earlier, just before we found the little house on 5th Avenue, I was driving west on Pender Street. Richard was sitting in the front, and Tony was holding court in the back seat, doing one of his now familiar monologues about how "the white man" had so terribly mistreated every single Native that ever existed. I had heard this story now many, many times. I was only half listening.

Suddenly his diatribe rang loud and clear. "So we Jewed him down." At this apparent triumph, he laughed heartily.

I jammed on the brake. "Excuse me? What was that? You 'Jewed' him down? Is that what you just said? You 'Jewed' him down?"

Ignorance doesn't necessarily suggest willful stupidity. It simply means not knowing. Tony, like many people using common epithets, had no sense of the history or import of an expression like "Jewed him down." Chink, slant, dago, wop—choose your throw-away. What's the big deal, anyway?

I blew my Jew gasket. "You ignorant asshole! I've been listening to you and Richard and all you jokers going on and fucking on about how badly you've been treated by the ubiquitous fucking evil 'white man.' And I've been nodding sagely and sympathizing with all this crap. Now, you talk about getting 'Jewed down?!' Well, screw you, cousin!" A short instruction on Shylock, money lending, the Rothschilds, banking and the myth of Jews owning or controlling all the money in the world followed. Call it Dave's Personal Protocol's of Zion Rap. Now, discovering that Richard had spent the night in jail and that Tony had probably known about it, I was smacking Tony around the room and yelling at him. For some people, "caring" must arrive in Technicolor, stereo, and IMAX projection or it goes unnoticed. It took me a long time and many mistakes to learn that there was a productive middle ground somewhere between caring passionately and indiscriminately, and keeping a frozen intellectual distance from people you are pretending to help.

A church group in North Vancouver had taken Richard home that morning. I drove over to get him. "This is the last time, Richard. I am never *rescuing* you again. I am officially out of the *rescuing* business, you hear me?" I never did choose to rescue him again. Or anyone else, for that matter. But that didn't mean that the troubles had stopped.

After a few months, I realized that Richard had been stealing from me. Small things, petty things. Maybe he felt too dependent on me, and this was his declaration of freedom. Maybe I was too dependent on his dependence. Maybe he was just an outright creep and a thief. Maybe he was an alcoholic. There's a thought, a thought I had carefully resisted. I drank at the time; I didn't give up my own drinking and pot smoking until almost two years later. So it hadn't yet occurred to me that for some unlucky souls drinking was more than a night out. For some people, drinking was a compulsion and a necessity. For some people, drinking is everything. It is life and it is death.

When I finally realized and admitted to myself that Richard had been stealing from me, I went into overdrive. Of course, I was terribly hurt, but I would never, could never admit to such a human feeling. I was thoroughly invested in my mask of self-sufficiency. Love, loneliness, vulnerability? Not for this master-of-the-universe! I was above such pedestrian concerns. Besides, I had a carefully calibrated first response for all emergencies—ANGER. Even today, almost fifty years later, I sometimes have to work very hard to leap past my favorite answer to all things—anger—and recognize some other human feeling, like sadness or grief.

Ever the dramatist, I chose a public intersection to confront Richard about his transgressions. We were standing at the corner of Broadway and Arbutus on a warm spring afternoon waiting for the traffic light to change. I was crying, playing to the balconies. I took off my shirt and threw it at this ungrateful thief. "Here, you want something of mine, all you have to do is ask. Don't you know that by now, you fool?"

If this was supposed to be an object lesson, it was wasted. Richard was testing behavior incarnate. Only two years later, we would have signs on our residence and clubhouse buildings that asked, "Are you suffering from T.B.? Testing Behavior."

If you are the mother of a two-year old, then you are more than familiar with the schemes and maneuvers of the child who must constantly be poking the environment to see how far he can go. Now, meet the adult alcoholic or addict—a child in long pants. Only a tad more dangerous.

Perhaps Richard was momentarily impressed with my over-wrought emotions. Perhaps he had a real sense of affection and friendship as a result of living and working with me for a few months now. But, as I was to see very soon, he was a drunk, self-pitying and violent, and his descent into hell was a vortex inevitable and unstoppable.

4 watching TV is good for you

Something happened on a lazy Tuesday afternoon in the early fall of 1967 that would change our lives.

Several of us were sitting in the house, watching TV. As people are fond of pointing out, television is often nothing more than furniture. So it seems unlikely that our futures could be so powerfully affected by something we saw on TV. But that is exactly what happened. A National Film Board documentary came on called, *Daytop*.

The movie was about the inner workings of Daytop Center, a rehabilitation community for addicts in Staten Island, New York. All of the people in the movie, except one, were resident clients and workers in the center. The one exception was the wonderful Canadian actor, singer, poet, and artist, Don Francks. With over one hundred film and television credits to his name, and still going strong, Mr. Francks is perhaps best remembered for his central role in the film version of the musical, *Finian's Rainbow*, starring Fred Astaire and Petula Clark and directed by Francis Ford Coppola.

Here in *Daytop*, Francks played a junkie coming in to the program and struggling in every way with the rigorous and brutally honest approach that he found there. Daytop was and still is a therapeutic community modeled after the grand-daddy of them all, Synanon. How were we to know on that afternoon that Synanon and its methodology were soon to play a major role for everyone in what would soon become The X-Kalay Foundation, Canada's first and longest-running treatment center?

What we saw grabbed us by the throat. We saw men and women confronting each other in therapy groups with courage and love and scalding forthrightness. We watched this and said, "That's what we should be doing!"

But how could we put this dynamic interaction into play, here in our modest bungalow in Vancouver?

It would take a few more months and a few more little learning experiences for the answer to reveal itself.

· · ·

Here is one little donnybrook typical of the struggles that visited us or that we often invited whole-heartedly through the front door. The Canadian Penitentiary Service had a policy. In truth, it had tomes and volumes of policies. One particular rule stated that no man who had served time in a federal prison could return as a visitor to that institu-tion, until he had been out on the street for over a year. No doubt the Penitentiary Service would have preferred that the ex-con had also amassed a personal fortune and become a deacon in a church and a member in good standing in a men's service club, a golf club, a curling fraternity, or other colossal achievements to that effect. The fear was that the inmate, still grooved in his criminal ways, might smuggle in contraband or deliver encrypted criminal messages from the outside. Fair enough. But what if the former inmate really had gone down that straight and narrow road? By the time he was allowed back in for a visit, he had become such a citizen square head that no inmates could identify with him or even hear a word he might say.

I wanted to bring Richard Sims back into the Pen within weeks of his release so that he could meet with the Indian Education Group. Perhaps, still bruised and raw from his own transition experience, he might confront his former friends with some of the harsh realities of making the shift from the regulated timetable inside the stone walls of the prison to a life outside—a life that demanded an internalized self-discipline. I thought this would be a valuable dialogue for all concerned. The prison authorities resisted this idea and the argument developed into a small bureaucratic skirmish. Meetings were convened; temperatures were raised and then cooled. In the end, the corrections authorities softened their stance and let us try this "unusual" visit on an interim basis.

Richard and I went into that same meeting room in the library where I had first met these men of the Indian Friendship Group. I was a mute witness to the phenomenon that followed. Richard talked slowly and very deliberately about his first few months on the outside. Maybe the prison authorities were right. I had the eerie feeling that Richard was, in fact, speaking in code, some Aboriginal con lingo known only to the men who had lived on the inside. This normally reticent, tough man had taken on the mantle of a country preacher. Here are the real goods, brothers. And here's how you will have to play your hand to survive. You could see in the eyes of his former jail mates a look of astonishment, and a new kind of respect. Was this the Silent Terror, the one we have known for three years to be avoided at all costs? Here was Richard, Crazy Horse, one of their own, not a social worker, not some do-gooder, but someone they knew very well, or thought they knew, looking and sounding very different. It was a small revelation.

What is amazing, and a testament to the slow march of progress, is that in the year 2009, I attended an event inside the Nanaimo Correctional Institution, a provincial prison, in which a fellow named Ernie, who had been out only two months, was one of the guest speakers. Hard to believe that forty years ago, such a meeting would have been an impossibility, and that Ernie would not have been allowed to participate.

. . .

The bungalow on West 5th Avenue had grown too small for us. Soon we found a bigger house and joined forces with a Native women's group. The women's group was having trouble paying the rent. What could be more perfect? We'd join forces and solve everyone's problems. Now there were men, women, and children. Still there were no rules, no plan. Let's talk problems.

I was standing in front of this second house one beautiful late summer evening when Tony came down the street with a gun in his hand. "I'm gonna kill the sonovabitch. Then, some cops, that's what." This was a Tony I had never seen before. Gone was Santa Claus; gone was the pouting little boy. This was Tony seriously flipped out, Tony coked on anger and revenge.

"Tony, where did you get that thing?"

"You did your big Superman act last time and got that knife away from him, but he can't stop no bullet."

"Ah, you mean Richard. What's he done now?"

"He's trying to fuck my woman, and I'm closing that book right now. Then, you know what I'm gonna do? I'm taking this little piece downtown, right to Main and Hastings, right in their territory, a block from their fucking jailhouse, and I'm gonna kill me a few policemen before they get to me."

"Good."

"You like it?"

"Very much. Absolutely."

"Good on you. Now get the fuck outta my way."

"Tony, just before you go and kill yourself and all these people, which by the way is just fine with me, I think, really, it's a very nifty uptown plan and all, just first, one little question if I may?"

"What?"

"So are you saying you'd really like to get even with all these cop bastards, is that the thing?"

"Don't fuck with me. You know what I'm saying!"

"Then try using your head for just once in your life, you idiot! You want to get even with all the white law enforcement officers who have done you such wrong all these years, I'll tell you there's only one way to do that!"

"Fuck you."

"You become a citizen, Tony. You become a successful law-abiding upstanding Presbyterian effing citizen beyond reproach, so the next time some traffic cop stops you for driving too casual, you flash him your driver's license and give him a lecture on being a public servant who should not be stopping honorable citizens when they are on their way to important, legitimate business and there are still plenty of real bad guys to catch! That's how you get even, pal."

We took a long and pleasant evening walk past Locarno Beach to Spanish Banks. We laughed and swapped silly stories, admitted a human frailty or two, spoke of dreams and somewhere near the University of British Columbia, we fed the little semi-automatic to the fishes.

. . .

A young man named Luis Molina was working at a social service agency in town. He was an American who had spent some time in Synanon, the California therapeutic community that was gaining so much attention those days both for its unusual methods and for its surprisingly good results in getting addicts off their habits and onto a better lifestyle. It was Synanon, in fact, that was the granddaddy of all the therapeutic community models that would follow—Daytop, Delancey Street, Phoenix Houses, X-Kalay and Portage in Canada, and even San Patrignano in Northern Italy. I met Luis and told him that I was looking for a way to start doing the kind of work we had witnessed in the *Daytop* documentary on television. How could we initiate these group encounters?

A few years earlier, such a question might have seemed like heresy. But the world was now well into a kind of spontaneous social revolution. Joseph Brodsky and his fellow poets were stirring a noisy little revolution in Leningrad. The Beatles, the Stones, and Bob Dylan were blasting out of speakers on every street corner from Columbus Circle to Marble Arch to Las Ramblas. Andy Warhol was painting soup cans and Liz and Chairman Mao. And on California's Monterey Peninsula, the Esalen Institute was spearheading something called The Human Potential Movement. Investigate yourself. Learn who you really are. Release your inner pirate, warrior, ballet dancer, gunslinger, or guru. In Vancouver, there was no one more identified with this phenomenon than a local clinical psychologist named Dr. Lee Pulos.

Luis Molina suggested that Dr. Pulos was the man I had to meet.

Lee was strikingly handsome and bristling with energy. A Greek, who had grown up above his family's grocery store in Calgary, Pulos had dropped out of school, joined the navy, and come back to the academic life on a veteran's package. He remains to this day one of the most brilliant men I've ever met and one of the most sought-after and dynamic public presenters. Google "Type A personality" and Lee's passport photo will appear. Everything about him is positive with a capital P. He was and is the poster boy for enthusiasm and science and mysticism and progressive ideas. Not too long after I met Lee, he and his brothers opened a chain of Spaghetti Factory restaurants in a dozen cities. All the while, Lee was writing and publishing self-help books and tapes, seeing ten clients a day in private practice, lecturing, running workshops, skiing, playing racquetball, and dating a seemingly endless string of gorgeous blond women. Early in our relationship, he taught me self-hypnosis, which I have continued to use in so many ways. In my mid-thirties, using Lee's technique, I beat a pack-a-day cigarette habit in less than forty-eight hours. When the Pulos Brothers sold the restaurant chain, Lee walked away with a considerable paycheck and a little plastic card that guaranteed him free meals with an unlimited number of guests until the year 3038. We still have dinner there every four months or so to catch-up on the latest gossip and laugh our heads off.

For our first meeting, Lee came up to the office that I was still using on occasion at the Company of Young Canadians. I yelled at him.

"Get your goddamn feet off my desk!" In his effort to appear cool and casual, Lee had begun our friendship—one that would last forty years, and counting—by swinging his loafers onto my desk. Two competitors, two territorialists, two dumb bulls. We huffed and puffed at each other for a few minutes, established our mutual bona fides, and moved on to the business at hand. I told Lee about the work we were doing and about how impressed we were by the group encounters we saw in the *Daytop* film. He knew the program and the technique, but wanting to go one step further, he immediately suggested radical intervention.

"I really like marathons these days. These are twenty-four hour group blowouts. You get everyone into a room. You stock up on food and coffee and cigarettes. No one can sleep and no one can leave except to go to the bathroom. It's way more effective than an hour here and an hour there. After about eight hours of bullshit, you get tired and the barriers break down. You pass the point where you can put up with all the crap. And soon the truth starts coming out."

A week later, on Sunday, July 23, 1967, there we were at eight in the evening, about a dozen of us gathered in big armchairs and sofas in the living room. The food covered the dining room table. Richard and Tony were the only house members beside me who joined in. Fred, Willie, Mary and her baby, all the others disappeared into the bushes long enough for this unholy ceremony to be done with.

To fill out the group, I invited several friends. One was Bob Hunter. If Bob, ever the intrepid adventurer, could sail into a potential nuclear detonation in Amchitka, Alaska, he could certainly weather the psychological storms of a little encounter group. Our mutual friend Terry joined us. Terry, also from Winnipeg, was now a social worker in Prince George. He had been one of my greatest friends during my college and university days, and when he and his wife-to-be, Chloe, eloped to Spain and Morocco, I was compelled to follow months later. Within a year of that exodus, our whole gang was living in London, England, laboring under the sweetest group delusion that we were a literary circle, each one of us more gifted than the last. The only question was whose book would win The Prize first. Filling out the room were among others, Dale Seddon and several volunteers from the Company of Young Canadians.

Dr. Pulos set out the rules and we began. You can say anything. You can express yourself in any way you like. You can use any language. You can comment on what someone else has just said. You can give them feedback, positive or otherwise. You cannot physically harm or touch or accost or even hug someone else without his or her clear approval. You cannot leave except for washroom breaks. You cannot sleep till it's over. Strive for truth and honesty.

The twenty-four hours flashed by in a moment. But what a moment it was.

Pulos began by asking if someone would like to begin by introducing himself or herself or telling his or her own personal story.

Following the customary shuffling silence, a young fellow named Allan spoke up. Allan was one of several Company of Young Canadians volunteer workers, along with Maeve, Bill, Allison, and Dale who had courageously joined us for this novel experience. Allan was a decent, straightforward, and earnestly dull man. He worked with low-income families who lived in a notorious public housing project in the east end of town. The neighborhood was scarred with the full jacket of urban disasters—poverty, unemployment, boredom, crime, and hopelessness. Allan was doing his best to help mobilize people into political or social self-help actions. Allan talked about himself for about five minutes. He drew a simple enough sketch of who he was, not much different from what you might hear in secondary school or around a board table. I'm this and I'm that, and I do this and that. One could hardly expect deep personal revelations in the first few minutes.

But that apparently wasn't good enough for me.

From the moment we had all gathered in the living room, I could feel my heart racing. I really, really, really wanted to dive into the pool of discovery. Who are you? What do you really want? Forget your masks and disguises. Show me the core. Show me the stuff of which you are truly made. I felt a mad urgency to find through the mirror of others who I really was. I remember vividly telling myself several months earlier, "If I can understand these guys I'm working with, maybe I will come to understand myself."

Allan finished his modest presentation and I jumped in with both barrels blazing.

"Well, isn't that nice? Isn't that cute? That's exactly the kind of bullshit we'd expect from a mealy-mouth wimp like you, Allan."

Where did this hostility come from, this cruel, unfocused rage? Every single person in the room, including Lee Pulos, jumped back a step at this seemingly unprovoked assault. Poor Allan sputtered some self-defense, but I pressed on in my outrageous attack. "You're such a namby-pamby clod, Al. Do you ever stand up for anything? How the hell do you do that work you claim you're doing? Do you really have the confidence of those people when you never really *say* anything?"

Somehow, Lee Pulos managed to have all of us soon engaged. I was challenged to talk about myself as was the next person and the next. People lit cigarette after cigarette. We strolled to the dining room for more coffee or a carrot stick or a salmon sandwich. Crunch, munch, slurp, burp. People wandered out to the bathroom and came back. We laughed ourselves silly. Some of us were terribly funny. Some of us were funny when we least intended to be. We were tough as nails. Nobody was allowed to say anything without query and challenge and opposition. Even Richard, the silent killer, was clearly astonished by this kind of freewheeling and open exchange. Here was a man who spoke with his fists. Here was a group of white people shouting obscenities at each other one minute, and then collapsing next in hysterics. White people are crazy; we all know that.

Tony Lavallee, ever the politician, rolled with the punches. He loved it. His Santa Claus act was out in full force. Everything we said amused him. Ho, ho, ho! Everything, that is, until Richard tentatively joined the fray. Suddenly the old rivalry between these two erupted. It had been clear to those of us who lived together in this house that Tony and Richard just barely tolerated each other. Their icy standoff clearly had a date stamp on it and you didn't want to be in the neighborhood when that date arrived. Something in the air had triggered for Tony a deep and painful memory. He tried to share with us the horror story about his mother's tragic life and death. We all sat quietly, listening with as much empathy as each of us could muster to Tony's efforts to tell his tale and to grasp its meaning. His tears fell easily and others in the room cried in response. But for Richard, something else was at play. Lee had warned us that, in the course of the twenty-four hours we would spend together, we might meet our "monster." We might also meet our "god." Lee's advice: "Step up and shake that monster's hand. Give that god a good hug. Recognize, with gratitude, the giant of your dreams and the dwarf of your nightmares." Fair enough. But for Richard, there was some secret element buried in Tony's dolorous narrative about his mother, some quality of shame or disgust that Richard alone knew or felt. This was some spook he simply could not abide and he was determined to end its sovereignty over him on the spot. We were never to learn or parse the deep wound that sparked Richard's explosive reaction to Tony's story, but we certainly experienced the result.

Suddenly, Richard leapt across the room at Tony, not only violating the Rules of the Game, but absolutely terrifying most of the group. The two of them struggled their way into the hallway. Fortunately, what began as a physical combat quickly decelerated into words, and miraculously, the words soon became softer. The two men returned to their seats in the living room. The entire altercation lasted about three minutes. It was terrifying and it was exciting. Later, as Lee had predicted, when the sheer passing of time had eroded most of our false performances and many of our shop-worn defenses, some very basic emotions began to surface. I still have a picture of someone leaning over Bob Hunter's chair and calling him every name in the book. Chicken and French fries flew across the carpet. When the session ended, when we stood on the front steps and said our goodbyes to one another, there was a strange feeling of exhilaration in the air. And just a hint of love. Most of us hugged and laughed and looked into each other's faces as if seeing one another for the first time. What was this, an acid trip without the grape juice? To this day, Lee Pulos says that this was the most powerful, overwhelming group he has ever experienced. Let's just say it was pretty raw. For several days afterward, we were all emotionally high as kites. We couldn't stop talking about this "peak experience." And we wanted more.

. . .

One night, Alvin Wallace came into my bedroom and woke me from a sound sleep. Alvin was the nineteen-year-old from Cape Mudge on Vancouver Island who had twisted his ankle jumping off the garage roof. He possessed the most seductively wicked smile I've ever seen. Once, we were having the inevitable who-do-you-like-better-the-Beatles-or-the-Stones discussion and I argued that the Stones were evil. "Yah," Alvin grinned triumphantly, "that's why I like them!"

"David, I have to talk to you."

"What time is it?"

"About two."

"In the morning? Get the hell out of here. I have to sleep. I'm no use to anybody without sleep."

"But…"

"FUCK OFF!"

This was an ugly little moment. It was also a great learning experience for both of us.

Alvin and everyone else had been taking for granted that Dave would always be available. I was the official helper and fixer. Anything that might go wrong—and practically everything *did* go wrong sooner or later, you could count on that—I would get it back on track. This was clearly a role that I relished and that I had seized upon. Talk about making yourself indispensable. I had been going out of my way for so many months now to always be helpful and available. But, if you are always on duty, if you are always prepared to serve, when do you rest? And, equally important, who helps the helper?

Mothers know this problem full well. And some women who make motherhood their entire authority and raison d'être are familiar with the withdrawal symptoms that can appear when the children become young adults and begin to leave the nest. What is my usefulness now? Whom do I serve? For many years, my son was the caregiver in his primary relationships with women. The first two truly significant partners in his life were beautiful, smart, and extraordinarily high maintenance women. Then, at the age of forty, he met and fell in love with a woman who was herself a real caregiver. Here was a partner who was direct, straightforward, and supportive. For the first time in his life, Sean could let someone else do some of the worrying and managing. More importantly, for the first time, relieved at last of the burden of the caretaker role, he could *allow himself* to be cared for. I was in my sixties when my son shared these thoughts with me. These notions were very easy for me to identify with as I had just been learning them myself late in life.

When I was twenty-five and still striving mightily to reorganize the world according to David, I hadn't yet learned those lessons.

So here I was at two in the morning freshly learning to define my limits and my territory. This kind of declaration comes, of course, with some risk. If I tell Alvin Wallace to fuck off at two in the morning, will he still love me at noon? Saying, "No," to someone is dangerous. You might lose him forever. Sooner or later, you have to trust that real relationships can survive arguments, disappointments and the occasional, "No, thanks." The stakes are high in these games. So, in this case, in this moment, egged on to the next level by sheer exhaustion, I said, "Wait. For once in your life, you spoiled little shit, just wait."

Later, the entire concept of waiting would play a central role in the therapeutic process of X-Kalay.

5 breaking bread with Malcolm

Geoff Cue had in fact never hired me on as a volunteer for the Company of Young Canadians. Even though my enormous salary of $235 a month was the same that the volunteers were paid, Geoff appointed me to a staff position, which allowed him to call on me for some input into other projects. What enormous faith he had in me!

I had begun working for Geoff and the Company in January. In April, he surprised me by asking me to fly to Montreal for a conference.

"A conference? About what? I don't want to go to Montreal. I have work to do."

The following year, Geoff and I would travel together to Montreal for a Company conference. It was on that occasion that I learned from him the three golden rules of business travel.

One: Conferences are, by their very nature, a complete waste of time. Everything is said. Little is done. Nothing of substance is ever accomplished. Blah, blah, blah. Don't go.

Two: If you must go away on business, always take your bathing suit. The hotel is bound to have a pool, or, at the very least, have an arrangement with the Y or fitness club across the alley. It is very hard to think about anything irksome, including annoying conferees, while practicing your free style. Similarly, if you're in a major city, buy tickets to a show or concert. Enjoy Yehudi Menuhin, Miles Davis, or Reba McEntire. Do not be visible in the hotel. Some rube will always want to debate the finer points of the day's proceedings.

Three: Never, ever discuss conference business over meals. It's bad for the digestion. If some passive-aggressive shmuck at the table starts in with one of those predictably polite respectful disagreements about the finer points of who knows what, just put your fork down, look him in the eye and declare, "Please. We're eating."

All Geoff would tell me about this first event he wanted me to attend was that I would be picked up at Dorval Airport and someone from the Company would take me to a retreat in the Laurentian Mountains.

Two days later, I was in a very beautiful and expensive resort in the village of Val-David, Quebec. The meals were lavish. The bread was baked fresh every morning before our very eyes in a brick oven in the dining room. The occasion was not really a conference. It was a training session for new Company volunteers, one of whom was a gangly young fellow from Ontario named Paul Windham, whom I would soon get to know in the most surprising way.

On the inaugural evening, after a magnificent meal, the volunteers all gathered in pajamas or après-ski clothes to sit and recline on the floor of the lodge's main living room.

One after another, the leaders and executive of the Company of Young Canadians made stirring speeches about the work ahead. Most of these captains and commanders were, as it turned out, Americans. Most had been a part of the civil rights movement in America. They were all personal friends of Martin Luther King and Stokely Carmichael. They strummed guitars and banjos around campfires with Joan Baez and Pete Seeger. They spoke proudly of marching into history, of bloodshed and sacrifice. They promised that a new Canada was on the horizon, a Canada of universal justice and resources shared by every citizen. No one could question their passion and zeal. All we had to do to make the dream come true was to seize it. They made every effort to stir the revolutionary juices lurking within the souls of these young Canadian wannabes.

I was completely baffled. I had no idea what they were talking about. Later I was to learn that each of these shepherds was drawing a considerable salary. In 1967, $20,000 was a substantial income for a single person under the age of twenty-seven. Moreover, each of them was doing something very fiscally clever with their loot. Keeping up a busy schedule of traveling across the great breadth and northern reaches of the Dominion, they were able to subsist largely on expense accounts and bank their paychecks. They were preaching the overthrow of government, while happily accepting handsome incomes from the very sovereign nation they sought to "correct." Classic Cadillac Communists.

I was asked to speak. I was, at the ripe old age of twenty-four, a staff member from exotic British Columbia and, after three whole months of service, a seasoned veteran of the wars.

"I'm afraid I am not sure exactly what the previous speakers were talking about," I began. "I am not an American, I am a Canadian. I grew up in Winnipeg and I've been living in Vancouver for about three years now. I didn't march on Selma, Alabama. I'd be lucky if I could find Selma on a map. For the past few months, I've been working with Native Indian ex-convicts. We're starting a post-release centre, a kind of halfway house and we seem to be making some slow progress. Sometimes it's hard to tell exactly how or where you're going, because you're right in the middle of the action. I do agree with the previous speakers about one thing—this work is about a kind of revolution. But it has nothing to do with bloodshed or riots in the streets. This is not America. This is Canada. We are not a gun country. We are tied to the Queen. We are polite and apologetic. If you think the Canadian government is going to pay you to foment public discord, you are completely mad. If there is a revolution at stake here, it is what I would call a Revolution of Gesture. Can we be more civil to one another? Can we smile at one another as we pass in the street? Can we surpass the Hallmark way of life and not 'care enough to send the very best,' but care enough to *do* the very best? The work you have chosen to do as volunteers can be honorable. You may make a small but important contribution. But do not think for a moment that what you are about to do is glamorous or exciting. Your work will not be the stuff of TV episodics. Often, the work is excruciatingly boring. You may spend hours having coffee with people who want nothing more than to tell you their troubles. Your clients' biggest ambition in life may be to own a Chevy Malibu convertible. Political or social action may take many months to formulate and put up on wheels."

When I was finished, the leaders and executive sent all the volunteers off to bed. I was about to leave the room, when they asked me to hang back for a minute. As soon as we were alone, the room exploded.

"You son of a bitch," they railed at me. "You are the most destructive asshole I've ever met." And so on. Apparently I had undermined all their good work. Understandably, it is a fundamental sin at team rallies not to sing the company song—and with gusto!

I was unmoved. "Mm. Thanks for your feedback. I have no interest in you, any of you, or anything you have to say. Frankly, I think you are all nuts. Have a good night."

The next morning, I was walking along the snowy front path with my suitcase. The Executive Director came running after me.

"David! David, where are you going?"

"I'm going home."

"What?"

"I'm going to Vancouver. I have work to do."

"But the conference isn't over!"

"It is for me, pal."

Geoff picked me up at the Vancouver airport and, on the ride into town, I gave him my summary of events, my impressions and my conclusions. "These guys are on a different page, Geoff. And it's not one I want to know about. I think they are serious whack jobs. And possibly petty crooks. The less we have to do with people like that, the better."

"Oh, thank god," was Geoff's response. "You've got to

understand, David, the reason I sent you to that thing is that I thought I was losing my mind. I had this real sense that the National Executive was on a completely different track than we were. Half the time I never know what they're talking about. They'll call and we'll talk and the words seem to be reasonable enough, but I'm always left with this strange feeling of dissonance. That something is just not kosher. I needed to see what would happen if you went there by yourself. If you had come back and told me that everything was terrific and that these guys were wonderful, I knew that I was sunk."

"Really?"

"No, I trust your judgment about people. I think you have an unusual insight and everything you've said just confirms what I've been feeling. Oh, I feel so much better now!"

. . .

At this point, heading into the early fall of 1967, we were still renting the big old house on West 6th Avenue that had originally been a refuge for Native women. There was no one in our house at that time using heroin or cocaine, although almost everyone drank, some way more than others. Most of us, myself included, smoked pot. Our first attempt at having any rules whatsoever was one of those half-measures that people take when they do not really have their feet solidly underneath them and their shoulders squared to meet the wind. We decided that no one should drink *in the house.* Oh, you could tear up the town all you wanted and close any number of bars, so long as you crawled home quietly and didn't disturb the sober few. Ha! What were we thinking?

Richard tested this first rule not once, but twice, and in the end, it was the last we ever saw of him.

Paul Windham, one of the volunteers that I had briefly met at the training session in the mountains of Quebec, was now working on a low-income housing project for the Company of Young Canadians in Vancouver. Whatever his assignment might have been, Paul was obviously not engaged. He took to visiting our house on a regular basis and hanging out. He asked me dozens of questions and expressed many times over a period of months that he'd really like to work with me. I thought he was a decent enough guy, but perhaps somewhat naïve and linear in his thinking. Often, while searching for the deeper meaning in things, he seemed to slip right past the obvious. My sense was that, in this setting, you had to be living truly in the moment, that you had to see clearly and exactly what was standing before you. Paul thought the guys were interesting and he wanted to help. I appreciated his fascination and while I didn't want to discourage him entirely, I also didn't have a role for him at the time and I just couldn't see him adding much to the environment. A year later, he would join the program and prove me quite wrong. Once he dived in, he worked tirelessly and with great good humor and became a solid contributor to the growth of the organization.

There was a particularly destructive notion floating amongst the spores of the West Coast those days, an idea that still has some traction in certain lofty circles. The theory is that pot is a more magnanimous and safer and altogether more benign drug than alcohol. That may or may not be so, but let me assure you that helping a drunk move from booze to gange is not exactly the swiftest rehab methodology on the block. Most of us were still drinking occasionally *off premises,* mind you, and all of us—Tony, Richard, Paul, me, and others—were enjoying a good regular smoke. Paul thought that smoking some weed with the boys might be a good way for him to get closer to them. I warned him that that was a dangerous idea. I couldn't offer much of a solid explanation when he would ask, "Why?" It was just an instinct that the mix of Paul and Richard or Tony and high-powered marijuana was not a great idea. Brilliant. What insight.

One evening, I arrived back at the house at about seven. Paul was lying on his back on the living room floor. Richard was sitting on top of him. Richard had his knees pressed firmly into Paul's chest and shoulders. There were bags of pot scattered about the rug and Richard was clearly drunk. Paul was crying and Richard was laughing maniacally. Oh, yes. One other small detail. Richard had a large knife in his right hand and he was waving it in front of Paul's throat. That would explain the crying part.

In my pressing urgency to help, I had conveniently tucked aside the reality that Richard's two best friends were a bottle of booze and a knife.

I tapped Richard on the shoulder. "Very nice, Richard. Get off."

"Hahahaha…"

"Yes, that's very funny. You've scared the little white boy. You're very scary. Now get off." What made me think I had the moral authority or the weight of our friendship allowing me to speak like this? When I look back on a moment like this from the vantage point of forty years, I don't understand how I summoned either the balls or the sheer stupidity to behave like this with such confidence.

Somehow Paul and Richard had engaged one another in the buying and selling of dope. Like these seemingly friendly and harmless negotiations often go, this one turned Deep South and Richard decided to let his Mr. Hyde out for an evening stroll. The happy result was the scene I had just entered. Richard rolled off Paul's chest. Paul crawled to his feet, grabbed his spoils, and heading to the door, tried to offer through his tears some explanations.

"It's OK, Paul. Just go home and don't try this again. You really don't know what you're dealing with." Did I know what I was dealing with? I must have believed that I did.

Richard quickly hurried off somewhere and when I saw him the next day he was sober as a judge. Dr. Jekyll had returned and all was well. Although, not for long. A few weeks later, I walked into the house and headed for the kitchen. I found Richard merrily destroying a large bottle of whiskey. I picked the bottle off the table, marched to the front door and, with all possible operatic flourishes, threw the half-full bottle smashing to the street. Richard just howled. Funny! He was a killer and I was some kind of social worker. He moved to the living room and collapsed in hysterics on a sofa. I told him to get lost. "We have a house rule. You broke it. Hit the road. Come back when you're sober." This pathetic litany went on for some minutes while he laughed.

Laugh at me?

I snapped and lunged at him. My fists bounced off his face three times. He was thoroughly unscathed and unimpressed. He rose very slowly to his feet. His face was a deranged smiling plaster cast. There were purpose and deliberation in his every move. He had almost killed me once before. Now, there was no question. He was going to finish the job.

Just as he reared back to begin his assault, Tony, Alvin, and Skinny Willy appeared from nowhere and, imitating a trio of skilled middle linebackers in a championship game, dropped Richard at once where he stood. Where had they come from? I didn't even know they were in the house. Why did they rescue me? Richard fought viciously, demonically, but the other three men overpowered him and threw him wholesale down the front steps.

I expected him to come rushing headlong back in to the house and create utter havoc. Instead, to my astonishment and no small relief, he looked at us with great sadness and skulked off down the street, like the great wounded grizzly he was. Not so much physically knocked off his stride as shamed by this show of force against him and deeply disappointed in his young friend, David. He looked abandoned and betrayed.

I didn't sleep very well for the next few nights, convinced that Richard would return and that I would be terribly harmed. This man was a Quasimodo. He was a deformed, hulking, terrified man; a killer, a drunk, a violent child lost in this violent world. He was also a castoff who had shown glimpses of tenderness, kindness, and love.

We never saw him again.

The next year I learned that Richard Sims had been killed in a knife fight in Prince George.

6 just sign on the dotted line

One thing had become clear. Ownership was the key.

We had now rented two separate houses since we began this experiment in January. Both places were pleasant enough and centrally located, but they weren't ours. Somehow, we needed that sense of having the title in our hands. Today, economists, like Hernando de Soto, will argue that the issue isn't whether Nike pays people a dollar a day to make $200 sneakers in Asia. The issue is whether they invite those workers to be part of the invested ownership. Give everybody a stake in the company, and work, morale, productivity, and profits will climb.

Here we were at the end of our first year, 1967, and we had had a glimpse of how we might continue. The structure that was to spring forward a year later was hardly in place at this time, but a feeling of coming to grips with the issues was there. We knew instinctively that we could make this program work and that, properly managed, it could serve many people well. Renting was out. Everybody was adamant. We simply had to own a piece of property. It had to be something we could call OURS.

Sometimes, to maneuver successfully through urban traffic, you have to head west for a block or two before turning abruptly and heading east as you intended all along. Jets leaving the Vancouver International Airport for Europe do exactly that several times a day, lifting off over the Gulf of Georgia and banking as they climb until you are settled comfortably in your seat with the set path due east and north.

We disbanded. The small group that had survived the melodramas and traumas of the first year agreed that we would leave our last rented house, go our separate ways for a few months and only come together again under a roof that had an ownership deed attached to it. There was a great risk inherent in this strategy. Momentum is everything. What if nothing developed? What if interest and enthusiasm flagged? I had good reason to fear that people might disperse, taking with them the future of our little enterprise. And where on earth were we supposed to find the money to buy a piece of real estate?

Richard was long gone. Tony moved in with his girlfriend, a blonde bombshell who was grooming him for greater things. Within a few years, we would see Tony sporting a red beret gracing the cover of a national news magazine and being hailed as "Mr. Red Power." All of the other house members disappeared into the mist.

All except Jimmy.

James Damon Augustine, like Richard Sims before him, was a Carrier Indian from Fort Fraser, B.C. No two people could be more unalike—at least on the surface. Jimmy was warm and charming and lovable. There seemed nothing dark or threatening or violent about him. It's true that he was an ex-con, true that he had returned to civilized life from the bleak shadows of the B.C. Penitentiary only recently. Make no mistake about it—he wasn't in stir on a research project. Like everyone else, he was doing time for some grievous crime. The details remained sketchy. There was a robbery. Someone was hurt. Jimmy is in a hotel room. The alarm bells ring and suddenly he's on the run. He's caught, charged, tried, and convicted. He does three years and then gets out on parole. Who knows what really happened?

His version went something like this.

"I got six years for Breaking and Entering. It was just the wrong hotel room. I went through the wrong room, that's all. The judge's sister owned the hotel. I was looking for this girl, Reevee, and because I was a little pissed and maybe I thought I was in love or something, I got this bright idea to shimmy up the back wall of the Canada House, and all these balconies, you know, looked alike, so…So I climb through this sort of patio door and this guy's sitting on the edge of the bed screaming bloody murder that I'm trying to rob him. Parka salesman. And the squaw who's blowing him doesn't even look up. Just tends to her work. You know, what injuns are always doing—servicing the white man. So this fool decides that she and I, we're a team and the whole thing's a set-up, right? Course, I don't know her from Christ, but by the time I shut him up and get past the front desk in the lobby, I'm on the Ten Most Wanted list. The Mounties, you know, not too subtle up in Prince George. They get off about five or six rounds and that was that."

You would never guess his history from his manner. His energy and his laugh and his smile were positive and utterly disarming. There are criminals who exhibit much of the same presentation, who are, in fact, sociopaths. Their smile and their charm are the hooks by which they conduct all of their compulsive bait-and-switch magic tricks. While they are tickling your balls with their left hand, the right is holding the shiv that is slipped so knowingly exactly between the fourth and fifth ribs. You never see it coming and you're enjoying the party enormously until you realize, too late, that you've just been had. This was not Jimmy. He was a genuine learner and a seeker. James Damon Augustine really did want to know what was going on around him. He really did want to know what made the world tick.

Where Jimmy was like Richard, where he was like almost all the men and women we were to meet over the years was this: He lacked internal structure. Where most reasonably successful adults have a sense of mission or ambition, large or small, the addicts, alcoholics, and ex-convicts with whom we worked had little or no focus. Without their gang-who-couldn't-shoot-straight or the Keystone Kops chasing them, they literally didn't know what to do next. The truly desperate cases went even further. They had no core, no substantial center. In later years, I would be warned by a famous psychoanalyst, Fritz Perls, known as the Father of Gestalt Therapy that, "if you are doing a dream workshop and the subject person speaks repeatedly of emptiness—empty streets and houses, for example, you must move on to another person. This one has no identity!"

One autumn night, Jimmy and I were driving back to

the second rented house on 6th Avenue. Jimmy was talking about a girl he was crazy about and all of the problems, real or imagined, that came with that territory. I listened valiantly for a while, but soon had to admit to myself that I was bored silly. What in god's name was he going on about? He didn't even know this girl? We parked across the street from the house and got out of the car. I walked over to the boulevard and picked up a very large, very wet maple leaf. Before Jimmy could see it coming, I lightly slapped the leaf across his face several times. Thwack, thwack, thwack.

He laughed. "Hey, what're you doing?"

"No, Jimmy. What are *you* doing?" I picked up a pile of wet maple leaves and thrust them into his hands. He felt them and then rubbed them in his hands as a child would until they all sifted back onto the lawn. "Give me your hands," I said.

"What?"

"Just give me your hands." I took his hands and placed them around the broad rough trunk of the tree. "Here, Jimmy. This is a tree. A maple tree. Those are leaves. These, under our feet, these are also leaves, maple leaves from this actual tree. Do you know where you are? Do you have the faintest idea? You've been out of prison for—what now? A week, ten days? *You are still in prison, Jim.* You don't have a girlfriend. You're not getting laid. But you're babbling on and on about some fairy princess you've been dreaming about for the last few years. You aren't in the least *here* in the present. Is this some monologue you used to tell your buddies in the prison yard? This is classic cellblock talk. It is pure bullshit and wet dream land. Wake up, man! You have to figure out how to stay out of jail. And to do that, you're going to have to have your wits about you. You gotta be sharp, awake. So cut the crap and get in touch with reality, will you?"

Cruel? Presumptuous? Maybe that and more. But it did the job. At least for that moment, and perhaps a day or two more. James Damon Augustine was a life-long dreamer. He could manage a few days or a few hours of concentration at a time, but he always came back to some interior life of his own. He once told me that his all-time favorite moment in the movies came from Dr. Zhivago. "Remember when he was in the train and he had nothing. He's lying on his stomach in this cattle car and he's peeking though the boards. The train was rolling across Russia, Siberia maybe, and outside it was just clear, white snow as far as you could see and he smiles because, even in misery, you can always find great beauty, you know?"

Of course, he also had a broad and sometimes vicious sense of humor. There was a time in Canada when movie theatres played "God Save the Queen" at the end of the evening after the last film was shown. On one occasion, Jimmy and I went to see Richard Brooks' great film version of Truman Capote's monumental book, *In Cold Blood*. The last shot of the movie is the moment when the killer, Perry Smith, drops through the hangman's trap door to be executed. The screen went black, then blank. The lights came on in the theatre and "God Save the Queen" began playing over the sound system. Jimmy burst into hysterics. I confess it took me several seconds to realize what he was laughing at and to appreciate his sweet maverick sense of irony.

· · ·

We abandoned house number two and Jimmy and I and a couple of other guys made what we hoped would be a temporary move into an old beat-up place in the East End. We thought we'd just sit out the winter until we magically came up with the keys to the new kingdom—a place of our own. We survived Christmas and New Year's without much incident. I had to struggle on a daily basis to figure out what to do that would in any way advance our cause. I wondered every day why I was drawing even this modest salary when we were accomplishing so little and what the future might hold for this funny little project?

Then in the spring, a small miracle happened.

Vancouver City Savings Credit Union, today Canada's largest credit union, was in 1968 about twenty years old and just beginning to feel its real strengths. The General Manager of Vancity was an extraordinary man named Don Bentley. He was a brilliant administrator, who was described in his official biography some years later "as an energetic humanitarian with a deep compassion and understanding for his fellowman and relating to people from every walk of life." Bentley had persuaded a number of well-heeled founding member investors to create a kind of social fund that would reach out into the community to help seed new and unusual social initiatives.

Well, if we didn't qualify, who did? Geoff Cue put a proposal on Don Bentley's desk and we were back in business. Suddenly, we had been gifted $5,000, which in 1968 was a heck of a lot of money, and certainly enough to secure a down payment on a house.

We found a beautiful, old, wood frame Victorian house at

1155 West 7th Avenue. Not a mansion, but hey, it was ours, and with a full basement and five bedrooms we might be able, in a crush to hold fifteen or more people. Ha! To add to our good fortune, the local Lions Club gave us a $3,000 loan, which allowed us to buy an option on an almost identical house next door at 1145 West 7th. Years later, as the Fairview Slopes became a très chic neighborhood, that second house would become the recording studio for the great vocalist, k.d.lang.

All of this had been unimaginable only a few months ago. Now, the very thing we had hungered for was a reality.

We moved in to 1155 and went to work. Soon, we found more money, exercised the option on the house next door and quickly filled 1145 with more resident clients.

It is said that life is what happens while you're making plans. Well, we didn't have many clearly formed plans, which was probably a good thing, because life was about to jump in from several directions at once.

. . .

Even before we had become property owners, we realized that we needed to legally incorporate the society. So we needed a name. Everybody wanted The Indian Post-Release Centre Society. Everyone except me. I thought it was a mouthful, unmanageable. But we were still at that point where I defined myself as "the helper," certainly not the leader or the boss, so it was not my place to make big decisions. We were stuck for the moment in that lovely, ineffective wasteland called consensus. So The Indian Post-Release Centre Society it was.

We filled out the necessary forms and sent them in to the appropriate government agency.

A week or so later, we were advised by return post that our chosen name, The Indian Post-Release Centre Society, was not acceptable to the Registrar of Companies. Not acceptable? Why not? Isn't this a democracy? Can't you choose a name for your company or society without the interference of some obscure government mandarin?

We made an appointment and took the half-day journey (drive, ferry boat to Vancouver Island, drive some more) over to Victoria to see the Registrar. There were Tony and me and two young resident clients who had attached themselves to the project in recent weeks.

The Registrar spoke to us as if we were kindergarten children. "Now, boys, this is just not a go, The Indian Post-Release Centre Society. I mean I'm sorry but that just sounds like Indian Prostitute."

"That's right." Tony laughed and flashed that wicked smile of his at the Registrar of Companies, that look that said, "Buddy, you just don't get it and you're never gonna get it, are you, you poor dumb schmuck?"

"That's right?"

"Yes, we *are* saying Indian Prostitute. That's the whole point, sir. I mean there *are* Indian prostitutes, very many Indian prostitutes. And Indian guys committing crimes. I was one such guy, and I was sent to jail many times. And now, I am not in jail. I am in The Indian Post-Release Centre Society house and I am going straight. So what we're doing, sir, is we're just calling a spade a spade, if you see what I mean."

"That may very well be, young man, but it still sounds awful. And I won't allow it."

"But, it *is* awful, sir. The reality is awful. That's the whole point! And if I want to call myself Betty or George, what the hell business is it of yours?"

"It's entirely my business, young man! That's my role here. I'm the Registrar of Companies."

"I'm the Registrar of Companies. I'm the Registrar of Companies. Big poop!"

I jumped in with what I thought might be a timely solution. "Look, how about the Leonard Nanaquiwitung Society?"

"Excuse me?"

"The Leonard Nanaquiwitung Society. How would you feel about that?"

The Registrar practically assaulted his fountain pen with excitement and relief. He began to write. "Leonard Nan…"

"Nanaquiwitung."

"How would you spell that?"

"N-a-n-a-q-u-i-w-i-t-u-n-g."

"…u-n-g! Yes, lovely. Nice ring to it. And who was Mr. Nanaquiwitung? Was he a great legendary chief? I think that would be wonderful to honor a revered leader from the past. That would be most appropriate."

"No doubt."

"So who was he, or is he?"

I turned my head and nodded at a nineteen-year-old boy, sitting behind me who just a few days ago had been released from Haney Correctional Institute. "That's Leonard over there."

Tony and the boys collapsed in hysterics. The Registrar

glared at me in disgust. Who likes to be the butt of bad jokes? In his own office yet! In front of The Unwashed, for god sakes!!

A few weeks later, we were granted full custody of the name, The Indian Post-Release Centre Society. Lucky us.

. . .

Shortly after we moved into the first house we owned in 1968, I challenged everyone to come up with a new name for the organization. "Look, the name we have now is just fine. I mean it's fine as a legal name or as something to describe what we're doing, but it's impossible to say. Try saying The Indian Post-Release Centre Society really fast three times. It takes a week to say it and it's completely unmemorable. We need something that people can latch on to right away. We need a name that they've never heard before, something really different that sticks to the roof of the mouth like peanut butter."

It couldn't have been more than a week later that Dawn, one of the young women in the program, approached me with a book in her hand. The book may have been the only copy of a Kwakiutl/English dictionary in existence. The Kwakiutl Indian Band has lived on the northeastern shores of Vancouver Island since time immemorial. Their language, almost driven into extinction by the arrival of Europeans, was being rediscovered and taught anew to their own people.

Dawn was part of the recent influx of new people to join our merry band. Since we opened our new home on West 7th Avenue and put out the word that we were in business, almost a dozen men and women had moved in. They were all

Native Indian and they had all been in some kind of hot water or another with the law. (This project began with Aboriginal men and, while it went through many shifts over the years in terms of resident client ethnicities, today, in its present form in Manitoba, it is almost 90 percent Aboriginal.) Dawn was a short, sexy, and attractive girl in her early twenties who had arrived at our front door with her common-law partner John. John was tall and slim and movie star handsome. He was polite and warm and pleasant, helpful in every way. Yet he gave off the unmistakable air of the proverbial used-car salesman, and a bit of the rounder. You always had the feeling that, John, no matter how sweet he was being at any given moment, was just a hair's breadth away from selling you something…or punching you in the ribs.

Dawn was equally warm and pleasant and accommodating. Yet in her case, you had the sense that she had only recently extricated herself from some dreadful tragedy.

Those of us who remembered the twenty-four-hour group marathon with Dr. Pulos were anxious to bring the experience forward to our new environment and somehow make it a part of our daily ritual. We began by establishing a one-and-a-half-hour session in the evenings, three times a week. None of us was a qualified expert at anything. None of us could boast the alphabet soup after our names that would legitimize such serious work. We were simply, naïvely perhaps, crazily determined to create an environment that would help ex-cons remain "ex."

Only a few days earlier, Dawn had been on the Hot Seat in one of our first attempts to run the regularly scheduled encounter groups that we were later to call The Game.

Dawn was telling us her life story. People in the circle were listening and listening hard. In time we were to learn by experience that no matter who was on the hot seat, the real focus of the group was The Group. Everything said and felt ricocheted around the room and resonated with people in surprising ways. Within a year, as the program expanded rapidly in numbers of people and in complexity and sophistication of activities, we would teach group leaders to watch the entire circle at once. Yes, concentrate fully on the person who is speaking. Listen not only to the words, but also to the sound of the voice. Watch the gestures, the body language. And at the same time, be a human radar machine. Let your gaze swivel around the room. Observe the reactions of all the other players, some startlingly visible, some a tiny flash in the eyes. Get in touch with "the group gut." What amazing experts our people became. They were the best therapists I ever observed.

At one point in her narrative, Dawn said something that seemed particularly self-defeating and I responded with an accusation that came entirely out of thin air.

"Well, that's exactly the kind of thing we'd expect from someone who's been raped by her own brother." To this day, I have no idea why I said that. I had no information of any kind to suggest it, and, all these years later, it seems like a brash and cruel thing to say.

Dawn turned absolutely pale and ran out of the house. Her boyfriend, John, chased her down the street. I remember clearly the tenderness he offered her standing out on the sidewalk in the early evening. This was a big, tough guy who had done federal jail time and here he was looking for all the world a kindly uncle or grandfather comforting the forgotten child. John brought her back to the house, shaken and sobbing. She took her place again in the circle and unraveled more of the dreadful story of her childhood. Everyone listened with great respect. In all the years I was to do this work, I found the same thing: when people speak honestly and from the heart, everyone truly listens. We seem to know instinctively when the bullshit has ended and the real goods have arrived. Everyone responds with due respect and love.

Dawn wanted to know how I had learned this part of her shameful personal history. "Who told you?"

"Nobody, Dawn. Who could tell me?"

She looked around the room. "Nobody. Nobody even in my family knows. So…?"

"I don't know. I just looked at you at that moment and I *saw* it."

From that incident on, I acquired the reputation of being a kind of witch, a magician who could see right through you. Of course, nothing could be further from the truth. I was a person with good natural instincts and a strong desire to communicate. Put those together and you might believe that I knew something. In fact, as I proved with comical regularity by making mistake after blunder after error, I didn't really know much of anything. I often just happened to be in the right place at the right time.

Oddly, this peculiar encounter, which might easily have ended disastrously, brought Dawn and me closer together. Even John, who might easily have become angry with me for "attacking" his wife, was more direct and up front with me after this evening. Several months later when the two of them moved out to an apartment of their own, the three of us remained friends.

Now, here was Dawn with her Kwakiutl dictionary stepping up to the plate for our contest to find a new name for our organization. "How about this, Dave? There is a wonderful word in my language, 'Kalay.' It means 'path.'"

"Put an 'X' in front of it and you've got something. 'X-Kalay—The Unknown Path.'"

"I knew you were going to say that." No question about it. Dawn and I had some strange psychic connection.

And that is literally how we found our name. The X-Kalay Foundation. The Unknown Path. Our logo was a black square around a white square, denoting a community within a community.

The name did exactly what we wanted it to. People may have mispronounced it or misspelled it, but they all remembered it. Above the door of the Shell Service Station we were to acquire two years later was a discreet white plastic sign that said, "The X-Kalay Foundation, Proprietor." Outside on the street were sandwich boards with the name, X-Kalay, proclaimed in bold type. "Come in and get gassed up by a junkie!" This was the seventies and the age of the bumper sticker. Thousands of local vehicles sported a sticker that said simply, "X-Kalay is..." People would ask, "Is...what?" And we'd say, "Come over to a Saturday Night Open House and find out." All of the businesses we began in 1969 and 1970—our beauty shop, our pen advertising company, our pizza restaurant, and our hotel on Salt Spring Island—they all waved the X-Kalay banner proudly and each business handed out X-Kalay corporate brochures vigorously. Every judge and courtroom and parole and probation officer came to know the name, X-Kalay, as, we suspect, did every street junkie. Certainly, the name became a staple to all the media, as X-Kalay appeared with great frequency in the newspapers and magazines and on radio and television. We gave the media great lead stories and controversies and all we had to do was call and they responded.

What's in a name? Everything.

7 blood on the walls

"Tom slashed."

The 'Tom' being referred to was Tom Tonquil, a very intense, very handsome Indian with a macabre, dark sense of humor. On the day he cut both his wrists, I had already known him for almost a year.

Richard and I first met Tom in the William Head Penitentiary, just outside of Victoria, only a few months after Richard and I had begun to work together. William Head is a minimum-security federal prison in a most beautiful and pristine setting right on the water facing Juan de Fuca Strait. It is a favorite jail for attempted escapes. Swimming or paddling away, although rarely successful, must be awfully tempting because it is tried with comic regularity. Not quite Alcatraz, but a jail nevertheless.

When Richard and I arrived for this interview with Tom, we got the expected befuddled and hostile looks from the prison staff. What is this? One little kid and one dangerous hombre? Are they kidding? An interview?

Of course, an interview was hardly what we had in mind. Tom's name had been given to us from Charlie Wass and the Native group in the Pen. He looked like a good prospect for our project. As would happen over and over again when I appeared in a prison setting, some helpful classification officer would rush to tell me all about the person or persons I was visiting. File and case history in hand, the prison worker would be ever so anxious to share with me all he knew about this fellow or that girl. I understand the officer's desire to be helpful. But, like anyone else, I have my quirks and one of them is that I don't want pre-information in front of me when I am meeting someone new. I appreciate that common sense assures you that it is probably a good thing to know if the person in front of you is really a serial killer or a doctor or a cellist. I am usually not interested. For the first encounter, I want no information in front of me other than the human being I am about to meet. I want nothing to prejudice my instinctive, natural response. I've maintained this attitude through my entire working life. If you tell me that the producer I am about to work with in radio or television is an asshole and I won't really like him, my auto-response is, "Thanks. Why don't you let me be the judge of that?" At concerts, I don't read program notes. Mozart is either going to speak to me tonight or he isn't. Ditto art galleries. Whatever those helpful little notes on the wall next to the paintings may say, I'm either going to get Jackson Pollock and Barnett Newman or I'm not.

One occasion a few years down the road was particularly funny. I was standing in a hallway in Matsqui Penitentiary, in the valley east of Vancouver. This was a maximum-security lock-down that went through numerous incarnations as Corrections Canada in its infinite wisdom toyed with approaches, inmates' lives, and the safety of the community. Under one hat, it was filled with women; under another it was the Regional Psychiatric Somethingorother. I will never forget sitting in the office of the headman during the "psychiatric" phase. He was a doctor, a psychiatrist, of course, and he was explaining to me patiently and in great detail that this was not a prison at all. It was a hospital, don't you know. I turned my head to the left, looked up at the bars on the windows and said, "Gee, Dr. Roy, it sure *looks* like a prison."

The day I was standing in the hallway at Matsqui, waiting to begin a group meeting with some inmates, the inevitable eager classification officer was hovering beside me rattling off a litany of crucial information. The steamy details were flying quickly in one ear and out the other.

Suddenly, this stalemate was broken by the surprise appearance of an inmate shuffling along the hall, someone that I knew quite well. Gary Cowan had been a resident client at X-Kalay for almost ten months. He was brilliant, with a measured IQ somewhere in the stratosphere. He was a black kid of about nineteen. He was funny and likable and a superb athlete and, as Dr. Perls had warned about some people, Gary was completely without a core identity. Hence, he was also a shiftless drug addict. When we first met Gary, his gorgeous mother had been hot in the middle of a secret tryst with a local politician. Gary himself was lovable, for sure, but a certifiable fuck up. Maybe you know such a person.

The time of this incident was the early 1970s, when we had grown to 125 resident clients in British Columbia and another hundred in Manitoba. I had no idea that Gary was back in stir. As far as I knew, Gary had been devoured by a whale or was writing his Ph.D. at Queens' College, Cambridge. All we could do once someone split from our little world was wish him or her luck.

What made this encounter in the prison hallway so funny was that Gary did not interrupt me and the prison staff by saying, "Hi, David. How are you?"

No, instead, in an uncannily perfect throaty impression of Eddie "Rochester" Anderson, Jack Benny's radio and television valet and sidekick for so many years, he said, "Oh, Mistah Berner! How are you? So good to see you, Mistah Berner, suh!"

Without missing a beat, I slapped my left palm on my cheek, and in my best Jack Benny, replied, "GA-ry! What are you *doing* here?"

Gary and I were terribly impressed with our own great good humor and we collapsed in howling laughter. The classification officer simply could not compute the scene that had just played out before him. He wandered back in the direction of his office muttering mystical incantations.

When Richard and I took the ferry over to Vancouver Island and drove out to the tiny community of Metchosin to see Tom Tonquil at William Head Penitentiary, there were no spontaneous comedy routines. Richard was never going to win the Bob Newhart award and Tom himself was a simmering kettle. Emotions of every kind, mostly dark, often hysterical and panic-driven, were always bubbling along just below the surface, so he was not someone you might quickly forget.

Ex-convicts, like most human sub-groups and minorities,

have a secret language all their own. Often that language is unspoken. In a glance or a nod, two men can size each other up, determine if they are of any use to one another and agree, in a silent conspiracy, to hold off for another day words that might otherwise be said. Tom and Richard glanced quickly and dismissively at one another. Richard closed down and Tom focused all his energies on me. He went on for ten minutes about all his parole plans. They were glorious and letter perfect. Over the years, I would come to hear hundreds of these stories, each an intricate little fairy tale designed like all good Disney epics to dazzle and amaze.

One winter afternoon a few years later when I was spending a few weeks at our Winnipeg facility, a guy started talking to me in the library. He didn't know who I was and the only thing I knew about him was what he told me. He was out on a three-day parole, sent to us to be in our care, and he had a marvelous plan for his full-time parole. He was going to stay at home every night with his wife and three kids and be a terrific husband and father. All the time he was telling me this, his right leg was bouncing up and down like a jackhammer.

"Cut the crap, will you?" was my warm and friendly take. "Look, buddy, that so-called plan is so full of holes you could drive a getaway car through it. You try to stay at home with the little lady and the brats and I give you three weeks tops before you break all the furniture, head out to the nearest pub, get ripped, start a fight, and end up back in the joint."

The guy froze.

"Now, on the other hand, you tell me that you're going to take that physique and all that nervous energy and natural born hostility, you take all that and teach kids boxing three nights a week or play hockey or do something physical and useful, you tell me you're going to do something like that, and I will personally recommend you for immediate parole."

My stock response to stories like this was born that first day with Tom Tonquil. "Hey, Tom, do I look like a parole officer? I'm just a guy like everyone else trying to get from A to B without crashing into the furniture. Forget all that stuff. If that's what it takes to get you out of this nuthouse, soldier on, buddy. But don't lay that track on me, OK? So, how the hell are you?"

Tom actually blushed. Then, he smiled. He looked relieved. The performance was ended. He could take off the clown's nose and the baggy pants and go back to being himself.

During that interlude between renting the two houses on the West Side and buying our first property on Seventh Avenue in 1968, Tom had been released from William Head and he found a job at a small logging camp near Squamish, the now rapidly growing village on the Sea-to-Sky Highway halfway between Vancouver and Whistler. Someone told me that Tom was in some kind of trouble, and I drove up to Horseshoe Bay one night to meet him. We sat in my car in the rain and talked for two hours.

Tom told me that he was going to kill himself. He told me this in the same manner that you might say you were thinking of going over to Sears to look for a good wool scarf.

"No, you mustn't do that."

"Why not?"

"Because I love you and I don't want you to die."

He looked like he'd just been hit with a brick. In time,

I would see this reaction thousands of times. In Game after Game, as people expressed their care and affection for others, those who felt undeserving of such kindness would practically go into shock. I remember one man sobbing uncontrollably. "I've never been showered with so much love and concern, and I don't know how to handle it. It's really overwhelming, just too, too much."

I didn't really know this man, Tom Tonquil, and I certainly did not know much about love. In truth, I don't think I came to grasp the first idea about love until I was in my sixties. But I felt honest and straightforward in saying to Tom on that night, "I love you and I don't want you to die." Looking back on that moment after all these years, this expression still feels right.

I grew up with my grandparents, Orthodox Jews, during the Second World War. I was born in 1942 and I saw photos of the concentration camps before I was old enough for grade school. I met people with numbers tattooed on their arms and I heard the stories. My grandparents had fled the pogroms of Russia at the turn of the century. They came to Winnipeg to escape genocide. As bleak as I could become, as depressed as I could be on occasion, the urge to Life has always remained basic to me. Survive first. Thoughts of suicide are not foreign to me. I've had them. Yet, I hate to hear people talk about suicide. I understand despair. I don't think you can be in the helping professions if you have not wrestled from time to time with the dybbuk of hopelessness. But suicide—short of someone choosing to not prolong the agonies of a fatal illness—is not an option I want anyone to choose.

So we sat and talked that night and Tom got past the

demons of another night. One more night. Sometimes that's all you can hope for.

Tom was among the first people to move into our new digs at 1155 West 7th Avenue on The Fairview Slopes. And he saved my life.

Charlie Wass, the leader of the Indian Friendship Group in the B.C. Pen, the originator of the idea that had become this living program, was released from the penitentiary to the house. He discerned at once that he had lost his power base. In prison, he was the kingpin of the group and the man who had breathed life into the embers of the inmates' halfway house dream. Here, on the outside, things were different. David, that little Jew-boy from Winnipeg, was supposed to be a volunteer, just helping us, you know. Well now, as everyone could plainly see, he was running things. Take the name, for fuck sake. Without even consulting Charlie or the boys on the inside, these bastards had abandoned their original name, The Indian Post-Release Centre Society. That was a good name. What was wrong with that? Now Charlie was a prisoner on parole to something called, The X-Kalay Society. X-Kalay! What the fuck?

I was very excited by Charlie's arrival at the house. I knew that he was a natural and charismatic leader. I was really looking forward to the contribution he was going to make in building the program. The weight of the program was often too heavy for my delicate shoulders. I welcomed the idea of someone to help soldier the load. It never occurred to me for a second that Charlie had another agenda altogether. I had also managed to conveniently forget that Charlie had a wee problem called alcoholism. Did I mention rage and violence?

It took Charlie only a few days to organize his palace coup. I walked into the waiting trap on a Saturday night. As others were helping themselves to some coffee from the huge silver percolator in the dining room, I wandered into the front hallway. Charlie Wass and two of his pals emerged as one from the basement bedrooms and attacked. They were drunk, and, in spite of their best efforts to hit me, their wild swings somehow missed their marks. I remember vividly a button flying off the front of my shirt. Oh, good. I'm a matador. Call me El Cordobés.

Tom Tonquil, the loner, the potential suicide, the gloomy dark presence from an Indian reservation in Kamloops, had been upstairs in his room. He heard something that caught his attention. Thank goodness. With one deft move, he planted his right hand on the banister, flipped effortlessly over the top and landed with a feather touch smack in the middle of the melee. Punch, punch, punch. Three quick hits. Lloyd Arnouse heard the noise and dashed into the hallway from the living room. I will never forget the sense of slow motion as I watched Lloyd make a major life decision. Lloyd looked at Charlie and his friends. He looked at me. He looked back at them. Which side? Which side? My fellow Natives or The House? Charlie or David? Past, present, future? The whole process of choice may have lasted about two seconds, yet it seemed to go on forever. And the entire dilemma played out on Lloyd's normally impassive face. Lloyd chose our side, thank goodness, and between them, Lloyd and Tom floored all three attackers. End of insurrection. Charlie and the two boys fled through the basement and out a back window just as the police came through the front door.

We never saw or heard from Charlie Wass again. That was the last time such a fight would ever occur at X-Kalay. Oddly enough, only a few months ago, forty years after the incident I've just described, I saw a small item in the local press about a man on Skid Road in Vancouver's notorious Downtown Eastside, a regular, who was making proclamations about what was needed to clean up the mess. The reports said his name was Charlie Wass and that he was a well-known local denizen.

. . .

Now, not long after the Charlie Wass uprising, Lloyd Arnouse was sitting in an armchair in the living room. Lloyd was not known for his loquaciousness; but, even for him, this set a new record for brevity.

"Tom slashed."

Not too many months later, Lloyd would make one of his short, cryptic comments that would become the stuff of X-Kalay lore. We had toyed unsuccessfully for a few months with operating a Chevron station on West Broadway. We didn't have enough manpower at the time to keep the business going for very long, but it proved to be a dress rehearsal for something that did work less than a year later.

Our friend Geoff Cue drove his powder blue Chevy wagon onto the Chevron lot. Lloyd Arnouse, all decked out in his spiffy uniform, proudly greeted him.

"Hi, Lloyd, let's fill 'er up, and also I think I'll need a new wiper blade on the driver's side here."

"No problem, Geoff." Lloyd examined the worn blade,

found the product number and disappeared into the garage. Some time passed before he emerged, with only a sorrowful shrug. "I guess we don't have that one in stock, Geoff." Lloyd looks up at the pleasant skies. He contemplates the heavens, smiles, and turns to Geoff, triumphant. "Oh well. It isn't raining now."

Talk about living in the moment!

So here was Lloyd sitting around the living room with several others on a rainy afternoon. "Tom slashed."

"Lloyd, what are you talking about?"

"It's a real mess."

John Tobin and I were up the stairs in a flash. The mirror on the old dresser in Tom's back bedroom had been shattered and there was blood everywhere. Great smears and swabs of blood decorated the carpet, the bed, the walls and what was left of the broken mirror. Tom Tonquil, who only a few days earlier had saved me from a very bad time indeed, was lying across his bed. He was in a kind of swoon; his wrists were raw, bloody wounds.

I'd witnessed this little horror show once before, when I was very young.

My mother, like all of us, was a mixed blessing. She was brilliant. She entered university at the age of fourteen and graduated with two degrees two years later. She was the only girl of her era that was invited to study Torah and Talmud with the rabbis. She was both a Hebrew scholar and an iconoclast. We ate kosher food at home, in my grandparent's home, and on Saturday afternoons, after I picked her up from one of her mysterious jobs, we ate pork chops at Josie's Grill. "Leopold Bloom ate with relish the inner organs of beast and fowl." She was a speed-reader, witty and funny, and passionate and caring, especially of infants and children. She taught school on an Indian reservation in Saskatchewan. Today my son coaches a community football team. His star quarterback and his best defensive ends are Aboriginal. Family themes? My mother taught me many great and wonderful things, hardly the least of which is the ancient invocation that goes like this:

If I am not for me, who will be?

If for me alone, what am I?

If not now, when?

She was also manic-depressive and, on occasion, suicidal. I saw her on her knees on the kitchen linoleum with blood flowing from her wrists. I was six.

Now here we were in Tom Tonquil's newly decorated red bedroom. Without exchanging a word, John and I pulled the belts from our own jeans and wrapped one around each of Tom's arms. He moaned when we tightened the belts to stop the flow of blood, and he moaned when we half carried him down the stairs and into one of the X-Kalay cars.

At the Vancouver General Hospital, emergency staff attended to Tom Tonquil with dispatch. Oddly enough, nobody mentioned the Indian Clinic or the Immigration Building. The early morning hours of the next day approached. Tom's condition had stabilized, and John and I were exhausted. We tried to plead to the hospital staff the special circumstances.

"He's a parolee, and he's just tried to commit suicide. We live only a few blocks from here, and we thought we'd go home and try to get a bit of sleep, but only if you feel confident that he's going to stay here for a day or two."

"No problem."

"The thing is we know you have a lot on your mind, lots of people, but look, here's our phone number, this is the X-Kalay Foundation, a kind of halfway house, so if for any reason, you're thinking of discharging Tom, I mean, say before noon today, just call us and we'll get right over. Because the last thing we want is for him to be wandering around, you know? But if he's sedated now, then we can catch a bit of shut-eye..."

"No, no, absolutely. You go right ahead. Not to worry, fellas."

We went back home and crashed.

At 6:30 a.m., with large, cozy white bandages adorning each of his wrists, and with no warning whatsoever to anyone, Tom Tonquil walked back into the house.

Maybe this half-drugged, naïve Indian boy from the wilds of the Cariboo had plain outsmarted the good doctors and nurses at the big city hospital. Maybe the weekend demands in Emergency were impossible, as usual. Maybe the new golden age of the modern god, communications, hadn't quite arrived.

Maybe we just had to count our blessings that he had received timely medical attention and that he wasn't sent to the Indian Clinic in the Immigration Building.

8 Sammy and the judge

Les Bewley was known locally as The Hanging Judge. Decent, broadly educated and passionate, he was nonetheless impatient with recalcitrance and stupidity. He once described plea-bargaining as "the venereal disease of the criminal justice system."

When Sam Scow was brought before him, Bewley was livid.

Sam Scow was waddly. He was a short, round Native from Alert Bay and he rolled on the outsides of his feet when he walked. Like most of the Namgis First Nations people, Sammy came from a large extended family whose livelihood was fishing. Sam was jolly and pleasant—most of the time. Like Richard and Tony and Jimmy and Tom, alcohol was the fuel that primed the Dr. Jekyll and Mr. Hyde dichotomies of Sammy's personality. Sober, he was a sweetheart. Drunk, he wasn't violent and dangerous like some of the others, but he was certainly out of control.

Now, head bowed, he was standing before the toughest judge in town.

"He was released only two days ago from the B.C. Penitentiary?"

"Yes, Your Honor."

"And now he is being charged with Theft Over Fifty?"

"He stole a tugboat, Your Worship, valued at over $50,000 and he was headed for Vancouver Island."

"Yes?"

"He lives there, Your Honor. We believe he just wanted to go home."

"Except that he crashed into Texada Island first, is that right? With somebody else's tugboat?"

"Yes, Your Honor. Drunk, Your Honor."

"Drunk."

"Yes, Your Honor."

We had just taken ownership and moved into our beautiful old house on the Fairview Slopes. I was wandering the old Police and "Public Safety" building at 312 Main Street on a Monday morning, when I ran into one of my mentors, John Webster of the John Howard Society, an organization concerned with the welfare of convicts and ex-convicts and their families.

John had built a successful career as the manager of Advance Taxi. When he learned that I had been a driver and radio dispatcher for Yellow Cabs, we became fast friends. He told me that one morning he looked in his bedroom closet and discovered that he owned twenty pairs of shoes. To John, this was a statement from the heavens that he was on the wrong path in life. He quit the taxi business and left his first marriage on the same day. He went to university to study social work and got a job with the National Parole Service in northern Saskatchewan. I never saw him wear anything fancier than clogs.

The first day on his new job, he asked his supervisor for a favor. "Give me a winner."

"What?"

"I need a winner. For my first client. I've got to start this with a home run, or at least a base hit. Give me a guy who's got a good chance of making it in real life."

When he realized that his supervisor and most of the good people at National Parole didn't have much of a connection to real life, he moved to the John Howard Society, where he happily remained to the end of his working days.

In World War II, John was stationed on a Canadian battleship not far out of Halifax Harbour. Off their starboard one morning was a German U-Boat; off their portside, an American ship. Soon the Americans were launching their best firepower at the Germans—across the Canadian boat. John and his mate were pointing their own guns at the German boat as well. After a blast whizzed past them from the American side, John turned quickly to say something like, "Boy, that was a close one." He never got to say that. The moment he turned he saw that his friend's head was gone.

John went completely berserk, swiveled his canon around, pointed at the Americans and let loose.

In quick order, eighteen-year-old Seaman First Class John Webster was airlifted from the boat to Halifax and from

Halifax to an army base in Saskatchewan, where he spent the rest of the war years playing hockey for the Canadian Armed Forces.

John was one of several wonderful mentors that I was blessed with in these first few years at X-Kalay. I was a young man and very often submerged way in over my head. I was a risk-taker, but filled with fears. I was subject alternately to melancholy and over-enthusiasm. I made mistakes by the carload. John Webster and his colleagues at the John Howard Society, Jack Lynch and Merv Davis, and, of course, Geoff Cue, championed the work we were doing and suffered hour upon hour of my angst and frequent threats to pack it in. How many afternoons did I sit in John's beat-up old Plymouth station wagon with the plywood floorboard and whine about the dreadful essential unfairness of life? John, like Geoff and Merv and Jack, would listen patiently, throw a few splashes of verbal cold water on my sorry head and send me back to the mission at hand.

On this particular, winter morning, John collared me in the hallway of the "Cop Shop."

"Hey, Berner, what're you doing here?"

"Nothing special."

"Well come with me. We're going into this courtroom. I've got a bit of a case here. Just follow my lead, OK."

I didn't know what John had up his sleeve. I also didn't know at that time that John was married to Gloria Webster, the daughter of the chief of the First Nations people at Alert Bay. He knew Sam Scow and Sam's family quite well.

Judge Bewley, as I said, was livid. His frustration was palpable. Day after day for years on end, silent, repentant natives stood before him. They faced serious criminal charges. The sober memory couldn't recall the deeds of the drunken fool. What am I doing in this courtroom, facing this angry man in black robes? I'm a good guy, no? Most had already served lengthy prison sentences. The carousel had to stop.

Bewley exploded. "But I can't keep sending these people back to prison every morning. I might as well send myself, send us all to prison for lack of imagination! There must be something else we can do! Will we never find alternatives for this madness?"

The silence had its own smell.

Bewley turned to John. "All right. Mr. Webster, then. What does the John Howard have to offer in this case?"

"Me, Your Honor? Well, nothing, really."

"Nothing? But isn't that what you're supposed to do? Come up with better ideas than sending people like this back for another round of jail time?"

"Well..." Now came one of Webster's patented carom shots, a magician's trick complete with a set-up, a sting, and a pay-off. "There is someone in the court today who might be able to help, Your Honor."

"There is? Where?"

We all looked around, myself included.

"Well, there is a young man here who is doing some very interesting work with Native ex-cons, and, with the court's permission, Your Honor, perhaps he could say a few words. David...?"

At this point in the young history of The X-Kalay Foundation, our program could hardly be described as sophisticated. But please understand that in 1968 in the city of Vancouver,

Canada, there was nothing in the way of legitimate com-
munity-based rehab work. The mere fact that we had more
than ten people living together in a house was considered
revolutionary. The fact that there were men and women was
for some observers an outrage. The fact that they were, at this
point, all Native Indians and they were living in a normal
house on a normal street and not on Skid Road was shocking
to many. At every stop on the road in those first few years,
we were challenged by doubters and naysayers. You can't do
that. Indian ex-cons living together in a house in the city?
They'll kill each other. Give it up, boy! Then you'll want to put
men and women, hookers, junkies, children, teens all under
one roof? Chaos. Insanity. That's not going to happen, kid.
Keep in mind that this was British Columbia and colonialism
was still very strong in Canada in 1968 in literature, music,
theater, and social niceties. We may have embraced American
culture in all its raucous, marvelous noise and vibrancy, but
we were still at heart members of the Commonwealth. The
Empire was a very big wheel and it moved ever so slowly.

To people in the John Howard Society we were a welcome
new player, a hopeful beacon to the future. To the National
Parole Service, depending on the individual, we were either
flat crazy or interesting. However we were viewed, there was
no question that, without our being aware of it, we were
pioneers. As the program grew in texture, range and detail
in the coming years, much would be said and debated about
what we were doing. At this point it was difficult even for us
to describe what it was all about.

My impromptu speech to the judge went something like
this:

"Good morning, Your Honor. My name is David Berner. I'm working on a sort of halfway house project with a group of men and women, most of whom have serious alcohol and drug problems. Some are ex-cons or parolees from both federal and provincial institutions. We've just moved into a marvelous old house near 7th and Oak. Now, the truth is we don't really know what we're doing just yet. We're finding our way, working on making our program a little more sophisticated every day. But, we can tell you that so far—at least this was true this morning when I left the house—everyone is clean and sober. And that means about fifteen people. We don't have any police or anyone playing cop to make sure no one is drinking or using drugs. Except that all the people are kind of looking out for each other. They all know that for most of them this is their last chance to get straightened out.

"Now, I don't really know this man, Mr. Scow. I've never seen him before Mr. Webster asked me to come into this courtroom a few minutes ago. And looking at Mr. Scow, I can't really claim that he has any redeeming social value. But I do know this for sure, Your Honor. If you send him back to prison, you will accomplish only two things and both of them are bad. First, Mr. Scow will cost this community about $50,000 in room and board. (This was 1968! Today, that bill would run closer to $250,000 when you add in the costs of construction, staff, psychiatrists, and social workers.) Second, what Mr. Scow will no doubt learn is how to be a better criminal. I haven't been at this very long, Your Honor, but my impression is that there's not much going on in prisons that is very helpful—either to the prisoners or to the community.

"So, if you let me take Mr. Scow home with me, no guarantees, but chances are it'll probably be a more productive move than the usual thing"

Judge Bewley was delighted and he sent us on our way. Next!

Sam Scow was ordered to the new Indian halfway house on one month's probation, with an injunction to return in thirty days. For the first two weeks, he smoked our cigarettes, drank our coffee, swept the front room of the house and did his best to imitate a block of cement. A pleasant, compliant, uncommitted block of cement.

A week before he was to reappear before the famous judge, Sam found himself standing in the dining room. He had been with us, at least in body if not in spirit, for three weeks and to date we had heard nothing, learned nothing about Sam Scow, Tugboat Thief. All the men and women in the program surrounded him. We were playing a game called, "Psychodrama" and Sam was "it." John and Annie and all the others had created a courtroom scene. We were going to give him a chance to rehearse his upcoming performance at 312 Main Street when he made his scheduled reappearance before the famous Hanging Judge. Sam as Sam was predictable; he hung his head in shame and confusion and uttered not a word. But then the moment came for role reversal and something astonishing happened. Role reversal usually is called for when the subject person himself raises some significant psychological question. Sam had muttered something like, "What do you want from me?" Now he was challenged to abandon his defeated Indian loser act and trade places with Lloyd Arnouse, who had been doing a passable job as the judge. Now, in the dining room of a sixty-year-old, wood frame Victorian house, silent Sam Scow became Judge Les Bewley. Damn it, he *was* Judge Bewley. And like the ingénue pushed by circumstances into the diva's gown on opening night, Sam Scow found his voice.

"You must speak up, young man. It won't do to have you standing there staring at the floor like a cigar store Indian. Come on, now. What do you say for yourself? Shall we keep sending you back to prison? Is that going to accomplish anything?"

For a moment, we all thought there was some kind of divine ventriloquism going on. It wasn't just that Sam Scow, the silent floor sweeper, was now speaking—and speaking eloquently—but also his entire demeanor had changed. Gone were the stooped shoulders and the hooded eyes. Were we seeing correctly? Instead of five foot six or seven, he now appeared to be a towering six feet tall.

The longer he spoke as the judge, the more articulate and insightful Sam became. "You are old enough now to know better, Mr. Scow. This isn't a life. Stealing, rotting in jail, drinking. You have a family, a family who cares about you. Don't you care about them, about what your family thinks about you?"

Pow! Role reversal time. Lloyd Arnouse went back to playing the judge, and Sam returned to being Sam. Only now, being himself again, Sammy Scow had a voice, a voice that nobody, perhaps even he, knew that he possessed.

"I do think about my family, sir. Yes. And I do care what they think. I…I care what they think about me. And…sir, I am ashamed." He cried very quietly for a moment. "But

I can do better, Your Honor, for sure. I don't need booze. I have many friends without booze. And I don't need those places, the penitentiary. I have a home. I can go home. I'm a fisherman. Everyone in my family, we go fishing."

We talked about that evening for weeks. None of us had ever seen anything like it. No one could have predicted it. The new Sam had arrived to stay. Sam, the granite block, had evaporated and been replaced by his angel twin, the talk show host. He was downright voluble now; we could hardly shut him up.

We went back to Judge Bewley's real courtroom at the end of the month.

Imagine the judge's surprise when nobody would come forth to speak for the defendant.

"Mr. Berner? Mr. Webster?"

We both shrugged our shoulders, as if to ask, "What do I have to do with any of this?"

Just as Bewley was about to blow a gasket, Sam Scow stood up.

For a moment, I thought the judge was going to have Sam arrested or constrained by the armed policemen in the courtroom. What's this? A Native standing up in our courtroom? What in god's name does he think he is doing?

Sam began his presentation.

"I can't say I've changed, Your Honor. I think maybe real change probably takes a long time. Yes, a long time. I've only been at the house for thirty days as you know, and I haven't really done very much. But I am sober. I haven't had a drop since I saw you last time. And I think I am learning some things. Some things about myself, and maybe what I've got to do. I'm not sure what exactly, but something. Not what I've been doing. That's no good. The people there, in the house, they're good people. They are like family. Really. They are family."

This was unprecedented. Judge Les Bewley had never before this day had an accused Native speak up for himself in his courtroom. Social workers, preachers, do-gooders, white people, they did all the talking. They made all the hopeful, false promises about the future.

"See, if you send me back to prison, well it costs lots of money to do that, lots, and I think I'll be just the same when I come out. Maybe worse. That can happen in a place like that. That's a bad place. Maybe I've done some bad things, sure. But that penitentiary, well it's a very bad place. Maybe if I stay with the house, I'll really learn something and stay out for good. It's what I've got to do. It's what I want. That's what I want to do now. Anyway, that's what I'm thinking, Your Honor,"

The Hanging Judge was crying. He sent this felon away on probation to a house in The Slopes. Sam Scow never once went back to jail.

Within a few years, Native Court Workers programs would become a staple in court rooms across the nation; but Judge Les Bewley would swear to his dying days that, in just this modest, accidental way, the seed for that great idea was first born.

9 a dozen streams; then a river

When we moved into our new digs on West 7th Avenue, most of our housemates were Native Indian male ex-convicts. There were also a few young Native women, like Dawn, the girl who had come up with our new name—X-Kalay. In addition, Paul Windham, whom we had last seen fleeing the knife and maniacal clutches of Richard Sims, had moved in. Apparently, he had not been sufficiently scarred by this traumatic incident. Something about our work continued to fascinate him; he persisted so long in trying to convince me that he had some useful role to play here, that I finally relented and said, "OK, hop aboard." He stayed with us for more than three years and did terrific work.

In the next few months and in very swift order, several things would happen that would change utterly what we were doing and give real shape to how we would approach our work for all the many years to come.

The first challenge was the arrival on our doorstep of a white—that is, non-Native—heroin addict. This man was looking for help and he thought he might find it here. Remember that this modest experiment that would soon be budgeted in the millions of dollars and cover two Canadian provinces began life in the Indian Friendship Group in the B.C. Penitentiary. It was originally incorporated as the Indian Post-Release Centre Society. Paul Windham and I were not Natives and we hadn't served any jail time, although many an ex-con over the years would swear that he knew me well on the inside. Paul and I were simply accepted as helpers, I, because I'd been there from the beginning and Paul, because I recommended him and he had been hanging around so often. Natives are by and large generous and inclusive people. They may have more than their fair share of problems and challenges, but, in my experience, they generally need make no great leaps to being open and friendly.

So what to do then with a non-Native house member? Here was a white heroin addict—a man who had done very little jail time and was, therefore, unknown to most of our ex-con residents—who believed somehow that there was something in this burgeoning program for him. Street junkie and white—would we let him dive in?

The group quickly decided that Mr. Dope Fiend could join us. Another soon followed, and another. The word had somehow spread on the street that there was this place where people were getting off heroin and staying off. That in itself was big news. Nobody had ever pulled off this amazing trick before. Addicts, clean? You gotta be kidding. Many people on the street and in corrections and in the police simply didn't believe it. Many assumed that our claim to have a clean and sober environment was, of course, a transparent front for drug dealing. What else could it be? After all, just before we began, exactly such a place had gathered headlines and been shut down. A notorious con man had opened a halfway house for addicts to much fanfare. From the beginning, he and his cohorts were both using and dealing drugs. When we came onto the public radar, people jumped to the obvious and incorrect conclusions. At one point, the RCMP sent an undercover officer into our midst. He tried to pass himself off as a drug addict in search of help. The group gut had unerring instincts. The poor fellow was exposed and laughed at in his first and last Game. After surviving an hour and a half of being alternately ridiculed and then applauded for sticking to his official story, the young policeman left the next morning. We wonder what he wrote in his official report. Was he promoted?

It wasn't long before the resident population was half white and half Native, men and women. There had been a few Native addicts, but most were alcoholics, so a double demographic shift was happening simultaneously and we were very aware of it.

Alcoholics and heroin addicts, we were learning, were very much birds of a feather in most of the basic mechanics of addiction. Loneliness, fear, and lack of self-belief were commonalities. Manipulation, dissembling, and play-acting were part of the shared coping toolbox. But there were subtle differences. Alcoholics were swingers, they were mercurial. They could be violent, funny, passionate, sexual, entertaining, weepy, self-pitying, and suicidal—sometimes within a few hours. Dope fiends, on the other hand, were often emotionally detached. They lived in the Land of Gray. They were *dis*passionate and more plotting in their social machinations. Marshall McLuhan had been talking about radio as a hot medium and TV as cool. He might just as well have been talking about drunks and dope fiends.

To make the contrasts in our resident clients even more distinct, most of our drunks were Redskins and most of our dopers were Palefaces. Make no mistake, people got along and worked together, but there was always a divide in the social fabric humming along not far below the surface.

By the third or fourth year of operation, X-Kalay was known everywhere as "that dope fiend place." Courts, probation, parole, psychologists, psychiatrists, social workers, and the street itself—the whole great borscht of the helping professions—turned to our peculiar enterprise over and over again as the place to dump the incurables.

. . .

The next big change was a redefinition of my own role in this story.

Geoff Cue and the Company of Young Canadians had hired me to help a group of disenfranchised people realize a dream. I saw my role as exactly that—a helper.

But I was an activist and a loudmouth and a white, urban, college-educated young man with ants in his pants who liked to get things done. So more often than not, I was acting in a leadership capacity. To make matters worse, I really did suffer from what Tony Lavallee had originally accused me of—my Superman Complex. Oh yes, I was often insecure and baffled and afraid and ready to hit the highway. But when the kryptonite wasn't nearby, I was convinced that I could pretty much solve any problem, leap any building in a single bound.

On the other hand, when it came time for formal structure, or for taking credit for any small thing we might accomplish, I demurred. "Oh, no. This is your project, guys. You stand for president. At most, I'll be the secretary."

Shortly after we took possession of our new house, we had a meeting and agreed on our first half-hearted rule: no drugs or booze in the house. Of course, you can't have a rule without having a rule-breaker; so within days, all hell broke loose. I had been out one evening and when I got back to the house I realized at once that several people had been smoking pot. I hit the roof. "What are you idiots doing? I thought we agreed that there would be no booze or dope in the house." It took me a few more months to understand that half-measures like these were doomed. "Doesn't anyone here ever honor his word?"

Of course, the pot people laughed. That's what you do on pot. Your arm could be falling off and you'd laugh at the spectacle. "Hey, dig this, man. My arm's falling off. Hahahahahaha."

There is simply no talking to someone who is high. You want to waste your breath talking to a drunk or a stoned addict? You go ahead. I guarantee you that the expression "in one ear and out the other" doesn't even apply. Nothing is heard, because nobody is home. You are talking to chemistry, plain and simple. There are people who give addicts heroin or methadone and claim that they then do counseling work with the buzzed client. They are more delusional than the addict. The addict, by the way, is laughing up his sleeve at the sorry Santa who is so addicted to "helping," that he hands out free poison.

I was completely frustrated. I had no idea what to do. Being the mature twenty-five-year-old that I was, I ran away. Fight or flight. Basic child behavior. I said, "To hell with you fools," and drove up to the Sunshine Coast for a few days to stay with friends. I felt that our program had reached a total impasse. I could see all our efforts dribbling out into the gutter. I had seen testing behavior before and I was to see it again many, many times in the coming years. Yet, in this instance, I lapsed into catastrophic thinking, a little trick never too far from the top in my personal grab bag of stupid coping mechanisms. Disaster. It's all come to naught. Why had we bothered to come this far?

I came back to town, desperately looking for an answer to the current roadblocks. What the hell am I supposed to do next? There must be someone who would know how to get this group of people to the next step, the place where they are truly dedicated to creating a clean and sober environment. There must be a way. I called Luis Molina, the American who had spent time at Synanon and who had recommended Dr. Lee Pulos to me the year before.

I asked Luis about the legendary Chuck Dederich. Charles E. Dederich, Sr. was the man who, beginning with a hand-ful of addicts meeting in a tiny place on the Santa Monica beach, had created this enormous and controversial therapeu-tic community called Synanon. When we had accidentally stumbled across that National Film Board movie of Daytop Centre, we were in fact watching one of a dozen offspring of the Synanon model. Today, although Synanon itself is long gone, residential treatment centers built on the Synanon therapeutic community model abound. They continue these days all over the world, in America (Daytop, Phoenix House), here in Canada (Portage and the Behavioural Health Foundation) and in Italy (San Patrignano) to thrive and produce clean and sober citizens who were formally dedicated users.

Luis had been, like many a Synanon devotee, a non-addict who found something compelling and deeply satisfying in the Synanon lifestyle, and his sense of how the intricacies of the program really worked was imbedded in his DNA.

"How did he do it, Lou? What was Chuck Dederich's secret? I've reached a stalemate. We seem to go three steps forward and two or four back."

"It's simple, David. Chuck took control. He declared himself. He had an epiphany one day and realized that he *was* the program. He gathered the troops around him one day and just told them that he was the boss and that they all worked for him. The rest is history."

You know how, amidst all the chatter, gossip, and gab that constitute our daily noise, if you are lucky once every three years or so someone says something that really pierces right through you? I felt like I was listening to Scripture coming down from the Hill. The truth of what Luis was saying was absolutely clear to me. I had been playing at helping for a year and a half now. Everyone in X-Kalay was hanging on my every belch and utterance, yet I was coyly pulling back and avoiding the responsibility of the obvious. I was the leader. It was time to step up to the plate.

"You will never move forward, David, until you do what

Chuck Dederich did. People want leaders. They don't want social workers or advisors. And the kind of people you are working with *need* leaders. They really want to take the next step, as you say, but they don't have the wherewithal to do it themselves. They need you to tell them, 'This is how it is. This is what we will do.' They are looking to you, David, for the next move. No question about it."

We were a legally incorporated non-profit society. There were certain requirements, like having regularly scheduled Board meetings, which, in itself, called for electing a president and a secretary and a slate of society officers. In our last formal Board meeting, the group had once again insisted that I be president, which, I once again refused. "This is your society, your organization. You should be the elected officers." A young man named Danny, who stayed with us all of two or three months, was elected president. No doubt he had a nice smile.

Luis Molina was absolutely right. I went directly back to the house. I called everyone together in the living room. "I have an announcement to make. As of immediately, I am the Executive Director of The X-Kalay Foundation Society. You are no longer the president, Danny. In fact, as of this minute, the entire Board is dissolved. As of immediately, you all work for me. Our lawyers will draw up the paperwork in the morning. It has been clear to all of us for some time, I think, that I have been running this program all along and that all of you basically wait for me to make the next move. Well, now that position is official. I will decide what we are going to do next, what kind of activities we offer here and who can be a member of X-Kalay. Finally, if you don't like any of this new setup or any decision I may reach, you can try hanging your hat somewhere else. Today, decision-by-committee is finished and the Benign Dictatorship officially begins. Like it or hike it, folks."

This was one of the shortest meetings we ever had.

Everyone was clearly relieved. People smiled, said, "Thank you," and went back to work.

Not so ironically, perhaps, Luis Molina moved into X-Kalay about six months later, stayed for many years, became a Foundation Director and did wonderful work in every area of the Society.

. . .

Themes and ideas seemed to be converging.

Dr. Lewis Yablonsky was in town to run a weekend work-shop at the University of British Columbia. The process was called psychodrama. Yablonsky had written a landmark book called *The Violent Gang*, during his years in New York. He was the foremost student of Dr. Jacob Moreno, largely credited as the founder/inventor of psychodrama. Yablonsky had moved to California, become a multiple award-winning professor at Northridge and become deeply involved in Synanon. He became an intimate friend of Chuck Dederich, married Donna, a Synanon ex-hooker, ex-junkie, and written *Synanon, the Tunnel Back*, the basic and original bible on the therapeutic community treatment model.

Merv Davis, my friend and advisor from the John Howard Society, encouraged me to take this workshop. Geoff Cue agreed to pay for this with Company of Young Canadians' money. The workshop ran over the course of two and a half days. There were about ninety people in a large and comfortable room on the University of British Columbia campus. Yablonsky was a big, lovable bear of a guy who brought you immediately into his world.

Here's the current Wikipedia definition of psychodrama:

> Psychodrama is a form of human development which explores, through dramatic action, the problems, issues, concerns, dreams and highest aspirations of people, groups, systems and organizations. It is mostly used as a group work method, in which each person in the group can become a therapeutic agent for each other in the group.

A central subject person is chosen to act out a personal issue or dilemma or to explore new ways of dealing with problems, challenges, and opportunities. The experience is often quite theatrical, with props and lighting being used to create a scene or change the setting or mood of the moment. The audience is completely involved. Audience members will often come "on stage" to act out not only other parts in the drama, but also other, unexpressed faces or voices of the subject person. I might become, for example, the Angry You or the Regretful You or the Sexual You. You might "play" the other man's brother, wife, or lover.

In the end, everyone present in the workshop has been given the opportunity not only to see and hear and fully experience the myriad sides and range of a psychological issue, but also to try on new, creative ways of responding to life.

In the early stages of the weekend, Yablonsky had tried to work with a renowned psychiatrist as his "subject person." This man was loquacious and oozing with manufactured charm. He was also quite powerful in local social and academic circles, often called upon by the press and the courts for his wisdom and insight. Yablonsky dismissed this crank after twenty minutes. When I asked Yablonsky a few weeks later why he had cut this man off so quickly, he said, "Oh, that guy. Completely fucking nuts. Forget it."

The key moment of this particular weekend happened in the late afternoon of the second day.

I was sitting in the front row, just barely twenty-five, still sporting my Viva Zapata moustache, long curly hair and Mexican sandals.

Yablonsky had chosen as his subject person a Presbyterian minister from the university church who said that he was experiencing a problem he'd like to explore. The man had a wife and children and a lovely, fine tapestry of a life, but he was deeply dissatisfied. His wife, he told us, was even more aggrieved with him. He lacked spontaneity and made little intimate time for them. To complicate matters, he had begun having tea perhaps a bit too often with a woman parishioner. Frankly, although he had done nothing untoward, he was smitten. To be blunt, the man was emotionally frozen. He was dead from the neck down. Everything he told us came from the cerebrum.

I raised my hand.

"Yes, David."

"May I make a suggestion?"

"Please."

"What if three marauders come into the church and perhaps threaten to run off with your silver candlesticks? Do you think you could summon up the passion to defend the church, to defend something you really love?"

Yablonsky loved this idea. But, first he made a significant adjustment. "Yes, perfect. But instead of taking your candlesticks, let's say they are going to steal away your lady friend right in the middle of one of your famous afternoon teas!"

Immediately, a woman was sitting at the front of the room next to the minister, and Lewis and I and Frank Mullally, a friend from the National Parole Service, were fluttering menacingly at the imaginary door to the church. I'm six feet tall; Yablonsky was easily six feet three inches and Frank somewhere in between.

The three of us began an increasingly obscene litany of threats.

"Hey, nice chick."

"Nice boobs."

"Real nice ass."

"I think I'm going to get me some of that."

As the invocation of verbal assaults mounted, the minister became visibly irritated, although hardly what you could describe as angry.

A chorale of disgusting possibilities rained down on him.

"I'm going to fuck her in the armpit, you useless piece of shit!"

By now, the audience was hollering for some action. "Come on, man, do something!"

"Defend that woman, you dough head!"

Lewis Yablonsky was standing in front of the seated minister, a large, red sofa cushion in his hand, matador to bull. "Come on, Reverend. Save your girlfriend. Hit the pillow."

When he finally let go, the minister hit the pillow so hard, he sent big Lewis Yablonsky flying clear across the room.

Frank and "the lady friend" and I returned to our seats.

Yablonsky caught his breath and walked over and whispered in my ear. "OK David, are you ready for the role of a lifetime?"

"Huh? Sure."

"OK. Just go with it."

Yablonsky turned to the Minister. "Well, Reverend. We have a rare opportunity for you. You've got a real problem, haven't you? You have a parish of decent people looking to you for guidance. And you have a good wife who is looking for more than a sympathetic smile over breakfast. The occasional dinner, perhaps. A movie. A convivial stroll through the neighborhood. But you feel unmoved by these demands. You know you aught to do more, to *be* more, but you feel everything is nice the way it is. Why rock the boat? Let's just keep things going the way they are."

"Right. Yes, that's right."

"All right. Well, as I said, we have a very rare opportunity for you today. Dr. Christ..."

I came over and sat down next to the minister.

Psychodrama is a fascinating process. It is a very profound kind of role-playing, with many subtle shifts and slides and techniques. But what is apparent to even the most casual observer is the hypnotic quality that overtakes the moment.

One scarcely begins to enact a possibility then the drama becomes more real than real. We slip readily through the mirror, into the make believe and take this new dream world for gospel.

"Hello, my son."

"Oh, Father." The Reverend was already completely inside the mirror.

"Thank you my son, for the good work that you are doing every day. Going out into the fields and tending your flock with care. You are truly doing the Lord's work. Bless you."

"Oh, thank you, thank you."

"But I sense there is a problem here, my son. Your people are suffering. Life is difficult. It is full of tests and challenges. Money, health, work; nothing comes easily, my son. And your people feel these pains. They need relief. They need someone who understands their suffering."

"Yes, Lord, yes."

"But for you, my son, there is no evil. Nothing is bad. Everything is sunshine and roses. Everything appears to be good. And bland. This is unrealistic, my son. How can you help your flock if you cannot sense their real suffering?"

"I know, my Lord, I know. It is a terrible deficiency. Sometimes I feel completely inadequate to the task."

"Would you like to learn? Would you like to know how to be truly of service?"

"Yes, please, my Lord, please."

"All right then. Come with me. Come with me today, now."

I took his hand. "It is cold where we are going. And foreboding. But you can get there. Climb, climb up this hill with me."

There didn't seem to be a soul breathing in the whole room. Yablonsky was staring at this tableau in disbelief.

"Come with me now to Cavalry. Close your eyes, my son; look deep, deep, deep into your own soul. Ask yourself the ultimate question."

I leaned toward the minister, my face almost touching his. His eyes were closed. I had been whispering. Now, with every power that I had, I screamed.

"FATHER, WHY HAST THY FORESAKEN ME?"

I was shaking and I could not say another word. People in the group were sobbing. Lewis Yablonsky was staring at us with a mad smile on his face. The Reverend was completely unmoved.

Later, Yablonsky would tell me that, as far as he was concerned, the minister was practically psychotic—dead and unreachable.

Yablonsky and I became great friends. I would often fly down to Los Angeles—on occasion staying with him and Donna and their son in Santa Monica—to do more psychodrama work at his studio on Fairfax Avenue. His clientele included movie stars, and it was often very strange to work with people you had been seeing on the screen for years acting out the archetypal roles of fathers and sons, mothers and daughters in a little theatre next door to a famous deli. Yablonsky always took great pleasure in introducing me to his participants. "This is my young friend, David, from Canada. He always flies down to play God for us."

Psychodrama, gestalt, and hypnosis became stock in trade for us at X-Kalay. The Game, which I will describe in a later chapter in detail, remained the central therapeutic tool for us, but these various techniques often jumped up spontaneously to help a moment along. We might be in the middle of a basic encounter group, when suddenly, acting out a conflict and its many unexplored and underlying implications, we found that we had slipped quite naturally into a psychodrama. A core operating principle over the next years was that we were not wed to any one approach, school, or technique in our therapeutic arsenal. Whatever worked, whatever seemed right at the moment was welcomed.

Now, in our second year, all of these influences were coming together, momentum was building. In addition to the Indian ex-cons, there were now many white addicts in the program. I had taken charge of the organization and declared myself boss.

And now we had brushed up against Synanon, the granddaddy of all the dope fiend programs, in several ways. At one point, Jimmy Augustine and I even drove down to Los Angeles to meet Chuck Dederich who was at the time headquartered at the Synanon facility in the Del Mar Hotel in Santa Monica. He wouldn't see us. Lewis Yablonsky, with great kindness, said, "Too bad. That's his loss."

The final piece of the puzzle, the ultimate hitch in the wagon that would propel us to the next level, was the timely arrival on our front door step of a Canadian Native Indian who was a recovering heroin addict, and, moreover, someone who had lived in Synanon for over a year.

His name was Earl Allard.

10 now you see him, now you don't

John Webster, my friend from the John Howard Society, had told me that there was this guy in town that I just had to meet. According to John, this guy might hold the Keys to the Kingdom. The guy had soaked up some personal experience with Synanon and he was looking for something to do. I was busy and the truth was I didn't really think much about the exciting possibility of meeting another new person. I was meeting new people every day. Everyone I met was a challenge, a case, a resident client, a friend, and an entirely original landscape. I needed more?

But John insisted. Earl appeared within twenty-four hours.

My first impression was "crisp." He was short and intense. He dressed neatly and conventionally. Conservative and wound up both came to mind. He looked you right in the eye. We stood in front of the house on West 7th Avenue and had a long talk. He told me how wonderful he was and how he knew just about everything there was to know about curing dope fiends. I was singularly unimpressed. I couldn't quite get a feel for this guy. The words were right, but some dissonance in the tone colored everything he said. There was that familiar mix of combat and deep need that you might find in an eleven-year-old kid who hangs around the community center every day after school, but never really engages with anyone. Choose me or fight with me—what's the message? Earl was hidden away, and I wasn't sure that I wanted to trust him.

The year was 1969 and we were the only game in town. The world of drugs, addictions, and recovery was neatly divided by the very few choices available. If you were on the street, you were using. If you were in our program, you were cleaning up. I gave Earl what was to become the standard X-Kalay response at that time to any and all addicts we might meet who were living outside of our program. "Look, Earl. You're an interesting guy, no question about it. And your experience at Synanon could be invaluable to us. On another day perhaps I'd love to pick your brain about your time down there. But, all of that is beside the point. The real issue is this. What are you doing these days? You're a dope fiend. And if you don't start working the program for yourself and for others, you'll be dead in a week. You know that. 'You've got to give it away to keep it.' Isn't that a core concept? It's not that you *want* to give us something. It's that you *have* to give us something. You need this. Your life as a righteous addict depends on moving in and getting back to the only work you have been put on this earth to do."

Less than two years later, long after Earl and I had become working colleagues and friends, we illustrated this point very effectively on another drug addict.

Earl and I were standing outside our clubhouse headquarters on West 7th Avenue during Saturday Night Open House. One of our residents rushed up to us with a hot bulletin, "Hey, Earl, Dave. Frank Burns is here!"

"Who the hell is Frank Burns?" I asked. Earl told me at once that Frank is a street junkie that Earl has known for years.

"So what's he doing at our Open House?"

"Exactly," said Earl. "Tell him to come out here. We want to talk to him."

Moments later this slim, smiling hustler appeared.

"Frank. What're you doing here?"

"Well, I'm visiting, Earl. It's an Open House, right? Everyone's welcome."

"Not dope fiends."

"No, no, I'm clean, fellas. Have been for a while." Our bemused smiles suggested we didn't quite buy his act. "No really, I am."

"We have a simple question for you, Frank."

"Anything, Dave." Why was he calling me 'Dave?' Did I know this guy? Classic addict bullshit.

"Did you clean up at X-Kalay? I mean, I don't really remember you."

"No, I...No."

"Well then you're not clean, Frank. Because we know every junkie in town and the only clean ones are the ones who cleaned up here and who live and work here. Guests at our Open House on Saturday night, welcome guests, Frank, are Square Johns. They're middle class people who want to support what we're doing or who maybe have a son or daughter here. Do you have a son or daughter here, Frank? Of course you don't. So then you don't really qualify as a visitor, do you? And you don't qualify as a clean dope fiend because you don't live here. For all we know, you're delivering smack to some misguided loser who's determined to fuck up our environment. Are you a carrier, Frank?"

"Oh, god, no. No, no, no."

"Well, you only have two choices, Frank. One is obvious. You can piss right off. Or...you see that chair in the hallway there, in the front office by the reception?"

Frank turned and looked through the broad set of windows covering the front, street-side expanse of our building. "Yah?"

"Well, the only real sane life choice you have, Frank, is go sit in that chair."

"Soon, someone will come along and take you into an interview. And, if you survive that, you can move into the Foundation and you can start living honestly as a truly clean ex-junkie. You can give up this tiresome and exhausting masquerade of pretending to be clean and living on the street at the same time, like you're some kind of unique miracle child or something. What are you, the first junkie in the history of junkies who just up and quit all by himself?"

This taunt wasn't, of course, strictly true as there has been a handful of exactly such people over the years. But, by and large, heroin addicts quit in those days because they were sent to prison (not that there isn't a good steady supply of drugs behind the walls, a supply often steadier and more reliable in quality than that on the street) or they were choked to death by an overzealous narco cop (Vancouver had one such infamous officer who was often described as totally high "on the chase"), or they overdosed. Today, the community offers a broad range of services including free heroin, methadone maintenance, clean needles and crack pipe kits, safe injection rooms, and whiskey on the hour for chronic boozers. Call me crazy, but I'll continue to believe that offering a life free of debilitating substances is a more compassionate approach. We ask our children to have healthy bodies, why not a healthy mind and spirit at the same time?

Frank sat in the chair. He moved in that night and stayed several years. I've run into him over the years and he's still an old smoothie, fast-talking salesman, and, as far as I can tell, he's still clean and sober.

On the very first day that I met Earl, when I laid this identical approach on him, he looked like he'd been slapped in the face. Who the hell was this young smart alec? How dare he talk to a righteous dope fiend like this? What I couldn't explain to Earl or anyone else for a great many years was that there was something about this setting and this work and my role that allowed me to think and speak boldly and creatively. I am rarely shy, but often in other social settings I am polite, political, and even silent. The world of addicts and alcoholics and therapy was a place I felt, and continue to feel, free to be totally self-expressive. No wonder I've enjoyed it so much!

Earl and I shook hands and said our polite goodbyes. I walked back into the house and went back to work. Frankly, I never expected to see Earl Allard again. Just as Geoff Cue never expected to see me again when I told him that I was going to Mexico and then showed up at his office months later, Earl had a surprise in store for me.

I had recently gotten married and moved out of the X-Kalay house. For the first time since the project had begun, Superman was in his private little cave. My goodness. Would the world survive? Would the center hold?

Geri was a very beautiful and smart woman and I was crazy about her. Marriage was what I think it must always be for most people—both a blessing and a very big challenge. Aside from the usual hurdles of getting to really know each other and learning how to embrace differences and idiosyncrasies, we had the test that must be familiar to doctors and other single-focus maniacs who are, before anything else, married to their work. How could I be married to both my work and my wife and family? How could she live with a guy who ate, slept, and breathed his vocation? Who would want to? I would go to work in the morning, come home for dinner and jump up promptly an hour later to head out the door and back to work, often until the early morning hours.

The inevitable solution appeared within a year of our marriage, and just in the nick of time, as it was clear that this arrangement was not going to work for much longer. While I was back at X-Kalay every night, Geri, who herself worked all day, was trying on hobbies to keep busy. She dare not think too much about her idiot husband who was off playing in his field. One night, I actually had my hand on the doorknob, leaving once again for more work after dinner. I looked back at her. I looked at the door and at my car waiting in front of the house. "Hey, Ger..."

"Yes?"

"Why don't you get on this bus with me?"

"I never thought you would want me to be involved."

Geri promptly quit her secretarial job, sold her car and became deeply involved in every aspect of the X-Kalay Foundation. She was amazing. And her qualifications were similar to mine—none. Unless you count a rich personal life experience, street smarts, overflowing energy, and a passion for building something that was making a real impact on people's lives.

In addition to being a natural, instinctive therapist and role model, she was easily twice the businessperson that I was. People adored her and followed her about like puppy dogs. She was also a feminist and she significantly changed the working and living environment of the Foundation to provide equalities of every kind for the women in program. She created, among other things, our landmark daycare program for the many infants and children that were to become a regular feature of our resident populations, and the Kirkus, which was a kind of quiet refuge for women in the program. (Men were verboten. So, to this day, I really have no idea what went on in there.) She also started and ran our beauty salon, one of our most successful client-run businesses. The eight years we worked together, bound by common purpose, were the best years of our marriage. We separated and divorced in 1986, but that is entirely another story.

When I got home later the same day I first met Earl, there he was lying on the sofa in our living room, reading the paper. He had asked someone where I lived and they had stupidly told him. He had knocked on our door, introduced himself to my wife, and she had invited him to make himself comfortable in the living room until I got home. I remember vividly that he still had on his black Oxford shoes. I remember those shoes because they defined one important part of his complex personality: the militaristic, by the book, my-way-or-the-highway side of his character that was often, for good or bad, at play.

Thus began three years of Earl and three years of enormous corporate growth at X-Kalay.

Earl stayed for dinner with us and then he moved into the X-Kalay house that night. He immediately dived in to every aspect of our work. He was tireless and determined. He was alternately stern-faced and raucously funny. He was by turns autocratic and child-like. He became my lieutenant.

Our relationship would have made good material for a PhD thesis. I'm not sure what I was for him, but for me Earl was an intricate cocktail of friend, confidant, brother, son, and father. He threw ideas at me by the dozen, most of which I was happy to adopt, most of which went straight into the environment and became a part of everyday life at X-Kalay. We were like a pair of echoing magpies. Half my sentences in those days began with the phrase, "Well, Earl says..." And whenever Earl wanted something done and done right smart, now if you know what's what, he'd start his pitch with "David says..." I picked his brain relentlessly about the Synanon methodology. He was always aware of status and protocol and was very careful to have me, as Executive Director, enact new policy. Keep in mind that I was still in my mid-twenties and Earl was almost ten years older than me. I suspect he saw me as a kind of "little genius." I'm also certain that many resident clients thought that I was a kind of puppet Othello to Earl's Iago. Tough as nails with those below him, with me he was too often fawning and obsequious.

It's hard to convey how deadly serious and passionate we were about our mission. Over the next several years, Earl, Luis, Paul, Geri, and I and many others as they developed within the program, would stay up half the night discussing exactly how we could best help this guy or that girl. "Yes, but if we do that, won't he think..."

"I disagree. I think our best plan of action with this sucker is to..."

The give and take between us was exhilarating. All of us, even Earl with his doctrinaire mind-set, were open to exploring new ideas if we thought they might help in a given situation. We were a living laboratory of human behavior. The shared sense of being on to something special was palpable. We were NASA; we were on the cutting edge. So many evenings, we would say goodnight to one another with the tiniest of smiles, as if to say, "You know, I think we've hit on something tonight. This is good. This will work."

Earl's insight into dope fiend manipulations was encyclopedic. His knowledge was matched only by his marvelously self-deprecating humor. Here is his favorite story of being a charter member of *The Gang Who Couldn't Shoot Straight*.

"I was living down on Skid Road, doing my petty criminal thing. One day, we figured out that we had landed easily the biggest score ever. We were going to be rich; we'd be in smack heaven for at least a week. We had learned the location of a show room for a major importer of expensive Italian shoes. Right in the alley there, behind the Ovaltine Café, you know? Better yet, there was a skylight on the roof. Easily accessible—practically an open door. What a gift! We shimmied ourselves up onto the roof. It was only a second story job, which was a good thing because we weren't exactly cat burglars, you know? Pry the skylight open and lower ourselves into this showroom. Man, gold! Hundreds and hundreds of expensive leather shoes. This'll easily fetch ready scratch on the street. So we go to work. We're heaving shoe after shoe up and over the skylight and down into the back lane. We're hysterical. This is the best number we've ever pulled. Finally, we're out of there, we're away, we're down on the ground, no one's the wiser and we haul our catch up to our digs in the Sleazoid Arms. Now, we start adding up the tally.

"Oh, my god! Small catch.

"This is a showroom, right? The shoes? *They're all lefts!*"

. . .

With Earl's intimate knowledge of what made Synanon tick, we finally adopted the single biggest policy that would define X-Kalay forever.

The Two Rules

No chemicals of any kind at any time anywhere as long as you are a part of the program.

No violence or threats of violence.

That's it. Two simple imperatives from which all else flowed.

This is a safe and clean environment and you carry it with you wherever you go. The moment we adopted these two inviolable rules, X-Kalay became a civil society. No chemicals meant everything. No aspirin, Aleve, Tylenol, pot, weed, gange, junk, smack, heroin, H, crack, meth, beer, booze, whiskey, or wine. It meant everything, tutto, the lot. If you had a headache, you would have to ask someone for clearance on a pain reliever. We had both a doctor and a nurse on call and one very dedicated nurse volunteer who practically lived with us and was available 24/7. Medications were possible, but you'd better have a solid, healthy argument if you expected to be given anything. No chemicals anywhere, any time. This rule did not have a geography, address, or location attached to it. If you had a sip of beer or a toke of a joint anywhere in the known universe, you were gone, finished. To belong to X-Kalay meant that you were making a covenant with a group of people dedicated to being clean and sober at all times. Break the rule in the slightest and you had just signed yourself out.

You say you're sorry, you want to try again? No problem. Come back the next day, sit in the chair, wait for an interview and plead your case to start over again. Good luck. Everything will be harder. We used to make people coming into the program for the first time this promise, "Satisfaction guaranteed—or double your misery back." Once you've experienced the joys of Clean, it'll be that much harder to get off on Dirty.

No violence or threats of violence was very serious, very important, and subtle in some of its ramifications. We now had men, women, and children at X-Kalay. We had teens, the elderly, the infirm, some physically or mentally challenged, and infants and toddlers, along with our demographically averaged twenty-six-year-old drug addict. We had children, old and young, because addicts had children, old and young. A girl would come to us at four in the afternoon, strung out and desperate. She'd have a babe in swaddling clothes in her arms. What were we going to do? Call Social Services? Social Services were sending us their unmanageable teens and old age, long-term drunks and guys with cerebral palsy who needed something more than a weekly visit. So were parole, probation, and the courts. As our reputation grew, the warm bodies simply materialized in greater and greater number and variety. We were becoming a kind of humane dumping ground for The Impossibles. Today, there is an old hospital site in Venice, Italy along the Giudecca Canal that is being refurbished as a school for the arts. Those ancient buildings were known for many years as the "Incurabili," and every time I've seen them, I've thought, "Oh, yes. Tell me about it!"

Safety and security were core values. Everyone not only had to *be* safe, everyone had to *feel* safe. The tolerance level on this matter was zero. If we were interviewing a particularly scary, tough guy, we would be very clear about this rule. "Just so you understand. We know you're a big, scary guy. Boo! We're not scared. We're a program full of big, scary guys. Listen carefully again to this second rule. No violence or threats of violence. If you come even remotely close to breaking this rule, if you so much as think about it and we can see the flicker of it in your eyes, six of our most psychotic goons will take you down the back steps and break your legs."

Of course, in saying something like this we knew we were violating our own rule; we were making a threat. It was rare enough that we offered this warning, but on those occasions it felt right. Sometimes, for some people, the reality must be spelled out in bold and large font.

What about other threats, verbal expressions? After all, at least three times a week, resident clients would play the X-Kalay Game, in which they were encouraged to be as wildly expressive as possible. Get it out. Let it all hang out. Put those feelings on the table. Scream, yell, cry. Won't bother us; we've seen it all. Well, here was the trick. You could not say in a Game, or anywhere else, "I'm going to kill you." That's a threat. You could say and you could learn the self-control to say, even in the free-flowing spontaneity and heat of a Game, "Sometimes, I feel like killing you."

It was also a given that you could not express yourself with the abandon allowed in a Game "on the floor." In other words, Games are a unique circumstance, a strange out-of-time place where you can let your mouth and your emotions run wild. The rest of the day is real life, work, play, and social interaction; and in these arenas only civility is allowed. Cheerfulness, intelligence, understanding, and support would be really helpful, but at the very least, please, civility. So many times we heard someone say to another during the working day, "Hey, pal, save it for The Game."

Amazingly, we never once had to carry out our threat of violence meeting violence. Many people used drugs and left. Many came back. Only on one occasion did we have to deal with someone actually bringing drugs into the environment. Did we cry or feel defeated by this breach? Not at all. We used this betrayal to bring more cohesion and even a grander sense of purpose to the whole enterprise.

A final personal note on these two basic rules. The first

rule states: No chemicals of any kind at any time anywhere as long as you are a part of the program. For me, that was easy as I had already determined in 1968 that it made absolutely no sense whatsoever for me to be preaching and encouraging sobriety if I was still drinking booze and smoking marijuana. I simply stopped. And because this move was effortless, I realized that I was not an alcoholic or addict.

. . .

In 1969, only two years after we had begun, we sold the two old houses in Fairview for a considerable profit and bought a red brick mansion in Lower Shaughnessy.

The house at 2025 West 16th Avenue was stunning. Hardwood floors, built-in cabinetry, a grand central staircase leading to half a dozen large bedrooms, chandeliers, fireplaces, and a very green front and side yard. We paid exactly $79,000. Today, a second house has replaced the side yard. The current real estate value would be well in excess of $2 million and the house itself is probably a strata title now with at least four condo units.

The simple act of buying that property, as we did then, could not be repeated by a nonprofit social agency today. We asked nobody for permission. We were bound to nobody. We were a legal entity, a nonprofit corporation with stated goals and a structure. We saw something we liked for our purposes; we had the means; we acted. Sounds simple, doesn't it?

But let me say this again. You could not do this today.

The microchip was a heartbeat away from turning the world on its ear. Medicine, the military, telecommunications, and practically every endeavor known to humankind were about to be simultaneously shrunk and expanded exponentially.

In Canada, in April 1968, Pierre Elliot Trudeau became the fifteenth Prime Minister of Canada, and, from the beginning, he dedicated himself to building a new Federalism. The result is that Ottawa, once a pleasant village, is now home to fourteen separate levels of government. It is known as a recession-proof town, and almost half the Canadian workforce is riding a government desk.

Today, everybody is intertwined, everybody is interfacing and liaising and meeting and agreeing and damn little gets done. Everybody is after government approval. More importantly, they want government funding. There are municipal bylaws to be upheld. Is there a sink in the basement of that house? One fellow operating a perfectly effective program for alcoholic men in Vancouver had to close one of his east end houses recently because the sink in the basement violated some obscure local bylaw. Are the hallways wide enough? Are there push-out emergency doors? In the municipal elections of 2005, Gordon Robson promised that if he were elected Mayor of Maple Ridge, B.C., he'd use his own considerable resources to open a treatment center for young addicts. He was elected Mayor of Maple Ridge. The next day he opened a house he had bought for this express purpose. He hired a team of psychologists and workers. They never got to see one client. The house was never used as a treatment center for young addicts. Why? Because some mandarin in City Hall declared that the hallways were too narrow. It was a house, not a purpose-built institution.

Today, cities and towns across the nation are crying for

treatment beds for the addicted sons and daughters of their citizens. As of this writing, Victoria, the capital city of the Province of British Columbia is reputed to have one treatment bed for meth-addicted youth. One. Health care and addictions are not a municipal responsibility; in Canada, they are entirely federal and provincial concerns. Moreover, cities and towns don't have the money. But they do have the enormous local power to *get out of the way*. Perhaps politicians could try to encourage their bureaucrats to look at the larger picture. There is a national, no, a worldwide epidemic. A push-bar here, a sink or stove there, these are small potatoes in the grand scheme of things.

More than satisfying obscure bylaws, today you must resonate with every bureaucrat and politician's personal belief systems. Do you complete the community plan that all the stakeholders have been mapping out for the last five years? Does everyone at the table feel comfortable with everyone else today? God forbid there should be a moment of discomfort for anyone. If a key player in these boardroom comedies doesn't really think that treatment works, you might as well move to the next town and try your program there. And there are many, many such bureaucrats with enormous power who will tell you with a perfectly straight face that treatment, in fact, *doesn't* work.

At the provincial level, every inattentive, failing, shifting ministry must be massaged and mollified. Children and Families, Health and Welfare, Education, the Attorney General—none of them has even begun to get a handle on this nightmare, and yet, all must be consulted, all must be at the table, all must sign off on the latest Big Plan. Consultation and cooperation is the thing. The Assistant Deputy Ministers of every department must open a file and hear the story. Meetings must be held and held again, minutes taken and distributed and we must all agree that what is written is what was said.

In the year 2011, while I was writing this book, I met with two such bureaucrats snuggled in their tiny windowless offices amidst a rabbit warren of such hellholes in a gray government building in the provincial capital. While I came to discuss the possibility of increasing support and funding for prevention and treatment programs, they proudly prattled on about their ten-year plan. Had I read it? Oh, yes. Then I could see that they had the whole situation firmly in hand, and that in ten years time, which will pass like nobody's business, don't you know, we will all live in a drug-free, crimeless Eden. Blessed are those who believe.

At the federal level, grant applications must be completed and sent off, each one heavier and more detailed than the last. Sponsors must demonstrate how this small marble fits in with all the other small marbles that constitute the next grand scheme. If it's not going to eradicate poverty, it's not worthy of attention. No politician wants to fund "band-aids." Only big ideas need apply. Politicians want silver bullets. Everyone wants to be the author of the "next great society." Where's my photo op?

We were fortunate. We were acting in a time before all the ribbons got tied on all the bright little boxes. We were working in the age when everything was possible. We bought our house as any private citizen would buy a house. Wasn't that our goal? To make of felons, finaglers, and fiends new citizens?

Shaughnessy is a particularly old and beautiful neighborhood in Vancouver, one of the original nesting places of the lumber barons and Canadian Pacific Railway board members who didn't want to haul themselves up the West Vancouver hillsides to the British Properties. It wasn't long before the local Ratepayers Association had their lawyer petition City Hall. What were all these drug addicts and alcoholics doing on our street? And many are Native Indians! When the matter came before Council on a raucous Tuesday night, one distraught mother kept calling out, "But they have Indian girls there! They have Indian girls!" It turned out that she had a teenage son, and she was utterly convinced that all her boy had to do was walk past those Indian girls and legs would spread, pants would drop and papooses would magically appear. She said this. In English. She had a boy.

Brian Calder was the youngest City Councilor in Canadian history, having been elected to public office at the age of twenty-four. He came to our house and had lunch and got to know our people. He came back regularly. When the matter arose that Tuesday night in council chambers, he was the first to speak eloquently on our behalf. "I have visited the X-Kalay house on West 16th Avenue now several times. I've had coffee and a meal or two and I've spoken with many of the people who live there, the resident clients. Unless I have been very cleverly fooled, and I don't believe I have, there are no drugs or alcohol on the premises. Everybody is clean and sober. In fact, I noticed a sign on the wall in the front reception hallway. It says, "Clean Man Days." And I think the last number I noticed the last time I was there was something like 5,953. What that means is that every day that one person stays clean and sober is counted as a Clean Man Day.

If forty people get through the day clean and sober, well, you've got yourself forty Clean Man Days. This brave little group of people has accumulated now almost 6,000 Clean Man Days. And what does that translate into in dollars and cents for the rest of us? Well, in terms of savings of public funds that might otherwise be spent on prisons, jails, police, courts, ambulances, hospitals, doctors, I don't know…maybe hundreds of thousands of dollars already. Add to that fact that these are real people and they are decent people. I saw no monsters, no horns growing out of foreheads. I saw men and women who are being almost ruthlessly honest with themselves and each other. I saw people who have strayed (and who amongst us has not strayed?) people who are now saying, 'OK I can do better. I don't need that old way of living. There's a better way and I can get on the bus right here.'

"To limit or close down the X-Kalay Foundation and its house on West 16th Avenue would be a tragedy and a disgrace for the City of Vancouver. Rather, we should be grateful it exists. We should welcome them and thank them for their public service. Their work is costing us nothing, but it is gaining us much. Now, I know many of you here this evening that are upset about X-Kalay being in your midst, many of you voted for me. And I know that many of you are listening to me now and wondering why you voted for me and maybe swearing to yourselves that you'll never make that mistake again. And I understand that. But this is what I ask you. Go across the street or down the street and knock on the door. Say 'Hello' to the people at X-Kalay and see for yourself who these people really are. Don't make judgments based on nothing more than rumor and fear and innuendo. I think that if you just take a few minutes to do this, you will soon welcome X-Kalay into your midst as the best possible neighbor."

Harry Rankin, one of the most beloved and smartest council members in Vancouver history, never missed an opportunity to get off a good, memorable line. The lawyer for the ratepayers hauled out the old saw. "That place will bring down the property values." Without missing a beat, Rankin stood and replied, "If the X-Kalay Foundation can do something to curb current runaway property inflation, I say we should give them the key to the city!"

X-Kalay won. We were allowed to live in peace and quiet like anybody else. Among other things, we had successfully argued that we were the *only* house in the neighborhood that you could be guaranteed was clean and sober. As far as we were concerned, it was our gin-guzzling neighbors who were to be feared—not us.

What was truly lovely was that Brian Calder's entreaty to the ratepayers took root. In short order first one neighbor and then another came by for tea. It wasn't long before people were baking pies and breads and donating goods and cash and in every possible way supporting our work.

· · ·

Earl got married in X-Kalay. He and his wife, Carole, with whom I am still good friends forty years later, had a son, to whom I was honored to be godfather.

If Earl was growing restless or dissatisfied, I was unable to see it. But something was clearly eating away at him, because in 1971, after three years of wonderful work, he precipitated a confrontation and a showdown with disastrous results.

One of the challenges that faced us at X-Kalay was how to accommodate female addicts who were also mothers. Many brought with them their infant or young children. It was tough enough making any sense out of an addict's scrambled life if she was on her own. But add in the cries of a demanding baby and you've got a real dilemma. On the one hand, the mother had to be responsible for her child. Personal responsibility was a core value at X-Kalay. But, on the other hand, the mother was herself an emotional child. How could one child successfully care for another?

My wife came up with a brilliant solution. She created a very special kind of daycare. You get up each morning and you handle the basic needs of you and your baby. Wash, clean, feed, attend to, hug, kiss. Then you take your baby to our in-house daycare, which is staffed by our nurse and by other women and other mothers in the program. One or two days a week, you will be one of those staffing the daycare. Today, you drop off your baby and go to your work assignment in the Foundation. During the day, you focus on your own growth and achievement. At four o'clock, you pick up your baby and go back to being a mother. Some days, you put in a morning or afternoon shift in the daycare, helping with the care of not only your child, but several others as well.

Geri initiated this program in our Vancouver Clubhouse and she worked very hard at it, balancing people's schedules and needs to make it work for everyone involved. Our almost full-time volunteer nurse, Fran Mullally, was invaluable in her advice and dedication to this new initiative. It was quite a challenge and quite an accomplishment when it proved over a period of months to work exceedingly well.

Meanwhile Earl had moved with his wife and son to our Winnipeg facility that we had opened in July 1971 to oversee the exciting growth that was occurring there. (The full Winnipeg story is in an upcoming chapter.) Not long after Earl's move, we got a call from a tearful and distraught resident client. This was a woman who was a senior management leader in our Winnipeg program. She advised us that, in spite of many people begging him not to, Earl had closed down the Winnipeg version of our daycare program.

I was dismayed at this information. I asked Earl to call me as soon as possible. "What's going on, Earl? I've got people calling me in tears like the end of the world has arrived. They're telling me that you've closed down the daycare."

"Yah. So?"

"So? So lots, Earl."

"What's the problem?"

"The problem is that you're asking me, 'What's the problem?'"

"Look, I'm running this facility. I'm a Director of the Foundation, and I don't like the daycare."

"You don't *like* the daycare? What is it about the daycare that you don't like, Earl?"

"It's just all part of that feminist bullshit. These girls get knocked up, they bring their babies in here with them, and it's their bloody responsibility to take care of them!"

"OK, Earl. Whatever you may think about women and their responsibilities, whether you approve of our daycare program or not, this was part of our corporate agenda. My

now you see him, now you don't

wife, who is also a Director of the Foundation, built this program and we're all very proud of it. I'm proud of it, Earl. Social workers and eggheads from the university visit every day to marvel at what we're doing here. It is a brilliant and workable accommodation for a complex human problem. It works."

"Oh yeah?"

"So you don't have to *like* this program, Earl. It would be a lot better for everyone if you did, because it would show that you have some basic understanding of what we're doing here, but that's OK. You don't really have to understand it. You just have to *do* it. And if you had some real problem with following Foundation policy, you at least would owe it to yourself and, more importantly, to the rest of us, to discuss your concerns before you go off shutting down programs."

"David, I'm running this show here, and if I can't do what I want, there's no point is there?"

"Well, you can't just do what you want, Earl. That's dope fiend talk. I do what I want. That's baby talk."

"Fuck you."

"Excuse me?"

"You heard me."

"OK, Earl. Here's the thing. Please listen carefully. You have three hours to put the daycare program back into play. If you haven't done that, please vacate the premises."

He was gone within the hour.

Is there a moral to this story?

I am not a bible-thumper, Old or New Testament, but I believe it is in Ecclesiastes that we can read, "Everything is vanity and vexation of spirit." Vanity and loneliness are the great killers. They are twins, joined at the hip.

You could say, "Once a dope fiend, always a dope fiend." Maybe. But I know hundreds who have never gone back to their habits.

You could say, "Earl was destined to fuck up. He was wound tighter than a three-dollar watch." Maybe. You could play shrink and argue that Earl had some unresolved authority issue that would rise and bite him in the ass no matter where he was or what he did.

People in Alcoholics Anonymous are fond of saying that alcoholism is "a cunning, baffling, and powerful disease." Myriad are the curved and wandering routes that drunks and drug addicts will take to undermine their own successes and hurry back to their bottle or needle or pipe. It is success, not failure that is frightening.

Years later, Paul Windham told me that he met Earl in Victoria shortly after Earl left X-Kalay. Earl was trying to promote a new program of his own and he had an appointment to meet a government minister about funding. But first, Earl wanted a good stiff drink. It was eleven in the morning.

Paul told me that it was then and only then, that he learned with blunt force that there were people who could and should graduate from X-Kalay, moving on to the next, more independent chapter in their lives. And then there were people who needed the firm guiding hand and the solid and clear social, spiritual, and emotional structure of the Foundation to make continuing sense of their journeys.

For too many years, the rumors persisted that Earl had died of a heroin overdose shortly after leaving X-Kalay. In the fall of 2011, I had coffee with Carole Dawson, Earl's widow, who cleared up the mystery once and for all. Earl died in 1974 and this is the discouraging tale of how that happened.

Only a few months after leaving X-Kalay, Carole (herself an X-Kalay graduate, who went on to be a highly skilled sexual abuse therapist, activist, and leader in B.C. Aboriginal communities) and Earl and their son (my godson) Jason were living in Campbell River on Vancouver Island. Earl had been hired by a local Native band to do some community development work. One morning he was crossing the driveway of the Discovery Inn Hotel on his way to a meeting. He was knocked down and badly injured by a truck that sped away. He was "treated" at the local hospital, but given no X-Rays and sent home. Carole and Jason took him upstairs to their new apartment. He was dead within the hour.

Almost seven years after Alvin Wallace was told to take his damaged ankle down to the Immigration Building and Tom Tonquil was allowed to walk unescorted out of the Vancouver General Hospital with bandages around the wrists he had slashed only a few hours earlier with a broken mirror, the official response to Natives in trouble was still perfunctory at best.

11 three women

Delphi, Carol, and Shirley are each totems in their own way for the chronology of The X-Kalay Foundation. Each of these women came to our program at very different moments in the Foundation's history, and their stories reflect both that history and the mechanics and principles that made the program work.

Early in our second year, we were living in the two houses on West 7th Avenue in Fairview Slopes. Delphi was one of our first non-Native residents and first heroin addict. She also had the distinction of furnishing us with the first real test of our resolve to provide a truly clean environment.

"She's stoned, Dave. That's for sure." It's ten in the evening and here is a committee of the concerned confronting me in the living room the moment I've walked into the house. "She's upstairs in the front bedroom."

"Are you sure?"

"Come on, David. We know when someone is high."

"Didn't she just move in this afternoon? I mean, when

did she have time to fix?" A posse was challenging me not only to enforce this outrageous ideal of maintaining a house full of clean and sober users, but also to live up to my new position of boss. (My unofficial title, by the way, was King Freak.) I got to the top of the stairs and turned left towards the single light coming from the bedroom. Fluffy slippers, a terry-towel robe, and her hair in pink, plastic curlers, Delphi was channeling the domestic perfection of a black and white television show. She was in her mid thirties and she truly looked like she belonged on *I Love Lucy* or *The Honeymooners*. "Hi, Delphi. How ya doing?"

"Oh, great, David. This is real comfortable here."

As I talked to her, I watched her eyes. Nothing. She wandered in and out of the light from the bedroom to the darkened hall and back again and her pupils were fixed.

"You're stoned, Delphi."

"What?"

"Come on, Delphi. You know the setup. We were very clear about that."

"I wouldn't do that to you guys!" Junkies lie all the time. They lie to their mothers and fathers. They lie to their children and their lovers and they lie to the police, the courts, the social workers, the therapists, the pharmacies, the government committees, and most of all to themselves. Junkies shoot junk. Drunks drink. Why is this so hard to understand? And drug addicts, hands down, are the master manipulators of all time.

"You would and you did. I'm afraid you're going to have to leave."

"Oh come on. You gotta be kidding."

"Kidding is exactly what I'm not doing, Delphi. I am dead

serious. This is a life and death situation. We're all going to be clean or we're all going to die. I'm sorry that you don't get it."

"No, no. I do. I get it."

"You're history, Delphi. Goodbye. You have five minutes to pack up, get dressed, and leave. Try not to steal too much on your way out."

Delphi was a prostitute and a heroin addict and she protested her innocence valiantly. I stuck to my guns, and by 10:30, she was gone. Now the very people who had demanded that I act, turned on me. Remember that at the core of all therapy—personal, group, couples, communities—there sits the hard egg of resistance. Nobody really wants to change. We love our sicknesses. Those bottles of beer, those caps of heroin, those blackjack tables at the fancy resort, they are all our friends. I will never forget a simple moment with my son. We were walking out of an afternoon of silly fun at the annual Pacific National Exhibition. Rides, games, farm animals, cotton candy, the whole package. Sean was six years old. As we exited the fairgrounds hand in hand and turned on to Hastings Street, I saw a young man walking across the street. He was carrying two boxes of empty beer bottles. Twelve empty bottles in each box. He was heading to the liquor store to cash in and get a few more refreshments. The truth of the moment struck me then and there with absolute clarity. *That is his friend. Those bottles are his friend. Sean is my friend. That man's friend is beer.*

We all say we want to change and improve and get better. Then we fight progress with everything in our power.

"You killed her, you bastard! What if she ODs? Sure she broke the rule. But maybe we shouldn't be so harsh. Why don't we give someone like Delphi a second chance? In Native culture, Dave, we don't judge."

The group stayed on me for well over an hour. They railed on me with every indictment they could find. I was unmoved. "You said you wanted a clean environment. You want a safe haven. Well, now you've got it. Are there prices to pay? Absolutely. There will be more, you can count on it. Live with it. Get over it."

The next afternoon, the R.C.M.P. found Delphi's body in a fleabag hotel in New Westminster. She had died of a heroin overdose. Nobody ever raised the subject again, except to make the story part of X-Kalay lore. Did you hear the one about one of the first junkies we ever had? How what happened to her only strengthened everyone's resolve to make sure the environment was truly clean?

It wasn't long before X-Kalay was known on the streets and in the courts as "That junkie place. That *clean* junkie place."

. . .

Carol was an extraordinary looking girl. She was a prostitute who gave off the air of a Sorbonne student working on a PhD thesis on the role of memory in the French symbolist poets. Silver hair cut in a perfect tight bob, pucker-petal mouth and a lisp that was all sexual innuendo. She reminded me of the first prostitutes I had ever met.

One summer, when I was twelve, my mother and I spent two weeks at a grand old hotel by Lake Winnipeg. We often took summer breaks like this, staying in a quiet cabin or a family style bed and breakfast kind of lodge. But my mother was somewhat of a manic-depressive personality and in her up phases she liked to be gregarious and modern and progressive. Very much in one of her "Let's-meet-the- whole-world" kind of moods this particular holiday, my mother introduced me to "Rex King" and his friends. I kid you not. Rex was a pimp, and this was his handle. Rex, extraordinarily handsome and well coiffed, was a dead ringer for Ronald Coleman. His two friends were the most beautiful and charming hookers a boy could ever hope to meet. They paid me twenty-five cents a day to walk their poodles on the boardwalk during the heat of the afternoons. It was probably important for the ladies not to get too exercised or mosquito-bitten. Better to sit on the well-screened porches of the hotel with Rex and my mother, sipping cool drinks and discussing the news of the day. In the evening, my mother took me around the back of the hotel to sit on the swings and watch the curious traffic of men on the fire escapes. This was one of her creative lessons in the birds and the bees.

Carol arrived at X-Kalay the very next day after we had moved into the red brick mansion in Lower Shaughnessy. This was about six months after the arrival and departure of Delphi.

Once again, the Posse of the Concerned was standing in front of me. "She's doing this whole *Man with the Golden Arm* number."

They were referring to the 1955 Otto Preminger movie starring Frank Sinatra as Frankie Machine, a heroin addict. Sinatra was nominated for an Oscar for his histrionics as a junkie trying to kick a habit cold turkey. Unfortunately, this utterly false image of the addict convulsing for days at a time in mortal agony has stayed in the public mind. The image has, of course, been repeated ad nauseam in film after film, TV episode after TV episode. Jamie Foxx in his award-winning portrayal of Ray Charles in *Ray*, and Joaquin Phoenix as Johnny Cash in *Walk the Line* are recent examples of continuing the myth. The great jazz singer Nancy Wilson did a memorable turn on an old Hawaii Five-o episode that I believe won her an Emmy. Playing an addict may be a good exercise for actors, but the reality is more pedestrian. Most heroin addicts, in getting off their drug, will experience about the same discomfort you will suffer with a case of the flu—headache, sore throat, elevated temperature, drowsiness. Addicts, due to the ugly circumstances of their lives, kick habits regularly as a matter of practical and unwanted necessity. It is part of the life.

"Do we give her an Oscar?"

"For sure, Dave. She's got the sweats. She's got the cramps. She's got every disease known to mankind. But mostly she's got The Gimmees. Give me this, give me that. A pill, doctors, nurses, what have you. Rush in the bomb squad. I'm going to lose it. I swear to Christ, if you don't give me something fast, I'm going to completely lose it."

"It's been explained to her that all we got is love?"

"Sixteen times to breakfast."

I found her upstairs chewing on a blanket. It was almost eleven in the morning and the Queen was still in her bed. "Hey, Carol. Do you think you could do something for me?"

"Eh?"

"The thing is I need your help. You got a housecoat or something?"

"Sure. What is it?

I took Carol downstairs into the dining room and handed her a broom. "You know we just moved in to this lovely house yesterday and we're kind of short-staffed. Some of the kids are already working on getting lunch ready, and we've got a gang over at a local high school doing a presentation. They're telling the kids about their own miserable dope fiend lives and hoping some of these kids might get the message and avoid all the shit."

"Yah?"

"So, I'm almost embarrassed to tell you, because we're usually pretty good about these things. But we didn't really have much time to clean up this morning."

"No problem, Dave."

Carol swept the dining room. Then she dusted the built-in mahogany cabinets. Then she climbed a chair and cleaned the chandelier. Eventually, one of the other girls wandered into the dining room and offered her a coffee and a smoke. They got to talking. Carol put aside her broom and joined everyone for lunch. She went upstairs and made her bed and showered and changed. That was the last anyone ever heard about Carol's killer habit. She stayed in the program two years and thrived. Carol was beautiful and sexy and possessed of a raucous good humor. She probably was a very good prostitute. I can't say. But I guarantee you she was one helluva clean and sober citizen.

Word got out on the streets that there was a clean house up the hill. It's a place run by junkies, by people who really know the score. The courts, the parole and probation systems, and the prisons were on alert. Within months of buying the mansion, we were replacing single beds with bunks. Our numbers went from fifteen to forty within almost as many days. Soon, one of the favorite lines around X-Kalay, especially when someone was getting cocky about nothing, was, "Oh yeah? Well, look where all your smarts got you, buddy—a top bunk at X-Kalay. Some sharp operator!"

People in the helping professions like to talk about motivation. The accusation was leveled at us with boring regularity. "You have such great success, because you only work with people who are really motivated to start with."

Ha!

Motivation is nothing. Charlie knocked on the front door because three dealers he had burned were trying to push him off the Burrard Street Bridge. He was scared shitless. Edith was running away from an abusive boyfriend. Would you like to stay with a guy who put elastic bands around his little thing? Almost everybody was hiding from something or somebody. I was reminded regularly by a friend of mine, who was a private detective, that fear and pain were great motivators. Courts and prisons sent hundreds of people to us over the years. Not one of these poor souls began their journey with us armed with a single good intention. One of the several titles I originally considered for this book was "The Graveyard of Good Intentions." Not a great selling point, but it certainly captures the fog of mythology that continues to snake around addictions.

Forty years later, academics are still arguing about whether enforced treatment will work. The answer is simple. It will work if the program works. If the government runs the program and it is filled with "experts," it will continue the history of failure. If ex-addicts and recovering addicts and people who know the territory run the program, it will do its magic. Peer programs consistently show the best day-to-day results. Even expensive private clinics, run by medical doctors and PhDs, are invariably staffed with clean and sober counselors who have been through the soup themselves. How people get there is sublimely irrelevant. Motivation is fluid. It changes and can be changed.

The environment changed the people in X-Kalay and it invested in them a new motivation. When my son was in grade five, he was struggling. We moved him to a different school, one with a more positive, trusting academic atmosphere and within days, he became a student. Environment is always responsible for at least fifty percent of the equation.

At X-Kalay, people were slapping newcomers on the back and thanking them for a job well done. Or they were hollering at these novices for bad behavior. We were giving addicts and alcoholics exactly what they needed—equal doses of loving support and a regular kick in the ass. The very language of the environment was fresh and energizing. There was never any talk about alcohol or drugs. Why talk about garbage? Talk garbage, *be* garbage. The chemicals were the symptom of the larger malaise. The chemicals were the pimples on your ass. BORING! You stopped using your poison of choice the moment you came through our doors. Now you need a new focus and you get it non-stop. There are music and acting and an in-house newspaper. There are bridge games and football and swimming and concerts and a daily cacophony of laughter.

. . .

Shirley came to us from the Women's Unit at Matsqui Penitentiary. Starting at ground zero, cleaning toilets, she became in two years a Director of the Foundation and eventually ran our entire program in Winnipeg.

One day I was sitting in my office in the den of the grand old house on West 16th Avenue. I was leaning back in my favorite leather chair, staring at the ceiling and no doubt thinking of something truly marvelous. Shirley, having only recently arrived at the Foundation, was on clean-up duty and was busily vacuuming and dusting all around me. When she couldn't get my attention with her more than vigorous housekeeping, she simply launched into conversation. "Is that all you do all day?"

"Excuse me?"

"You sit in that chair and daydream?"

"Pretty much."

"Nice job."

"I like it. This is a problem for you?"

"No. It's no big deal. I could care less."

"So why am I getting the third degree from you?"

"I dunno. Everybody's doing something, and you're just sitting there."

"What should I be doing, Shirley? What would you like me to do?"

"I could make a suggestion."

"I'm sure you could. But how about this? If I don't sit here and daydream sometimes, you don't have a place to clean and someone to harass."

"You know, you're just about the most foul-mouthed bastard I've ever met. Not now. I mean not now, but the first time I met you, oh man! You don't remember? Oh brother. In the joint, in Matsqui."

"Matsqui…"

"You came in with a few other people, Bev and some others, to demonstrate The Game."

"Right, right. Yes, we've been doing a lot of that lately, but I'll tell you I'm not sure it's worth the effort. There's a whole argument we're having these days about whether you can really do anything productive in a prison setting. I don't know."

"Well, it got me here. If that's worth anything."

"Wow! Really? Well, that's worth a lot, believe me. I'm really glad you told me that."

"You completely turned my head around that day. Don't you remember what you did? How you ripped me? I'll never forget it. I really hated you. But you made me think more than I ever thought in my life. I was sitting there in that group minding my own business, thinking I never heard such a load in my life, and you're going on about who knows what. All of a sudden there's like a quiet moment and you turn to me and you say, 'So, that's it? That's all you got?' What the hell? I had no idea what you were talking about. Then you go into this big number about my shirt."

"Your shirt?"

"My tie-dyed T-shirt. I was sporting this psychedelic tie-dyed T-shirt that I'd made in the prison kitchen. A bunch of us made them. We were proud of those shirts. I was real proud. Till you asked me if I had a husband. Or kids or a fence or a mortgage or tickets to the hockey game. No, sir. I didn't have any of those goodies. I had a girlfriend in the joint and I had a tie-dyed T-shirt. First you laughed your crummy head off. Then, you got real sad and quiet and you said that it was real pathetic that all I could show for myself after all these years was this shirt. I was pretty convinced that you were altogether the biggest asshole I ever met. The only thing is I couldn't stop thinking about what you said. It disturbed the hell out of me. I didn't argue with you anymore. I didn't say a word after that, but I went back to my drum and the truth is I didn't sleep one minute that night. I didn't cry or anything like that, but I couldn't stop thinking that this stupid shirt was all I got to say for myself after all these years."

"Where are you from, Shirley?"

"I grew up in Steinbach."

"Manitoba?"

"Right on. Mennonite family. Holier than the Pope. Righteous in every way and wall-to-wall abuse. Big moral standards. Big phony bullshit. Everybody's doing everybody. 'Incest is best; leave the rest.'"

"Very attractive."

"Ran when I was thirteen. Spent most of my life on the streets. Winnipeg, Calgary, Vancouver. Hooking. Doing. Fixing. The whole shiteree. You know the script."

Shirley was the real deal. There was an immediacy about her that was winning and irresistible. In a Game, she could turn on someone with demonic fury and moments later be cradling that poor soul in her arms. As we worked together and came to know each other, we became wonderful friends. I trusted her judgment about people implicitly. When I would visit her in our Winnipeg facility, we would play bridge, go to movies, and dash off into the winter night to hang out at the local Boston Pizza. More often than not, we were laughing so hard, we could barely eat. On one occasion at the bridge table, she watched in disbelief as I confidently bid a grand slam and played the only card at the outset that could blow the contract. I went down six tricks. She laughed all that night and well into the next week. All you had to do over the next year was mention that game to send her off the deep end.

Like so many of the people we've worked with over the years, Shirley was a discard. She was part of the social flotsam and jetsam that is whipped into the gutters by the cool autumn wind. If she had died in her late twenties or early thirties, her passing would not have warranted even a line in the local papers. What we did with her may or may not be construed as some kind of miracle, but the process was anything but divine. It was steadfastness, above all, consistency. We looked Shirley in the eye and smiled at her very existence. We let her know that we were happy she was here with us at this place in this time. We also let her know when she was being an ass. When her dope fiend ways stepped forward from the shadows, hijacked the party, and dominated her behavior, we were there to say, "Oh no, kid. That's not the Shirley we need today."

Sports writers and coaches are fond of repeating that football is a game of inches. Well, say hello to rehab. A pinch here, an adjustment there, a little insight for the day, a meditation before bed, and a dedication in the morning, these slowly add up. The accumulation of small gains made through awareness and effort—there's the miracle!

12 sci-fi blues

This wasn't the Betty Ford Clinic.

So being graced with an A-list movie star, barfing out his bottomless shame for bedding more women than Wilt Chamberlain (all the while cooking his charms on the nursing staff), was not a huge likelihood at the X-Kalay Foundation.

But we can claim one major league celebrity guest client, whose influence did not emerge until twenty years later.

Shortly after we'd settled into the red brick mansion on West 16th Avenue, a man moved in and told us he was a writer. We laughed. We howled. We did back flips. All we asked of him were his poisons of choice—pills and booze—and could he clean the toilets? I have no memory of this man at all. I have since seen his photograph several times and I wish I could seize the dinner conversation by boasting that I recognized him at once, that we enjoyed many spirited games of handball together, and that we often talked long into the night. Not so. The good fellow serviced the washrooms, kept his nose clean, and split for the hills after three weeks. Writer, whoop-a-tee-ay-oh! Who gives an authentic old Canadian hoot?

But here's the thing. According to all that we have since learned, from official and unauthorized biographies and from the man's own writings, his three weeks with X-Kalay earned him a lifetime Gold Pass. He never used again.

His name was Philip K. Dick.

He published forty-four novels and 121 short stories in his lifetime. Films based on his works have generated well in excess of $1 billion in box-office receipts. *Blade Runner, Total Recall, Minority Report*, and *The Adjustment Bureau* are just a few of the familiar titles. Steven Spielberg, Arnold Schwarzenegger, Tom Cruise, John Woo, Ben Affleck, Harrison Ford, Robert Downey Jr., Keanu Reeves, and Matt Damon are only a few of the mega-stars associated with Philip K. Dick movie projects.

Mr. Dick's writing has long been considered not only super sci-fi, but also great literature by any measure and in 2007 Dick became the first science fiction writer to be included in The Library of America series.

None of these extraordinary accomplishments, of course, have anything to do with us and our brief association with Mr. Dick. That's all on him, his native talents and his dedicated work efforts.

But he did descend from the heavens one afternoon some years later with a surprise gift.

It is 1990. I am living in Toronto, and not doing very well. My kids are thousands of miles away in Vancouver and I am out of work and low on funds, with little or no immediate prospects. I am almost fifty years old and drowning—at least for that day—in the familiar sludge of self-pity. Woe is me. Will I ever get anything right?

An old high school chum had just picked up the check for lunch. This is good. Having nothing better to do, I stroll into a famous bookstore at Yonge and Bloor. Opposite the cash is a low shelf with all the new titles. There, staring back up at me, with the gaudiest and most garish jacket of all is *Divine Invasions: A life of Philip K. Dick*, by Lawrence Sutin.

"Really?" say I to my sorry-is-as-sorry-feels self. "Well, let's see if these folks got the whole story." I turn to the index expecting the comfort of disappointment. And there it is! Page 190, X-Kalay Foundation.

Three entire pages are devoted to Dick's stay with and his reflections of the experience. He found our little seminary to be infused with a Protestant work ethic and what he felt was an arid devotion to simple ideas. It wasn't really his cup of tea. Nevertheless, some extraordinary spore in the environment drifted into his inner ear and stayed. He became clean and sober and remained in that peculiar state until his death in 1982, which gave him a pretty good run of almost a dozen years.

So I am reading all of this standing at the counter in the bookstore on a day when I am being haunted about questions of my next meal and my general usefulness on this earth, a charter member of the Catastrophic Thinkers' Club.

I put the book down and look up at the heavens.

"Thank you. I did something. Life goes on. Next!"

13 all aboard! launching in five

I was sitting in my office one morning, when three of our resident clients came in to see me.

"Hey, Dave, there's an empty gas station on Broadway."

"Really? Whose flag?"

"It's a Shell station."

We had tried our hand at a Chevron station also on West Broadway the year before. That effort hadn't worked out, but we knew the concept was sound and this was an opportunity to redeem ourselves. What made this a more timely moment is that we now had almost a hundred resident clients and many of them were already running several good businesses. Here were three very able bodied men pointing us to a possible new activity. Today, committees must be formed, proposals must be written and submitted, and the assembled have to endure mind-numbing PowerPoint presentations. That's a today in which everything must be documented, not for the sake of history or research or study or to encourage others to model success, but simply to cover backsides. All parties must be singing from the same hymnbook and all three levels of government must be present at all the tables. Before you know it, $250,000 has been spent and nothing real has been added to the pool of human activity.

Here's what we did. "When you say this station is 'empty,' fellas, what do you mean exactly?

"Well, it's all boarded up and there's no one there."

"Where is this place?"

"Corner of Broadway and Collingwood. You know, just this side of Alma Road."

I picked up the White Pages. Shell Canada's Vancouver offices were on West Georgia in the West Coast Transmission Building. I found the regional manager and explained to him on the phone who I was. "I have a simple proposition for you that I think might be to our mutual advantage and I'd like to come by and spend a few minutes with you, if I may."

The next Tuesday at nine o'clock, I marched into the man's office with My Three Goons in tow. "You have a gas station at the corner of Broadway and Collingwood that is boarded up. I have lots of resident clients in our program who are perfectly capable of pumping gas, changing oil, rotating tires and even fixing cars. These men are not able to work a full eight- or ten-hour day just yet. They've either just come out of prison or they've just come off a booze or drug habit. Most of them don't own an alarm clock. Never have. They can't work a full day. Not just yet. They've got a low threshold of almost everything. If one of these guys tries to work an eight-hour shift, he'll get mean and short-tempered and punch somebody out. But they can work a four-hour shift and I've got dozens of these guys back at the house. The rest of the day, they'll be involved in other program activities. What's more, I don't have to pay them. They are already being paid in room and board and a very sophisticated and demanding social and therapeutic program. All you have to do, sir, is remove the hording from the windows, put our name up above the doorway as proprietors and open that hole in the ground so your truck can fill the tank with gasoline. We'll sell Shell product, we'll both make money and you'll be helping an important social cause by just doing exactly what you always do."

The hording was removed and the underground tanks were filled with Shell gasoline *the next morning*. Our guys were in Shell uniforms and selling product before noon. Can you even imagine trying to do this today? You'd be "in process" for three years before you even got out of the starting blocks.

For many years thereafter, motorists were drawn into our pump islands and our garage bays by sandwich boards at the curbside that advertised:

COME IN AND GET GASSED UP BY A JUNKIE
The X-Kalay Shell Gas Station

. . .

The gas station was the first of several successful businesses we ran. The second, a specialty advertising company, was a project that Earl Allard brought with him from Synanon. The concept was simple enough. You are William "Bill" Smith, insurance agent. We will imprint a thousand pens with your name and logo and telephone number for a very reasonable price. (Sorry, no web address, since they didn't exist in 1970.) Of course, if you'd like to order 2,000 or even 5,000 units, the price will be even that much cheaper, sir. It was only a few months after Earl's arrival that we found a machine that could imprint company names and logos on pens. Then we found a number of pen manufacturers, ink suppliers, and rate card printers. Before you knew it, our pen advertising business was up and running and employing sales staff and warehouse producers and drivers. We consistently made money. But the greatest joy for our ex-cons was in answering the telephone.

"Good morning, B.C. Pen!"

. . .

My wife was a real entrepreneur. It was entirely because of her that we opened Hair, our beauty salon at 41st and Cambie.

When Geri suggested that we open a beauty shop, I had only one question—did we have enough women to make it work?

Within weeks, she had negotiated a lease on a wonderful space directly opposite the Oakridge Shopping Centre and somehow filled it with all the accoutrements necessary, most donated. We looked at the three girls she had selected to begin this venture, Wendy, Alice, and Bev. All three were recovering junkie hookers. All three had studied hairdressing while serving time in Matsqui Penitentiary. Why couldn't they find success tending to middle-aged, middle-class women in a largely Jewish enclave in south Vancouver in the early 1970s? Anything was possible. Hadn't we already proven that?

Because we madly believed that we always knew everything about our people, Geri and I confidently predicted that Wendy would survive this challenge and flourish. We expected that Alice might hang around for a few months. We were certain Bev wouldn't last much longer than a day or two. Her full name was Bev Wing, and she was well named—truly wingy. Giggly, flighty, flaky. Take your pick. Bev didn't stand a chance.

Of course, we were completely and utterly 180 degrees wrong. Alice did in fact hang in there for a month or two. But Wendy, our star and the one my wife and I were betting on, split within the first week. She couldn't take the responsibility and the freedom and the success. Remember that more people are defeated not by the fear of failure, but by *the fear of success.* God, what'll I do with all my favorite excuses if I'm a winner? To whom can I whine? What will I whine about, what? Over the years, I came to call this syndrome the Fear of Flying. What it amounts to is nothing less than avoiding the full responsibility of adulthood.

When we are children, we are cared for, sometimes not very well, sometimes not at all, but very often we are cared for to some satisfactory degree or another. Our little faces are washed, our bottoms are dried, and we are sent to sleep in our little beds. Mortgage, deadline, feeding the kids, publish or perish? What's all that? We are eager in our adolescence to be independent, to try out our wings solo and we are skeptical of what has come before, what our families tell us is the truth. We move on. For some of us, many of us, the child and the adolescent remain alive and active not far from the surface. We may be bigger, stronger, and older, we may have bank accounts and much-stamped passports, but we don't really, really want to grow up. It can be argued that much of North America is an adolescent culture. Blue jeans-sporting, beer-guzzling hooliganism too often seems the norm. If only the world would take care of me. If only someone would manage my affairs so I can play in the fields. If only, if only. And please don't bug me when I am just having fun, OK? However, success, as an adult, arrives only by abandoning the expectations of childhood. We can still dream and hope and we can be beautifully childish in moments of joy and sorrow. But to fully embrace adulthood, we are willing to take life on as it is, as we can fully discern it.

Bev, the woman we had pegged for a quick exit, took to the salon like salmon to a stream. She thrived and grew in that role. She ran the salon herself in time, and a few years later, she and Amy, one of our other resident clients, traveled to Italy together to stay in a castle owned by the father of one of our wealthy alcoholic residents.

· · ·

Amy played a key role in the story of our Salt Spring Island Hotel.

For some time, Luis Molina and Earl and Geri and I had been thinking about the Foundation's need for a rural retreat. We envisioned some lovely hideaway where clients could repair for a few days or weeks after they had been in the program for at least six months. We did not share the notion that X-Kalay itself belonged in the countryside, away from city temptations. We welcomed the availabilities that only exist in an urban center—the concert halls, gyms, playing fields, businesses, charities, and churches. Nor did we believe it was possible to do our work in the midst of the madness, right on Skid Road.

One morning, one of our Foundation Board members picked me up for a bit of a surprise. Geoff Massey was a renowned architect, the business partner for many years of Arthur Erickson, Vancouver's most famous and celebrated architect. Geoff was also a member of the Massey Family, who had produced a Governor General of Canada (The Right Honorable Vincent Massey) and the Oscar nominated actor, Raymond Massey. Geoff was himself a member at that time of Vancouver City Council.

We drove to Main and Hastings. He had the keys to a magnificent stone building on the southwest corner. Inside, it was all dust and bats and rats. This was the Carnegie Centre, abandoned and looking for a purpose. "Wow! This is some building, Geoff."

"Yes, isn't it great?"

"It is. But why are you showing it to me?"

"It's yours. You can have it."

"What for?"

"For X-Kalay, of course."

"But, Geoff. We would never run a program at Main and Hastings. This is the dead centre of Bad. What's the reward for cleaning up? You get more of the same? No. Our people have to live in beautiful houses in great neighborhoods. We need trees and plants. We need some quiet and grocery stores and coffee shops and community centers. Why would our people want to stay in the midst of buildings and people that are falling down? There have to be some payoffs for all the hard work of cleaning up."

Today, the Carnegie Community Centre is home to dozens of social programs. Outside, on the front steps and on the corner sidewalk, Honduran dope dealers ply their trade in the open. The centre itself and its leaders have won numerous awards and citations over the years for meritorious service to the community. The Downtown East Side, in which the Carnegie Community Centre is considered a beacon, today boasts over a hundred social service agencies. Over a hundred social services in four-square blocks—which make the Downtown East Side the most serviced neighborhood in North America at a cost of one million dollars, we are told, each and every day. Yet for all those efforts, many of the core problems of poverty and addictions seem intractable. Theft, drug overdoses, prostitution, and misery seem built into the very stones of the buildings and alleyways.

One provincial government in the 1970s offered X-Kalay Ocean Falls, a remote coastal community, accessible only by boat or seaplane. Ocean Falls is noted for its abundance of rain—about 172 inches annually, and its roughly one hundred residents are referred to as the "Rain People." Just what we all wanted—a gray, wet prison on the outer edges of the rain forest. Thanks, but no thanks.

No. Our program could not survive downtown or on an ice flow. It worked best in the city, near enough to social, artistic, recreational, educational, health, and economic resources, but away from the daily hard scramble of drug dealing and pimping. What we could use, however, was a retreat.

My wife and I were on our way to Calgary to conduct a

weekend workshop for a corrections group. I handed Luis an obscure ad I had found in the back pages of the *Vancouver Sun* newspaper. "Island hotel for sale or lease." When we reached Calgary, I called Luis and asked about the hotel.

"Yes, it's on Salt Spring Island."

"Where's that?"

"It's in the Georgia Strait, between here and Vancouver Island. You get there by ferry boat."

"OK. How much?"

"$400 a month."

"WHAT?"

"And each month's rent goes towards the purchase price."

"MY GOD! Did you take it?"

"David, we haven't seen the place yet."

"I know, I know. But I don't care if the windows are broken, $400 a month and it all goes to the purchase!"

"OK. I made an appointment. You'll see it next week."

We got back to Vancouver and a few days later, Luis and I took the ferry from Tsawwassen terminal to Long Harbour on Salt Spring Island. To this day, some forty years later, I still believe that there is something inherently curative about making this journey. In spite of the fact that the numbers of travelers has at least doubled, perhaps tripled, and the ferry service is often suspect at best, something magical still happens every time I arrive at this dock. The terminal is at the end of a long spit and you have the distinct sensation that you are already a part of the Strait of Georgia. With no protective barriers of trees or buildings, the terminal is marvelously wind-blown and, if you are a foot passenger, just dragging your luggage from your parked car to the departure gates can be an adventure in itself. The trip from here to Salt Spring Island is a most leisurely three hours. The ferry stops at three islands en route, Galiano, Mayne, and Pender Islands, and with each stop there is much toing and froing, unloading of cars and reloading of new cars. It is useless and self-defeating to be in any kind of hurry on such a trip. Of course, the natural scenery is stunningly beautiful, but the simple facts of the time line and the water bring on an unavoidable and welcome calm. It is difficult to be upset about anything on this trip.

From Long Harbour on Salt Spring Island, we drove the corkscrew country roads to Vesuvius Bay. We pulled into the government parking lot at Vesuvius Bay and I fell in love at once with the old farmhouse that had, over the years and through many additions and revisions, become a hotel.

The owner was a Czech immigrant with a heavy European accent. I rushed over to him. "We'll take it."

"Firzt is lookink, then takink."

"OK, I'll look, but I'm telling you right now, we'll take it."

"Goot, but firzt is lookink."

In addition to the coffee shop and the dining room facing the bay and the living room and a dozen bedrooms upstairs, the property included five cabins on a hill behind the hotel and an oyster beach immediately in front.

We signed the deal with the owner at once. We agreed to both a monthly rental fee and a final buyout price. Each month's rent was being applied to the ultimate sale. Less than six months later, we found the difference and bought the property outright. A week after our first look at the hotel, about ten of us arrived and dived into the work of making the place shipshape. We had no plan other than to enjoy ourselves. As luck would have it, by eight o'clock that evening, another X-Kalay business was born.

The dining room had four-place tables along the windows facing the water and deuces against the wall that separated diners from the large and well-equipped kitchen. We were sitting at dinner when an elderly British couple walked in and sat down by a window.

I called Amy over. She was an attractive and likable girl in her early twenties whose older brother, Paul, would in time become a Director of the Foundation. "Amy, just go over there and be your usual charming, jovial self and invite them for dinner."

Amy approached the couple.

"May we have a menu, please?"

"Well, you see, we just got here today. This is actually our first day here. So we haven't had time to create a menu just yet, but we are having a lovely fresh salad and then pan fried oysters, which we picked up right here on the beach below us, and some vegetables, and Jim has made a wonderful apple pie for dessert. So, would you like to join us?"

"That would be lovely."

We charged them $2.50 each and they left us not $5.00, but $10.00. "That was delightful and delicious. Please keep the change. We'll come by again soon."

We all watched this lovely older couple leave. Then we looked at each other and began to laugh. I said, "Well, I guess we've just opened another business."

The next season, with the gracious help of a local crafts-man, we knocked out a set of windows, installed sliding glass doors and built a forty-foot butterfly deck reaching out to the ocean. For seven months of the year, with the good weather, that coffee shop, dining room, and deck were packed all day and night long. The profits from that operation not only paid easily for the hotel, but also helped subsidize our Vancouver programs.

Our fifth business in Vancouver was a pizza restaurant. We signed a standard franchisee agreement and ran the restaurant successfully for several years.

There are at least two things to note about these businesses.

The first is that they all made money—the gas station, the pen advertising company, the beauty salon, and the hotel eateries—and that all the profits were funneled back into the Foundation. Having said that, the amounts made were hardly fortunes or enough to carry residential programs for 125 people, but they certainly helped, and they were invaluable training grounds for hundreds of recovering addicts who came through the program in ten years.

The second may seem a little unreal, but it is the truth. Both our pizza restaurant and our Vesuvius Bay Hotel had beer and wine licenses. You would think that this would be a nightmare or impossibility with all our staff being recovering alcoholics and addicts. But, we did not have ONE untoward incident in which our resident clients misused their proximity to what might have been temptation. Not one.

How could this be?

When you have the large and powerfully structured and constantly re-enforced environment of the therapeutic community, discipline becomes internalized. All good discipline is self-discipline. There is no other kind that works. The therapeutic community model works on peer-to-peer support. Government programs are often expensive and ineffective because they run on a medical model. You are sick and only we professional doctors can fix you. The accepted mantra for many years now has been that addictions are a medical problem. You have to understand where that came from; only then can you understand where it should go.

For ages, alcoholism was in the closet. It was a family or personal problem drenched in shame. Nobody would speak of it. Spouses and other family members covered up and "enabled" their offending father or sister by providing excuses for bad behavior. Sorry, Alex has a bad flu and he won't be able to come in today. Everyone at the office knew damn well that Alex's flu came from a bottle of gin the night before and it was the shakes and the hangover that was keeping the poor sod at home.

Then, in the last decades of the twentieth century, after many years of great work by Alcoholics Anonymous and a few others, a corner was turned. Eager to get alcoholism out into the open where it could be faced and dealt with, many progressive people began to speak of the problem as a medical issue. There is no shame here. This is a disease and it needs to be treated. That sea change did some real good. More and more drunks were able to step forward into the light of day and begin to wrestle their demons to the ground. Alcoholism was no longer seen as a scourge or a plague or the work of the devil himself. Corporations and unions began to work together to create Employee Assistance Programs in which addicted workers could attend treatment programs without losing their jobs and without incurring bankrupting expenses. These programs are the norm today and all of that is to the good.

The only problem is that too many doctors took this medical model seriously and saw a career path for themselves. The doctor will help you. The doctor knows best. The doctor will cure you. Unfortunately for them and for us, addictions are in fact not a disease or a medical condition. Addictions are complex conditions, sure enough, but they begin with choices, bad choices.

At X-Kalay, the approach is this:

You're not sick. You're not even chronically stupid. You've been making some really lousy choices. You can learn to make new choices. It took you a long time to become such a fool, so don't expect to be a saint by morning. You've strayed and you can do better. You can start getting on your best track right this second. It will take you at least as long as you spent being a fuck-up to become an honorable, decent citizen. But that's OK. "Today is the first day of the rest of your life."

Now, if addictions are still seen as a disease and a medical issue, we are stuck with an enormous and insurmountable political problem. The "solution" is prohibitively expensive. Doctors and nurses are expensive. If we need doctors and nurses to straighten out drug addicts, we are looking at $250,000 per bed per annum in current dollars. You want a facility for one hundred addicted youth? Fine. That's $25 million a year for programming alone, and that's after you've already spent twice as much for a building and real estate.

And you wonder why Canadian governments have avoided treatment like the plague. But what if treatment were available at one fifth that cost, treatment that actually works?

Then it would be a bargain and an unavoidably sensible and humane choice for government budgets. Well, treatment programs that are run by ex-addicts and recovering addicts and a few enlightened social workers and psychologists cost about $50,000 per bed per annum. That's what Jean Doucha spends today at the Behavioural Health Foundation in Manitoba. Brenda Plant, the Executive Director (and for thirty years the guiding force field behind Turning Point, a Vancouver treatment center) pulls off her daily small miracles at $27,000 per bed! How's them apples?

Your government has no excuse not to act. And we as a community have to say goodbye to the medical model. It is not only wrong, it is priced out of reach. Addictions, properly understood, are an emotional, psychological, social, behavioral, and spiritual problem.

As of this writing, a medication has been found and proven remarkably effective in conquering nicotine addictions. It is entirely within reason that similarly targeted pharmaceuticals might soon appear on the horizon to defeat heroin and cocaine addictions. There is no question that Big Pharma is very busy looking for exactly this silver bullet; it is one of the holy grails of pharmaceutical research and development. But when that heraldic day arrives, the need for substantive treatment programs will be as strong as ever. Removing the poison of choice is only step one in recovery. Then the entire gestalt of destructive social habits, associations, and pay-offs must be addressed. The substance of choice is the pimple on the ass of addictions. It's *everything else* that takes all the hard work.

The next time you hear some "expert" carrying on about

heroin or crystal meth and they never get past the poison, just change the channel or read a good book.

Solutions are available. We have only to choose them.

. . .

And speaking of Jean and the Foundation in Manitoba let me tell you how in the summer of 1971 we suddenly leaped across the prairies and doubled our numbers and our impact.

One evening at about eight o'clock, we called five people into the den of our red-brick mansion on West 16th Avenue. I handed one person an envelope and another person a set of keys. "You're going to like Winnipeg."

Everybody stared at me. "In the envelope is $500 in cash. The keys are for the blue VW microbus. Don't race and don't dawdle. Driving at a reasonable speed, it should take about two and a half days to get there. Don't stay at the Banff Springs Hotel or the Roach Motel. Find reasonable, comfortable accommodation. When you get to Winnipeg, check into a hotel and call the number on the piece of paper in the envelope. That's our Winnipeg lawyer. He'll have the keys to our house on Montrose Boulevard, which is just off Wellington Crescent, a very beautiful and expensive old street. The house is very much like this one, a little smaller, but still beautiful. You should feel quite at home there. I'm going to arrive about two weeks from now. When I get there, I'd like to see the X-Kalay Foundation Manitoba Inc. up and running. Have a great trip and a great new adventure!"

The year was 1971. We were in our fourth year of operation, and we had made many friends in all walks of life, including many politicians of every stripe. One of the most important of these was Grace MacInnis. Grace was a lovely, bright, and committed social activist. She was the first woman from British Columbia elected to federal Parliament, representing the successor to the Co-operative Commonwealth Federation (CCF), the New Democratic Party. Her father, J.S. Woodsworth, was one of the founding members of the CCF.

It was Grace MacInnis who petitioned a sympathetic Manitoba government for help in establishing a Winnipeg branch of The X-Kalay Foundation. The province approved an establishment grant of $7,000 and we were off and running.

Two weeks after our gang of outreach pioneers set off in that VW bus, I arrived at the Winnipeg airport. I rented a car and drove straight to the grand old house on Montrose. The first thing I saw as I walked up the steps was a sign above the front door—The X-Kalay Foundation (Manitoba) Inc.

I let myself in. There was a young woman sitting at a desk in the hallway. I'd never see her before. On the wall to her left, was an "In-Out" board with many names that I didn't recognize, about fifteen in all. Next to it was a schedule of school speaking engagements for the coming weeks. Various familiar signs greeted me. "This is the first day of the rest of your life." "God grant me the SERENITY to accept the things I cannot change, the COURAGE to change the things I can, and the WISDOM to know the difference." "Are you helping someone? Why not?"

That night, I sat with old and new friends in the basement of the Montrose house for a raucous, lively X-Kalay Game.

In two weeks, our advance team had moved in, furnished the house, met court workers and parole and probation officers, and more than doubled the resident population. They understood at a gut level our core business. We were body snatchers. Find warm bodies and get these struggling human beings into action and on the road to sobriety and self-respect. The only direction our team had needed was, "You're going to like Winnipeg."

I flew back to Vancouver. Less than two months later, I was called back to Winnipeg for something truly amazing.

As lovely as the house on Montrose was, it was very soon inadequate for our purposes. Our program was a "Community within a Community." It was large and diverse and complicated. We made music, we acted in plays, we exercised, and we published our own newspaper. This was not a sit-around-on-the-sofa-and-daydream kind of place. We used to say, "This is not a half-wit house. It's a lifestyle." Our gang was always on the lookout for a bigger and better facility. One day Luis Molina discovered an Oblate Mission in St. Norbert near the University of Manitoba campus off the Pembina Highway.

He marched up to the front door and knocked. A nun answered. "Yes? How may I help you?"

"We'd like to have your property."

"One moment please."

Within days, I'd received the call. "David, we have a fantastic deal on the most amazing facility."

"Really, Luis? What is it?"

"Well, it's an Oblate Mission. The property is right on the river, over a hundred acres. A few cows and a pony."

"A pony."

"Patches. That's his name. Patches, the pony."

"Okay…"

"Wait. The building can house over one hundred people easily. There's an industrial kitchen, private and group dining rooms, a library, and a woodworking shop. Well, the priests want to give it to us. For a dollar a year."

"Sorry, Luis, there must be a bad phone connection here. I thought you said they wanted to give us this Disneyland for a dollar a year. Hahahahahaha."

"That's right. The only thing is, Dave, the head honcho, he wants you to come out and sign the papers and all."

The next day I was sitting in the good Father's office in St. Norbert. He was a friendly, robust man enjoying a great, fat cigar.

"Father, this is such an extraordinary act of Christian charity, giving us this entire property…"

"Don't forget, David, that there is a catch."

"You mean Father Dominic?"

"Yes, it would kill him to leave that woodworking shop of his after all these years. It's his life really and he would be heartbroken to move on. He'll not be a bother to you, I'm sure."

"No, he can probably teach some of our people some skills."

As it turned out, under Father Dominic's tutelage, we began producing the most beautiful homemade furniture and selling it under contract to a major department store. When my daughter was born, we brought her home to sleep in a maple cradle the good Father Dominic had made especially for her.

"But, why Father? I know I shouldn't question such a generous act, but…?"

"Let me ask you a question, David. How old is your average resident?"

"Twenty-six."

"Well, the average age of the people in our Order is sixty-six. We have scarcely half the novitiates we used to have even a few years ago. Frankly, we've been at this for almost 2,000 years and we've had a pretty good run."

"Right."

"We believe that you are doing God's work."

You are doing God's work.

Oh, my. I've never forgotten this moment. I signed the papers, we shook hands and the good Father walked out the door. We moved in on September 26, 1971. Within months we had over 125 people in residence.

For several years, I flew back and forth every month or two between Winnipeg and Vancouver, overseeing both programs, as well as our hotel on Salt Spring Island. At one point, my wife and son and I lived in a private apartment on the St. Norbert site while we got the operation into shape. By and large, however, X-Kalay Manitoba was managed by various Directors of the Foundation, each of whom had come up through the ranks.

Forty years later, the program is still running and it is stronger than ever.

The name has been changed in the intervening years first to The St. Norbert Foundation, and most recently to The Behavioural Health Foundation Inc., Holistic Addictions Treatment. The style has shifted somewhat, but the basic principles are the same. The program has achieved accreditation from a host of governing bodies.

Over the years, The Behavioural Health Foundation has been proud of its many firsts, including the following that once appeared on its website history page:

> The Foundation over the years and continuing today has evolved to suit the needs of the "client" base to which it provides services. The X-Kalay Foundation was the first halfway house in Canada. The X-Kalay Foundation/St. Norbert Foundation was the first residential addictions treatment centre in Canada and, in some cases, North America to:

- Provide long term residential treatment services to teenagers of both sexes

- Provide co-ed services to adults

- Accept families including dependent children in residence

- Provide Adult Basic Education as a part of treatment services

- Provide Special Education classes to teens in residence for substance abuse

- Provide provincially licensed infant, pre-school and school age child daycare services to persons in treatment, staff and the public

- Initiate and implement a Fine Option program

· Be accredited by a review conducted by an external
  accrediting agency

More than forty years after Richard Sims, Tony Lavallee, and I moved into a two-bedroom bungalow on West
5th Avenue in Vancouver, the program is humming along
in top form serving the community and helping alcoholics
and addicts get clean and sober and stay that way. And in
spite of the focus on addictions and alcoholism, more than
80 percent of the resident clients today are Aboriginal men
and women who have wasted years in prisons. When I speak
to groups like the Behavioural Health Foundation today,
I point out that each person is there not only for himself or
herself, not only for the brother or sister sitting beside them,
but also for the person who is not even aware that he or she
needs this safe place. All residents are setting a place at the
table for the next generation of people who are ready to leave
their miseries behind.

14 playing 'the game'

Ten or fifteen people sit in a circle of hard backed chairs for ninety minutes.

They cajole, poke, enquire, admonish and challenge one another. They also laugh and cry and clear the air.

At its simplest, this was the X-Kalay Game. The Game was, in essence, an encounter group. But it was so much more than that. This was the most renowned and most controversial part of the X-Kalay program. If people in the media or in social or psychological services admired the work we were doing, they would speak in the most glowing terms about The Game. If they questioned or distrusted us and our work, they would point to The Game and label it barbaric, attack therapy, crude, ill-advised. At X-Kalay, all resident clients, regardless of corporate status, attended at least three basic Home Games a week.

The Game is an emotional aerobics class. Your emotions are flabby, without tone, control, or self-discipline. Your feelings are submerged most hours of most days, with the potential to explode irrationally at the slightest and most innocuous provocation.

Perhaps for middle class, highly educated, even intellectual readers this seems a wild exaggeration of their realities. And that may or may not be so. But, even though addictions favor no particular social strata, most addicts are gut-driven, emotionally immature people. Their greatest skill is manipulation of others, and the single reason that they are so good at it is that they function almost solely on an instinctive, almost pre-social level. They are great natural therapists. So the first focus of The Game is your feelings. Express yourself. Get it out. Say what's on your mind. Better yet, say what's in your gut. Feel completely free to laugh and cry. Take the plunge and call your boss, your co-worker, or your lover an asshole. Or tell someone how deeply you care for him or her. Express rage, gratitude, puzzlement, fear, love, affection, and kindness. Don't worry about the meaning, the results, the reactions of others, the conclusions—there are none. It's now. It's of the moment. Just spit it out, fool.

But there is more.

The Game is also an exploration, an enquiry without end. Who are you? Where do you come from? What imprints have you allowed to be stamped on your soul? What are the bonds that you are bound to honor? How are they different from the ties that bind? What do you really want? What new life script dare you initiate? What have you always wanted to do? When will you get on with doing it? How do you rate yourself in terms of courage and kindness and fortitude?

What score do you give yourself as a friend, a colleague, a son or daughter, a lover, a companion, a parent, a leader, or simply a good neighbor and citizen?

And more.

The game is a workshop in which to try on new strategies in coping with the people, places, and things around you. You've fought with your best friend for the last fifteen minutes. That's fine. Now, what are you prepared to do to clarify this communication? How, if at all, will you accommodate? Will you compromise? Do you acknowledge the other's point of view? Do you hold a map for the future of your relationship? Will you put it into action? Do you have the guts, the stamina?

The Game took on a number of different forms and shapes.

Remember that this was the seventies, the height of The Human Potential Movement, an era that fostered an explosion of styles, techniques, and methodologies in discovering oneself. The X-Kalay Foundation had acquired a certain fascination for and cachet amongst the trendy set. Always looking to do more good, always looking for revenue sources, we soon initiated weekly Games for non-residents. This was known as the X-Kalay Square Game Club. Before long, our Games rooms and video room were packed night after night with teachers, poets, playwrights, nurses, mail deliverers, landscape gardeners, priests, rabbis, musicians, university students, actors, and movie makers—especially actors and movie makers. These Non-Resident Games, run—or "cooked"—by senior X-Kalay staff, were great fun, and at a mere $15 per person per evening, mildly profitable for the Foundation.

The real profit for us, however, was not so much in dollars

and cents, or even in the work accomplished in the Games. The payoffs came after The Games, when, at 9:30 in the evening, dozens of visiting Game players streamed into our main lounge for coffee and dessert and intermingled with X-Kalay resident clients. Friendships were forged and no doubt a romance or two began. Most important, however, were the natural bridges of understanding that are built when people gather together over food, especially in a somewhat heightened and charged atmosphere.

The X-Kalay resident client Games, however, were different from Square Games in one crucial element and they ultimately served an entire other purpose—social harmony. How do 125 people live together, work together, socialize, and involve themselves in psychologically demanding therapies without resorting to murder and mayhem? As much as we worked at all times for the good and the health and the progress of individual people, we came to an early conclusion in this work. No one is more important than The Group. A dangerous concept, we realized. Taken far enough, this is communism, totalitarianism, or fascism. But, for our purposes, in this setting, the idea was central and it worked. Do everything possible, reasonable, and constructive to aid the unique individual in his or her recovery and growth. Never forget, however, that no one is indispensable. No one can be helped if the whole organization totters.

Thus, The Game was also a hissing steam valve, a place where petty differences and idiosyncrasies could be exposed, beat up, laughed at, and put away for the night. People who worked together could say things to one another they would never dare say, nor should say, during the day. Couples struggling with the mysteries and demands of relationships could cry out for help. The perfectly competent employee, who suffered from lingering depression, could express his pain or the longing for his old friend, my favorite drug.

We soon came to refer often to the group gut. How are we *all* doing? How is the living organism of the institution doing? Corporate decisions were not made in Games, but soundings were heard loud and clear. One person's rant and rave would bounce around the circle and in quick order a battery of similar expressions might emerge. The group gut asserted itself time after time.

So The Game was all these things: community and corporate steam valve, emotional workout, psychological investigation, and bargaining committee. But there were two distinctive qualities that consistently made it different from a typical encounter group: language and intent.

The expressed intent of a Game was never therapy or help. Oh, yes, those necessaries were regular, welcome attendees, but not by design. The intent of the Game was to *have fun*. That's right. You walked into a Game three or more times a week, you took a seat, and you could feel your heart beating with anticipation and excitement and fear. But more than anything, you looked forward to the sheer silliness of it all; here was a chance to be anything you wanted for ninety minutes—a clown, a gangster, a chanteuse, a supplicant, or a saint. Nothing on TV or on the stage could match this. And what truly made this fun? Why the words, of course. The outrageous flights of verbal fancy, the barbs, insults and witty attacks, the side cracks, the bad jokes, and salacious stories became the stuff of in-house legend.

An X-Kalay mantra went, "What you hear in a Game, you leave in a Game." Nevertheless, human nature being what it is, one could regularly expect to hear at the coffee pot after a Game night, "Did you hear the line Paul got off on Bob tonight. Oh, man, hilarious!" The whole point of playing a Game was *to play*, to let fly with your creative genius, to guess and probe and demand and attack and seek out and challenge and, above all, to invent. If, by some wonderful accident, growth and understanding fell out as it often did with the rest of the mess, well, thanks and good luck.

In addition to the regularly scheduled House Games and the non-resident Square Games, there were several other versions that appeared quite often.

The first was the Emergency Game. This did not mean that the house was on fire or that someone needed medical attention. But, often enough to not be an enormous surprise when they were called, Emergency Games might be announced when a group of older resident clients or people in leadership positions discerned that someone in the program was in dire trouble. Is this guy drifting?

The 1962 David Lean epic, *Lawrence of Arabia* is one of my favorite movies. It tells the story of T.E. Lawrence, a British soldier, who led Arab forces on many successful campaigns against the Turks in World War I. Lawrence's first major coup involved seizing the city of Aqaba by attacking inland from the Nefud Desert. The Turkish cannons were pointing out to the sea and they never would expect anyone to cross what was a deadly, forbidding stretch of land.

Lawrence, dressed in Arab garb is, like his Arab army, riding a camel under the equatorial sun. He keeps dozing off, drummed by the heat and the camel's rhythmic gait. The Saudi Prince, riding beside Lawrence, smacks him with a hickory stick or a bamboo swatch. Lawrence snaps awake on time to hear his friend say ominously, "You're drifting! You are drifting!"

This is a great cautionary tale for people in recovery programs. Are you daydreaming about going back to the old life? Drugs? Booze? Crime? Your old friends in failure? Is the guy sitting next to you drifting?

One of the great strengths of the Therapeutic Community model is that it is forever vigilant.

Perhaps a pattern of behavior was being exhibited that said this guy or gal was reverting to old dope fiend thinking without ever actually using drugs. The X-Kalay philosophy was clear. The actual drugs and booze were the least of your problems. They disappeared the moment you moved into our program. The problem was stinking thinking. The problem was the way you approached almost every challenge or opportunity in life—with cynicism or defeat or soul-destroying self-pity. Maybe Jack or Betty had simply been resting on his or her laurels and was not proactively working his or her program. Maybe there had been no recent signs of reaching out to others, helping the newcomer, or participating energetically in available activities. Yes, everyone needs down time and solo time. But being a loner is what got you in the soup to begin with and if your housemates and colleagues see you slipping back into negative mode, you might soon find yourself the focused subject of an Emergency or Special Game.

Then there were the Stews, Psychodramas, Gestalt workshops, and Trips.

When we bought an old warehouse at 7th and Ontario and converted it into our Clubhouse, we built a number of new spaces, including our Video Room at the back of the second floor. Here, as in the several other Game rooms, there was a permanent set of chairs in the requisite circle. In addition, there was a raised platform for the Peanut Gallery and the video equipment. The Peanut Gallery was a kind of observation deck for house members and special guests to watch the drama of the Stew in front of them. Classes from social work and criminology and nursing programs of the universities in town could be found regularly in the Gallery. Video equipment recorded the event as a learning tool. Days after a Stew, resident clients might gather in a room and watch the interactions of the players and discuss what they were seeing. The Stews were reserved for experienced and skilled Game players. They were basically Games played at a heightened level and every manner of technique might be thrown into the pot, including hypnosis, psychodrama and gestalt. Psychodrama and gestalt workshops often were stand-alone events and they were highly anticipated and much attended.

A Trip was a very special event and it took us right back to our beginnings, with our very first group therapy experience with Dr. Lee Pulos. A Trip was a twenty-four-hour marathon blowout. We didn't hold them often, but when we did, they were very powerful experiences. We always felt it necessary to warn all the participants—who were often a mix of resident clients and non-resident visitors—that the journey they were about to take was a little unreal.

"Look everybody, what you're about to experience is a lot

of fun. It can be exhilarating and sometimes terrifying. It will certainly be a powerful experience, not readily forgotten or overlooked. But you must understand that it is also a somewhat false and artificial experience. When it is over, you will be high, over the top emotionally, and so we must issue this one cautionary note. Do not—repeat, DO NOT—make any life changing decisions in the days or even weeks after The Trip. Do not get divorced, separated, or married. Don't up and quit your job to open that hot dog stand on the Kona Coast of the Big Island like you've been dreaming about for the last four years. Don't schedule the sex change or put up the For Sale sign in front of the house. Don't run for public office. For sure, don't run for public office; we've got enough trouble as it is. DO take your time. DO allow some time, a week or two or even a month to come down off the wall and get a sense of what's just happened. Take the time to put it into perspective. It's not that what you are about to be a part of is not legitimate or full of insight or spirituality or whatever you may feel that it is. It's just that it's a dramatically heightened and unusual moment in a life full of moments. OK?"

. . .

What follows now is an almost verbatim—or at least the very best that I can recall it—transcript of an X-Kalay Game.

The woman on the hot seat was Maureen. Maureen was a dangerously obese woman in her late twenties. Her usual costume was a floral-print frock and $1.98 shower thongs. Her profile was almost prototypical of so many of the women in

X-Kalay. She was an addict and a prostitute. She could be marvelously kind and thoughtful. Not two minutes later, she could be a colossal, foul-mouthed, hate-spewing bitch. Not too many months after she became a resident client, she gave birth to a perfectly beautiful and healthy daughter whom she named Kalay. Her children from previous engagements were in foster care. In spite of her own personal struggles, Maureen proved to be a loving and attentive mother with her new child. She took great pride in her baby, and she was especially gracious in sharing her motherhood experience with the other women. Many of the X-Kalay women, some of whom would never have children, some of whom had lost children, tended and cared for baby Kalay as if she were their own. When another gal held Kalay in her arms, Maureen positively glowed.

Here is a dramatic, but not so atypical Game.

ERNIE: You're so fucking thick, man. Of course, she's a drug addict!

CAROL: Why don't you just say it, Maureen? "I'm a drug addict. I'm a drug addict."

PAUL: Librium, Valium, heroin, Quaaludes—what's the goddam difference?

MAUREEN: The *difference* is my *doctor* gave them to me. (*hoots and hollers from all the others in the room*) I was *specifically* instructed by a doctor to take those pills.

CAROL: Well, la-dee-da!

ERNIE: Specifically! Now, that is special.

SHIRLEY: I never got instructions. What a gyp. Where was the "instructions" line anyway? Damn, I must have missed it, babe.

BOB: Not just instructions, Shirl. "Specific instructions." That's where our Maureen stands apart.

ERNIE: Oh, Mo stands apart in a lot of ways, brother.

SHIRLEY: It's kinda funny because I just figured out all by myself that dope makes you feel reeeal gooooood.

BOB: All I get out of that bullshit, Maureen, is that you think you're better than the rest of us.

MICHAEL: Or worse.

JIM: But the reality is...

ERNIE: Oh Lord! Stand way fucking back, folks. Mr. Reality is about to lay it out for us.

JIM: The reality is, Maureen, you're even more screwed up than the rest of us.

ERNIE: Speak for yourself, punk.

BOB: He's right, Maureen. At least we got some clue what's wrong with us...

CAROL: We do?

BOB: I mean we got somewheres to start anyways. But what's your excuse?

ERNIE: For example, you could start by admitting some small thing about yourself.

MAUREEN: Like what, smart ass?

ERNIE: Like how you're the fattest cunt outside of a circus freak show!

SHIRLEY: Hm...nice, Ernie. We'll get to your "respecting women" issues later.

CAROL: She *is* a freak show. Look at that frigging tent she's always wearing. She's not just one of the freaks. She's the whole goddamn sideshow.

MICHAEL: Why are you choking yourself to death, Maureen?

PAUL: How about that?

MAUREEN: How about what?

PAUL: How about you are not satisfied with being hands down the most obese human being on earth…

SHIRLEY: I don't think you even look at half the goop you stuff in your face all the time.

MAUREEN: That's right, Shirl. You don't think.

ERNIE: It's not enough being the Square John Junkie of the Year…

SHIRLEY: Or a mother who can't or won't deal with her kid…

MAUREEN: Fuck! Talk about projection. Listen to Agnes Abortion here.

CAROL: Or a total wipeout as a person of the female persuasion…

MAUREEN: If you assholes didn't have someone to yell at, what would you actually do all day? I mean, really!

CAROL: We'd fuckin' shoot junk and guzzle sterno till we were blue in the face, that's what we'd do, like you don't know.

MICHAEL: Have you even spoken to the kids this week, Mo?

MAUREEN: I have seen or spoken to my children every single goddamn day for the entire eight months I have been here, as if you didn't know. Give me a break, will you?

MICHAEL: Tell you what, Mo. I'll give you a break if you will.

MAUREEN: What?

SHIRLEY: "If I am not for me, who will be?"

BOB: How are we supposed to support you when you spend most of your day shitting on your own head?

PAUL: Then, on top of all that other drek, you've got this world famous asthma condition, or whatever you're calling it this week.

MAUREEN: It's not asthma.

BOB: (*passing it around the circle*) It's *not* asthma.

CAROL: It's not asthma.

ERNIE: It's not asthma.

SHIRLEY: It's not asthma.

MICHAEL: It's not asthma.

JIM: It's not asthma.

MAUREEN: They think it may be a bronchial condition.

CAROL: Perfect! Have another menthol while you're at it.

ERNIE: Who's "they?" The fucking Plumbers and Pipefitters Union?

BOB: Her high-class doctors.

PAUL: Allow me to introduce myself. Harvey Handout, M.D. at your cervix, Ma'am. Drugs by the bagful sanctified by the tongues of the Romans! Quack omnibus quack!

MICHAEL: (*pretending to write this down*) "Omnibus quack…" Very nice, Paul.

SHIRLEY: (*getting up and doing a parading stroll around the backs of the chairs*) "I've got a bronchial condition. Hooray! I've got a bronchial condition."

MAUREEN: Lovely.

SHIRLEY: "I get so much mileage out of my bronchial condition, I may just never let it go."

MAUREEN: I think your driveshaft just came loose.

SHIRLEY: (*waddling and coughing*) "I don't need children or Tupperware…"

BOB: Hi, Mo.

PAUL: Phew! What a stench! Must be the old shitbag herself!

SHIRLEY: "I don't need anything, folks, cause I've got…

(*trumpets*) ta-da-da-da-ta-da! My World Famous Bronchial Condition to keep me warm!"

PAUL: Hooray! Let me embrace my bronchial condition. It's the bestest friend I ever had!

CAROL: Or was it the asthma after all? Oh, I'm so confused.

PAUL: I say, whatever it is, let's bottle it and sell it to the masses. There's a fortune to be made here.

ERNIE: Let's count the pay-offs, shall we?

CAROL: You get to whine about it.

JIM: And visit social workers...

PAUL: And Doc-tors!

MAUREEN: So, your old man's a rich doctor and you're an ungrateful, pothead, acne-faced jerk! So I got to pay for your misgivings? Work it out on someone else, Paul.

CAROL: And shrinks...

BOB: And most of all, you get a lot of dumb needless attention—for all the wrong stuff.

SHIRLEY: (*back in her chair*) Bottom line is you don't even know for sure what you've got.

ERNIE: If, in fact, you got anything, other than chronic attention deficits.

MICHAEL: Why are you choking yourself, Maureen?

MAUREEN: You really get off on these twisters, don't you, Michael? Ever considered sex as a healthy alternative?

BOB: Why don't you just answer his question?

MAUREEN: Pardon me, Bob. I forgot. Krishna speaks. Everyone genuflect real fucking fast.

SHIRLEY: You got the jam to confront that question, Maureen?

MAUREEN: And what are you hooked on, Mike? Game playing? Power?

JIM: (*suddenly standing*) SHUT UP!

ERNIE: Sit down, Kid. You might hurt yourself. (*JIM sits*)

PAUL: Come on, Maureen. What are you doing here?

MAUREEN: What are *you* doing here?

PAUL: Nya, nya, nya. I asked first.

MAUREEN: Well, what is your scam exactly, Paul? Insurance? VEGOMATICS? IT SURE AS HELL ISN'T PEOPLE!

MICHAEL: (*topping her in volume*) MAUREEN!

CAROL: Oh!

MAUREEN: (*looking away*) What?

MICHAEL: (*one-word-at-a-time*) Why … are … you… choking… yourself … to… death…Maureen?

MAUREEN: I…look, I…I don't know. (*chorus of 'come off it,' 'oh, shit,' etc. from the others*) We've been through all this before. God.

PAUL: Not really, Maureen.

CAROL: For sure all the surface bullshit, Mo.

MICHAEL: But we've never really gotten close to that monster or frightened little girl or whoever it is that's rummaging around inside your basic Maureen.

SHIRLEY: Let us meet the geek that's really running the Mo Show.

MICHAEL: Exactly.

BOB: Come on out, Maureen!

PAUL: Hey! Can Maureen come out and play?

ALL: We want Maureen! We want Mau-ree-een!

SHIRLEY: (*picking up an apron from the back of CAROL's chair, in*

harping mother's voice) She'll be out in a minute, children.
Now finish your lunch first, precious. There's a good girl.

MAUREEN: Oh, please...

PAUL: (*mother's voice*) What are you doing, dear? You know
you can't play in your new outfit...

CAROL: (*mother's voice*) Now, where is that adorable little
corduroy jumper I laid out for you?

MICHAEL: (*mother's voice*) Whatever will your teachers think
of me, sending you out in public like that?

MAUREEN: Yah...

CAROL: Now get off those cold, cold steps. Do you want
every single one of your friends to get piles, darling?

MAUREEN: God...

PAUL: What's the matter, pumpkin. Are you having trouble
breathing again?

JIM: I know. Let's get her to a doctor.

PAUL: Yes! Professional intervention, that's what we need.

ERNIE: (*standing in front of her*) This won't hurt, Maureen.
It's just medicine. Just like candy.

SHIRLEY: See what the nice doctor has for you today.

MICHAEL: Such a nice man. Reminds me so much of papa.

CAROL: Or what papa could've been like.

SHIRLEY: Should've been like.

PAUL: Take it angel. (*starts humming, "Rock-A-Bye, Baby..."*)

CAROL: This sweet candy will make you breathe better,
Maureen. Take it, take it...

SHIRLEY & CAROL: Come on, Maureen. Come on, now...

MAUREEN: (*rocking back and forth, her hands locked under her
armpits*) It's all right. I'm...Just...just leave me be. OK?

PAUL: What a shame. We've got a bad connection here, pumpkin. I can hardly hear you…

JIM: You'll just have to speak up!

MAUREEN: No…no…

MICHAEL: (*pretending to struggle past SHIRLEY & CAROL who won't let him through*) Maureen, Maureen, please! Why won't you let me know you? You've got all these damn barriers up all the time, Maureen, please…

JIM: (*on his feet*) Maureen, listen to me. Please. Listen. I…I'm just like you. I've been trapped inside for years. Here, Maureen, not in prison, but here. A "memory sack." That's what I've been, Mo. For a long, long time.

MAUREEN: Oh…

JIM: Show me the way out, will you? (*extends his hand to her*)

MAUREEN: (*so quietly*) I want…

OTHERS: Yes? You want..?

MAUREEN: I want …out…

OTHERS: (*backing off, with encouragement, gently*) Hm? You want what, Mo?

MAUREEN: (*exploding*) OUT! I want out of …this tomb! I AM SO TRULY SICK OF BEING A FREAK! (*right to JIM*) I…you see, I made myself…fat.

ERNIE: What did she say? Fat?

MAUREEN: An obstacle course…

BOB: Yes?

MAUREEN: What I am, who I am at heart is so awful, so unattractive that I have made it impossible for you or you or you to get close to me. Who would bother? Who would want to? I am…FAT! FAAAATTTT! I am drowning…

PAUL: And..?

MAUREEN: That's my challenge to the world, Paul. Wade through the shit. I dare you! I give you fat and smells and smoke and coughs and…

JIM: And..?

MAUREEN: And…and, you know. If anyone knows, Jim, you do. I want someone who will slug past all the…dross…

ERNIE: "Dross." Very good.

MAUREEN: A person…well…

JIM: Well..?

MAUREEN: I mean one good person, eh?

SHIRLEY: Will you meet one good person halfway, Maureen? Will you? Look at Jim, Maureen. He is reaching out to you.

A moment of stillness. MAUREEN is crying softly, looking up at the ceiling. JIM takes another step toward her, smiles. Tentatively, she rises from her chair, takes his hands and accepts his embrace. MAUREEN crosses to SHIRLEY, who stands. They embrace.

MAUREEN: Thank you, Paul. Thanks, Carol. Everybody. I…I've got to practice letting the world in a bit. Everybody…thank you.

People are crossing to give her a kiss or an embrace, as The Game ends…

15 the fabulous flying brothers m

"First time they let me out of Prince George jail, I swore I'd never go back in. That's it for me, man. Can't do that again, no sir. Won't. Oh, yah. I was rearrested two days later. I was thirty-three years old and now I was truly shit scared. No skills, no scams, no gimmicks to work. OK. So, I buckled down, took the chef's course, and when I got out this next time, I grabbed the first bus straight to Vancouver and the front door of The X-Kalay Foundation. Maybe they need a good cook, right? Never occurs to me maybe I need them. Ha! I didn't even last one whole day.

"My read off the top is these people are crazy. One minute they're telling you to shut your face, the next they're offering you a coffee. And all this is happening just while you're waiting in the fucking hall for an interview. So I hightailed it up to this friend's place. She was an anthropology teacher at the university. She listens to me whine for about an hour and then she tells me that she heard this X-Kalay place works and it's probably what I really need. Like, I should get my sorry butt back there toot sweet. Well, she was usually pretty good at giving me what I needed, if you know what I mean, so I went back. Smartest thing I ever done."

Meet Bob.

. . .

Entry into the program involved two crucial and demanding first tests—The Wait and The Interview.

Depending on who you were, The Wait could take anywhere from one hour to an entire twenty-four-hour day and night. You might come through the front door and say something like, "I'd like to join the program," or "I need help," or "Could I speak to someone?" If you were an eighteen-year-old boy, just released hours ago from a six-month stay in the Haney Correctional Institute, we would understand that you are full of piss and vinegar, not to mention hormones, anxiety, and hysteria and that keeping you in a chair in the front hallway for much longer than an hour might not be very productive. Chances are you'd bolt for the nearest trouble you could find.

If, on the other hand, you were a street-wizened, mid-thirties heroin addict and all-round general asshole, accustomed to playing everyone for a rube, we'd be content to let you stew in your own juices for a good, long time. We'd offer you coffee and cigarettes, and, as we wandered by, we'd either ignore you or say, "Hi. How're you doing?" Odds are that one of us already knows you from another movie—the street or jail.

What was the point of The Wait?

You're an addict. You are an emotional infant. You must have instant gratification. You always want what you want when you want it, which is *now*. If you can't get drugs or a room or potato chips immediately, you begin the Train Wreck, smashing everything and everyone around you at will. So, our goal is to begin treatment at once. From the first breath, from the moment you venture that hesitant stumble through those doors for all the wrong reasons filled with all the worst intentions, we are on your case and working your file. "Today is the first day of the rest of your life." Wait. For just once in your life, you child, wait for something. Do you want this? Do you really? Well, wait. Show us; show yourself that you mean business. Wait.

The Interview looks like this. One chair facing four or five chairs. You, the prospect, are facing people who have been in the program two months and six months and a year and a half and three years. You may know some of these people. You certainly recognize them for street people. But...well, there is something different about them, something kind of hard to pinpoint.

The Interview sounds like this.

"Hi. I'm Dave."

"Hi. I'm Judy."

"Hi. I'm Dennis."

"Hi. I'm Clare."

"André."

"And what's your name?"

"I'm Ken."

"OK, Ken. What can we do for you?"

"Well, I'm a junkie."

"You collect scrap metal?"

"What?"

"You're in the salvage business, Kenny?"

"Kenneth is into antiques, don't you know. Sweet."

"No, no. I'm a junkie. A heroin addict."

"Oh. A heroin addict! Why didn't you say so in the first place?"

"'Junkie.' It's so confusing, so indeterminate."

"You see, Ken, how your laziness with language keeps getting you into trouble? Nobody knows what the fuck you're ever talking about. No wonder you keep having a tough time getting what you want out of life."

"Not that he knows what he wants out of life."

"Not that Kenny ever wants anything more than his next score."

"OK. So we cleared that up pretty quickly. You're a heroin addict. Congratulations. So, what can we do for you, Ken?"

"Well, I'd like to stop. I need to get off."

"I need to get off too, buddy, but that's a whole other story."

"You're saying you'd like to stop shooting heroin into your veins, is that it?"

"Yes, exactly. What the fuck?"

"No, you what the fuck, sunshine!"

"Let me ask you something, Kenny."

"Ken."

"Ken. Kenny. Kenneth. Sunshine. Asswipe. Pukeface. Mr. Nowhere Man."

"He's a real nowhere man, sitting in his nowhere land, making all his nowhere plans for nobody..."

"Nowhere man, please listen…"

"You don't know what you're missing…"

"You said you'd like to quit using junk, right?"

"Right."

"So I was about to ask you—before the Beatles dropped in—how long have you been sitting in that chair in the hallway, soaking up our oxygen?"

"Uh, I got here before noon."

"And now it's about 9:30, so you've already been in our clean and sober environment for almost ten hours, is that right?"

"Sounds, uh, sounds about right."

"So what's your problem? You say you want to stop using heroin. And you've been here for most of the day. And you didn't shoot any junk in that time, did you?"

"No.

"Well, you could have, you sneaky thief."

"That's right, you used our bathroom about four times since you've been here, so you could easily have fixed in there."

"Hey, wait a minute!"

"No, you wait a minute, princess."

"Well, Ken, did you use our bathroom to get one last, little taste?"

"No! I wouldn't do that."

"Hahahahahaha…"

"And you wouldn't do your mother and your sister and your brother, but you have your whole miserable life, so what's to stop you now?"

"Well, I didn't, no matter what you think."

"And you know what, Ken? We agree. We believe you.

You probably *didn't* shoot up in our bathroom. And for that we are mighty glad. Not only that, but we congratulate you. You see. The program is working already."

"So, the whole point is this, Ken. You want to stop using and you've been here for ten hours and you haven't used, so we've solved that problem right smart. So say, 'Thank you,' and tell us please, now that we cured you of your mighty fucking famous heroin addiction what can we do for you tonight? Try to understand, Ken, that most of the people in the world are *not* shooting heroin as a regular vocation, so for folks like us it takes a bit of an effort just to work our miserable way back to zero!"

Over the next three hours, the covers will be ripped from Ken's façade. He has a construct, a presentation that he offers to the world. He's a tough guy one moment, a sorrowful victim the next. Tough guy, victim. Tough guy, victim. The Fuck-up Two-Step Tango. He avoids the truth like Venetians avoid the canals in the heat of summer. It will be made clear to him that the least of his problems is heroin. That his real problem is he has no season's tickets to the opera or the Canucks hockey team. He has no library card or mortgage or insurance policy or children or spouse or partner or real friends. He doesn't own a bicycle and he doesn't want one unless he can sell it for smack. He is emotionally, fiscally, and morally bankrupt and bereft.

He is dying of the single greatest human motivator, the one commonality that throws us into addictions of drugs, alcohol, sex, work, books, food, and madness—loneliness. He has made consistently lousy choices. He has created a downward spiraling vortex of lousy choices that have narrowed his concerns to a tiny piece of silver paper, a tenth of a gram of inert white powder, a match, some water, and a needle.

In his life, a scant and paltry and vacuous life he has *chosen* every day for years with a hundred tiny bad choices, there is no room for Mozart, for crossword puzzles, Mandarin lessons, vegetables, travel, laughter, tears, horticulture, astronomy, drama, swimming, or any projects that might be saddled with a beginning, a middle, and an end.

The "helpers," the good folks who focus on the white powder and the wine are as narrow and self-defeating as the addict they think they can help. The real job is the slow and steady injection of the myriad shapes and colors of real life. The addict is not sick. Sick people go to doctors. Doctors who waste everyone's time and their own training and talent trying to help addicts might more profitably go to a doctor themselves. Or, at the least, attend to people with tuberculosis or cancer or a bad cold.

The addict is not sick. He is not even congenitally stupid. He makes lousy choices. He can learn to make better choices, one tiny step at a time, over time. It has taken him so many years to screw up this badly; he can't expect to get right overnight. There are no magic bullets, no miracle cure. This will take time and time is on his side. He is afraid. We understand this. We are all afraid of something. We know all this, because we are he, we are the same; we've been there. We're still there. We're learning, we're emerging from our cocoons.

Finally, we will ask him what he can do for us.

"You see, Ken, we're not really here to help you. We are busy helping ourselves. And we're having a blast doing that.

We're busy day and night. We're doing work that's important and personally rewarding, and we're having fun, more
fun than we ever knew was possible, without a needle or a
bottle or some con on the go. So what can you contribute
to the enterprise? Are you a cook? We have a lot of mouths
to feed. Are you a great speaker? We're at public schools
every day, talking to the kids about the idiot lives we've
been living. Can you balance a set of books? Running an
organization like this costs a lot of money and requires a
good set of accounts."

Invariably, Ken will start out by cleaning the toilets. From
there, the only way is up.

. . .

Bob, the graduate chef from the Prince George jail, was
not a heroin addict. He was an alcoholic, a thief, a liar, and
a dedicated jailbird. He was also curiously sympathetic and
charming. These, of course, are the greatest weapons of the
anti-social underachiever: charm and sympathy. And Bob
had them in spades.

He survived a particularly long and grueling interview
in which he cried and swore allegiance to a process he knew
nothing about. We set him to work and dedicated ourselves
to keeping a close watch on this guy. We knew instinctively
that he would be both a valuable, energized addition to the
program and a handful of regular, petty nightmares. We
were not disappointed on either score.

He worked hard and he dived into all the interactions
of the Game. He was fearless in these encounters—funny,

clever, insightful, obscene, empathetic, and supportive; in short, a good creative Game player.

Three weeks after Bob arrived at our front door, he huffed and puffed his way into my office. He was in his now familiar indignant mode. When Bob felt that the world was once again, with striking regularity, treating him unfairly, handing him the short stick, he would thrust out his pouting lower lip, stare at the ground, shake his head and speak in a husky dramatic whisper. "You, you know, you've really fucked me up."

"Glad to hear it. That's my job."

"Yah, well, you've really done it now."

"OK, Bob. Why don't you just tell me in plain English. What have I done to you now?"

"I'm nothing."

"Sorry..?"

"I'm nothing, man. I came in here I was somebody. I had an identity."

"Which was…what?"

"Well, I was something."

"You were a loser."

"I was a crook. Not a super crook, what the fuck, eh? Bob, the Safecracker. Something. Then, sometimes, I was Bob, the Bootlegger. That was nice. Very sociable, you know. People needing me. Three, four in the morning, guy needs a place to get out of the weather. Sit quiet by the kitchen table. A little schnapps, a little bullshit…real nice, cozy. Maybe the guy's visiting from out of town. Tells some neat stories. I had some really good friends there. Then I fall in here, see, and you keep telling me things like, 'Hard work, Bob. No chiseling. Keep your nose clean, play it straight ahead and before you know it, you'll be Town Clerk or something.' Right? 'Honesty is the only policy. Change is the only constant.' And like that till I'm mumbling this crap in my sleep half the time. 'Forgive yourself. Give yourself permission.' Christ, man, I've been forgiving myself till I'm fucking purple!"

"Ha! I love it!"

"Sometimes I'm up at two, three o'clock pacing around, repeating these things like nursery rhymes. I make extra pastries in the kitchen just to have an excuse for being awake so early. Pretty soon I'm standing by the stove lecturing the apple turnovers, you know, holding court over the cinnamon rolls. 'Go through the motions. You are what you do. Everyone is redeemable.'"

"So now what are you, Bob? A park bench? A bran muffin?"

"That's what I'm telling you. I am nothing. I have no identity."

"Congratulations, Bob, and welcome to Phase Three."

"What the fuck?"

"Hey, you came in here maybe twenty days ago and you were Mr. Stupid. Phase One. Now, we've done some brain washing. We've literally washed your brain and emptied it considerably of Mr. A-Hole. So now you are a clean slate. Phase Two. Excellent. We've done our job."

"Great."

"No, great is Phase Three. Phase Three is welcome to my new identity."

"Which is..?"

"Whatever you want it to be. How about Mr. Accentuate the Positive? How about Joe Citizen? How about Call Me Responsible?"

"When does all this kick in?"

"It kicked in ten minutes ago, Bob, when you lumbered in here with that thorn in your paw. Have a nice new life."

Bob climbed the organizational ladder quickly. Within a few months, he was the head chef for what was now upwards of forty residents, planning and delivering three great meals a day. In fact, he threw himself with passion into every aspect of the Foundation, showing interest in how we raised money, in the Supply Crew, the Morning Concepts, and school speaking programs, music, and sports. He took an active, perceptive, and concerned interest in how others were progressing. He was respectful with the people who worked below him in the kitchen. He was very funny and a wily and dogged competitor in our Sunday touch football games.

On the other hand...Bob was sycophantic in the extreme, playing the good butler to the hierarchy at all times. In short, he was a major suck hole. And his libido was running way faster than his brain. Girls were either drawn to him or repulsed. Several truly despised the guy. And he was possibly the greatest melodrama queen in the history of X-Kalay. A week couldn't pass without some enormous personality conflict or procedural ruling needing to be adjudicated—Bob always at the sweaty, intense center of it all.

But, Bob has his own special place in this book because of one incident, an event that speaks volumes about the entire and mysterious process of rehabilitation and the seriousness with which we approached our work at the Foundation.

On a sunny summer afternoon, Bob and I strolled up to the neighborhood café. I can't remember what I ordered, but I remember vividly that Bob had a strawberry milkshake.

I remember this detail because it lies exactly at the heart of the story. As we walked back to the house on 16th Avenue, Bob started laughing to himself. "Boy, I really screwed that girl!"

"Pardon me?"

"Ha! The waitress. She short-changed herself."

"Our waitress?

"She gave me back twenty-five cents more than she should have. Ha!"

"Oh."

We walked back into the house. Bob headed into the kitchen and I went into the den, which, when not in use as a Games or Interview room, doubled as my office. I assembled a group of five people, and we summoned Bob to join us. He was now about to experience a ritual known as a "Haircut." The next several hours changed his life. Bob found himself sitting in a chair facing five other chairs, just as he had a few months earlier in his Interview. One of the women started things off in high gear. "So, hot shot, stealing from the little people again?"

"What?"

"And what a score, what a take, what a haul!"

"Mr. Criminal Mastermind strikes again."

"What are you going to do with this bounty, genius? Don't spend it all at once."

"What the hell are all you people talking about?"

"SHUT UP, YOU ASSHOLE!

"We're talking about the twenty-five cents you couldn't help but brag about that you stole from the waitress at the Ridge Coffee Shop, that's what we're talking about, you faceless prick! That's right, suck hole. Start gagging on your little pink milkshake. You should only choke to death."

"Do you even know who that waitress is? Do you? Do you know anything about her?"

"Well, I'll tell you, Bob. This is who that woman is that you so gleefully ripped off for twenty-five whole Canadian cents. She is probably a single parent, a mother who stands on her feet eight hours a day, while her kid is in daycare or being minded by grandma, so she can make ends meet."

"AND…she is paid minimum wage AND she depends on tips AND if she's two bits short on her tally at the end of her tiring shift…"

"Tiring from putting up with garbage like you all day, you puke…"

"Then she has to take the two bits out of her tips to make up the total or the creepy owner she works for who is trying to hit on her all day…"

"Just like YOU are trying to hit on each and every one of the girl's who work for you in the kitchen, you perv…"

"OR the creepy owner will fire her or demand a blow job or something or maybe just a quick feel in the back room to make up for the twenty-five cents you stole, motherfucker!"

You get the idea. Now multiply this harangue by three or four hours, delving deeper and deeper into the shoddy and suspect value system that motivates the petty criminal. His essential belief is a profoundly twisted rationalization that justifies all his bad acts. And it is this: *Life has screwed me and therefore I have the right to screw everyone else—first.* The core of his value system is in fact self-pity. It is self-pity that drives his every play. Today we speak glibly about *entitlement.* Many have observed the social stain in recent times of people who seem to feel that the government or their families or their communities or the world at large *owes* them something. This is exactly the mechanism that propels the small-time crook. You owe me. I am entitled to my revenge, to my twenty-five-cent triumphs.

"Weren't you the guy who sat in this very chair in this very room about four months ago and swore that you were so frightened of what your life had become that you would do anything to change? Wasn't that you, crying big crocodile tears?"

In the end, Bob was asked if he really wanted to stay at X-Kalay. "Do you really want to put in the hard work?"

"Yes, I do."

"How can we know that? You've been role-playing at being a citizen the last few months, but all the time, Bob the petty thief was alive and well and just looking for the opportunity to strike out at the world again. What can you do to prove to us that you really mean business? What can you give us as a sign of your serious commitment?"

"I dunno."

"Well, what have you got? You got a car we can have? A bank account? The house in the Hamptons? What about that? Maybe you could get a mortgage on that?"

Bob had nothing to give us but the hair on his head. That's right. The hair on his head. Bob agreed to have his head shaved. Hey, it's only hair; it'll grow back. And he lost his job and status in the organization. He went back to square one, cleaning the toilets. *And he walked back to the coffee shop and returned the twenty-five cents to the waitress and apologized for his grievous mistake.* And he was a walking, bald role model and object lesson and teacher for all the other resident clients about the meaning of commitment. *This* was truly the first day of the rest of Bob's life. His hair grew back and he regained his job as head chef.

Forty years later, a woman stopped me on the street.

"Say, aren't you David? Didn't you do that work with drug addicts way back when? Yah, I was running group homes for kids at that time and the very best house leader we ever had was one of your graduates. He and his wife were terrific. They just did great work."

Bob.

. . .

Archie was Bob's older brother.

We found Archie holding up a lamppost right in the mean old heart of Skid Road at Main and Hastings. He was a one-armed Native Indian alcoholic, epileptic, jailbird, and mental institution habitué. Remember that description; it's the first half of the Archie sandwich. Bob and Archie both came from Kenora, Ontario, for so many years one of the most desperately ugly places for Aboriginals in all of the Americas. Poverty, drunkenness, violence, illegitimacy, and institutional confinement were the norm. Archie lost his arm when he was eighteen and drunk. He tried to hop a freight train and missed. Train, one; Archie, zero.

The key point in Archie's interview came right near the end. The Interview was relatively short. It was evident to everyone in the room—except Archie, of course—that this was essentially a good man, a very good man. He was a sweet, lost soul. Moreover, he was smart, lugging around under all the other dead weight baggage, some basic smarts that he had rarely had the courage or self-belief to put to use.

The subject of Archie's epilepsy came up.

Someone jokingly held out a palm, televangelist style. "Arise, my child, and medicate no more. Throw away that poison, my son."

Archie had spent so much of his life in institutions of one kind or another, so much time being dictated to by doctors. We had a doctor and a nurse on call if the need arose, which it rarely did. Something told us instinctively that this man needed to be drug free in every possible way just now. All right. If he had a fit or something, we'd have to deal with the consequences and change our strategy. I worked with Archie for four years. I watched him marry and father two children. In all that time, he never had a grand mal seizure. He had one small seizure, which passed in a matter of minutes. We used to call him our miracle man.

Archie's first few days in X-Kalay didn't look that promising. He was vacuuming the hall carpets. The vacuum cleaner began to overheat and smoke. Archie's solution was to hurry the machine into a cold bath. Fortunately, the vacuum was unplugged at the time.

But it didn't take long for Archie to find his true calling.

Within six months, Archie became the head of our Supply Crew. He kept that position for several years. He ran the department all through the tremendous period of growth when we went from forty people to over 125 people in residence in Vancouver. At the same time, we added our hotel on Salt Spring Island and our almost mirrored duplication of programming in Winnipeg, Manitoba. Most of the goods and services that came into X-Kalay were donated by businesses, church groups, and individuals. Stoves, clothing, cribs, beds, mattresses, food, office equipment, cars and trucks, tickets to concerts of every kind, building materials, and party favors were all a part of the daily Supply Crew inventory.

I once stood in the office of the CEO of Finning Tractor, telling him about our work.

"That all sounds great, David. I like it. What can we do to help? What do you need?"

"A truck."

He looked out over the acreage of his yards works. "Take the yellow GMC."

Our Supply Crew people were, in effect, professional beggars. And nobody came close to Archie in terms of hard-core results. Put him in a tweed sports jacket and tie and trousers (one sleeve of the jacket discreetly tucked into the pocket) and send him out with a mission and a good story to tell, and Archie could hustle almost anything from anybody. We don't really know how he did it. All we knew was that he was sensational. We called him the King of the Hustlers.

In 1971, Central Mortgage and Housing Corporation, a federal government department, dedicated, among other things, to finding housing solutions for the poor, gave us a 110% mortgage so that we could buy an old warehouse building at 26 West 7th Avenue and fix it up.

We had dubbed the building The Clubhouse, and with an industrial kitchen, a dining room, a stage, a dance floor, a daycare center, and the offices and other rooms we were soon to build, this became our headquarters. Our 125 resident clients would bed down at various homes around the city, including our old mansion on West 16th Avenue and several former fraternity houses on campus at the University of British Columbia. But The Clubhouse became the beehive and heart of our program. Intake, interviews, Games, lectures, schoolwork, administration, medical, daycare, meals, entertainment, and house meetings all took place in this building.

The two great floor plates, each about 2,000 square feet, back of the street front offices were undeveloped. We needed to build offices and Games rooms and meeting rooms. "Archie, we need some Gyproc."

"Sure, Dave. What's Gyproc?"

"Well, it's a kind of plasterboard that you use to make walls. We're going to need lots of it to finish the two warehouse floors."

The next afternoon I was sitting in my new office on the third floor of our building. Suddenly, there was an excruciating, grinding noise echoing through the building. I had forgotten that just below me there was a two-story, corrugated metal, industrial door that hadn't been opened in years. Now, it was shrieking to life. I leaned out the window. There below me was an eighteen-wheeler flatbed backing into the building. It was loaded with *tons* of Gyproc! Yesterday, Archie didn't know what Gyproc was; today, he came home with a truckload of the stuff.

The next day, I told Archie that we would need some paint for all these new walls we were going to build. That's all I said. *Some* paint. The day after that one of our guys drove our bright red three-ton into the building filled with gallons of paint—pick a color, madam, any color. Do you fancy russet, perhaps?

But there is one story about Archie that defines the beauty of X-Kalay. Recall what Archie's rap sheet looked like when we first met him: a drunk, an epileptic, chronic jailbird, and a mental institution patient. Well, here's the other side of the Archie sandwich. Here's how I will always remember him.

One spring, we came up with the idea that we should open our Salt Spring Island facility to young boys and girls whose parents could not possibly afford to send them to a summer camp. We had the hotel and the five cabins up back and a couple of boats and the dock sitting right on the protected waters of beautiful Vesuvius Bay. We had enough resident staff to easily care for eight or ten kids at a time. All we would need really would be a few dollars to cover the cost of B.C. Ferries transportation and the extra food to keep the kids going during their stay with us.

We approached the City of Vancouver for help. "We're going to take some Vancouver kids over to Salt Spring Island for a week a time. We're thinking eight to ten kids for a week, times eight or ten weeks over the summer. All of these kids will be from families on welfare. We're hoping you can give us a few hundred dollars to help defray the costs."

The ready response of the city bureaucrats was creative and stunning. "But you're taking these kids out of our jurisdiction."

"Excuse me?"

"Why should we give you money? You're taking these kids out of the city to another jurisdiction."

"Perhaps we weren't clear. These are *city* kids, you see, with no resources. We thought it would great if they could be exposed to a summer camp experience."

"Well, that's all well and good, isn't it? But you're taking them out of our jurisdiction."

End of conversation. Who has the patience for this kind of blindness?

In the end, Archie and his Supply Crew hustled more hot dogs and buns, eggs, cereal, fruit, and cocoa—whatever it took to feed the children.

We put an ad in the *Vancouver Sun* newspaper.

> Are you on welfare? Would you like your child to have a summer camp experience? The X-Kalay Foundation is offering a free one-week summer camp to a limited number of Vancouver children who qualify. X-Kalay will take groups of eight to their Salt Spring Island facility for one week at a time. If your child is between eight and twelve years of age, please appear in person on Wednesday morning, May 12th at 9:00 a.m. to register at the X-Kalay Foundation, 26 West 7th Avenue, Vancouver.

I drove up at 9:30 that morning. The line started at our front door and wound around Manitoba Street at the far end of the block. Mothers, fathers, and children. Mostly, I'm sorry to report, mothers and children. A few questions of eligibility were asked. Medical problems, if any, were noted. Names and phone numbers were taken. I recall no one being turned away. Ten weeks of summer camps were set, dates and times and transportation confirmed.

It is important to remind the reader that this initiative

was performed entirely by resident clients, all of whom were recovering drug addicts, alcoholics, prostitutes, bank robbers, thieves, ex-cons, hippy potheads, and acid burn-outs. I was the Executive Director, but I have no memory of doing anything on this project, in fact, on *many* of our projects. It was all done in house. No social workers or recreation specialists. This was one of the principles of twelve-step programs in living action. *"You've got to give it away to keep it."* The best thing I often did was to give the green light to other people's endlessly inventive ideas and stand back and marvel at how it all unfolded.

And here's what I saw, what I will never forget.

One afternoon that summer, I was standing on the cliff behind our hotel overlooking Vesuvius Bay. I heard some happy commotion approaching below. Look. There's Archie in the most dreadful purple cotton cut-offs. He has no shirt on. And we can see that with the one arm that he has, he is pulling some sort of a big rope. At the other end of the rope, twelve or fifteen feet back, is a raft, a log raft strung together in quick-build, haphazard fashion. And on the raft are a pile of young boys and girls hollering and laughing and urging Archie on to go faster, go faster.

Where's Archie, the Disposable One, the social pariah? Search me, because, look, here's Archie, the camp counselor, Archie the surrogate parent, Archie the boy-at-heart coach and role model for children.

Moral of the Archie story? There are several.

The first is the ironclad rule that you just never can predict who will shine and who will fold and slink off into the night. Coming out of the gate, Archie was the most unlikely candidate for success one can imagine—a one-armed, alcoholic, epileptic mental patient and chronic jailbird. To society at large, he was entirely dispensable drek. Lock him away; forget him. Yet, his personal success was monumental. He was also one of the kindest, sweetest persons I've ever met, sunshiny and positive in almost every circumstance.

The second lesson is that, on face value, one would think that "saving" Archie would have taken a phalanx of professionals from a dozen fields. The truth is his recovery, like everyone else's, remains mysterious. But we do know that a constant steady dose of two elements of a seemingly disparate nature were key. On the one hand, he was loved and liked and praised and thanked every day for being exactly who he was and for doing the good work he did. On the other, he was scolded and harangued for and confronted by the small stupidities he let go by. We loved him and we kicked his butt. We loved him and we kicked his butt. Say it with me—we loved him and we kicked his butt. In short, we spooned out for him just the two magic marmalades he needed—love and discipline.

And after all the rigorous studies about this kind of work are written up, bound, submitted, read, and put back on the shelf to gather dust, this is truly the core process—love and discipline. The love is kind and embracing but not weekkneed; and the discipline is not cruel or punishing, but guided and instructive.

Archie was accepted whole-heartedly as an integral and important part of a small, complex community. He was a one-armed guy who played a clever round of bridge and a vigorous Sunday afternoon of football. He sang at the concerts and he played with the children.

This mysterious process takes time and focus and knowledge.

And it works.

16 a day in the life

By 1971, the X-Kalay Foundation had become a complex organization. Resident clients included not only the Native Indian ex-convicts with whom we had begun four years earlier, but also an increasingly diverse array of characters. Of course there were recovering drug addicts, alcoholics, and ex-cons. That's what we were known for. But there were also muddled housewives, terminal hippies, and a scattering of philosophical seekers with an eye for communal life. This was the full dress Flower Power West Coast in the 1970s, a time of great social upheaval and exciting bursts of creativity in the arts and the humanities.

Ken owned a vacuum store. He had the Red Skelton good fellow laugh. He was a good businessman and an attentive and caring father to his two adult children. He was also a silent, secret drinker. He put the shop on hold and moved in for two years.

Brenda and her husband were both falling down drunks. They owned a spectacular, architect-designed, West Coast cedar-and-glass home near the water in West Vancouver. Like many of her neighbors, Brenda began her drinking day as soon as the kids had been packed off to their private school. The party fell into full swing when her husband returned home for pre-dinner cocktails. By mid-evening, they were either out cold in the laundry room or slapping each other around the marble stairways. Brenda moved into X-Kalay; her husband didn't.

Nina was escaping her creepy lover. Shelley had three young daughters, no current husband, and a fatal attraction to selfish, emotionally unavailable men. You'll understand that she struggled with the demon depression. Dirk felt right at home in Shaughnessy. He had grown up in privileged circumstances, angry, and afraid of his own shadow. He was also terribly bright and funny, and not long after he left X-Kalay, he began a career in journalism, which sent him eventually to the editorial board of one of the largest daily papers in Western Canada.

Ted and Margaret were addicts. They were also dear friends of mine from my early years in Vancouver, long before I had heard of the Company of Young Canadians or the Indian Friendship Group in the B.C. Penitentiary.

Margaret was a warm and charming, sexy gal who was a waitress at a local jazz club. Ted worked at odd jobs, but at the time, he was my hero. He dressed in the most mod fashion and looked a dead ringer for one of the Beatles. Both Ted and Margaret had great raucous laughs. One day, just a year or two before I walked into the Offices of the Company of Young Canadians and met Geoff Cue, Ted and Kerby, another friend, took me downtown to Main and Hastings to hang out with them while they scored some heroin. I had no idea what they were doing. I knew that heroin was illegal and therefore dangerous to procure, but that was about it. We loitered about in front of one of the many bars in the neighborhood, with Kerby and Ted looking for the world like a couple of characters out of a comedy about guys trying to score heroin. Eyes darting furtively in all directions at once, shushing me and each other if anyone strolled by. In those days, the local narco-cops were ferocious in their dedication. They'd just as soon choke you to death than bother with the paper work and the pesky court appearances resulting from an arrest.

When Kerby and Ted finally landed their prize, we dashed into an alley. They rolled up their sleeves and went to work. They were kind enough to offer me a taste. I had no interest in sticking a needle in my arm. No thanks. A week or so later, I accompanied Ted in mid-afternoon when he went to collect from a friend who had burned him on some small-time drug deal. I will never forget Ted kicking in the door. I was terribly impressed. I thought these peculiar experiences were all very romantic and colorful.

Now, less than five years later, Ted and Margaret were my clients, living at our treatment center and trying to come to terms with their drug habits.

So here's the challenge. You have 125 people living in half a dozen locations around the city and working in or from a central Clubhouse. You are also running several small businesses, therapy groups, and social programs both within the organization and out in the community. How do you keep everyone busy and active and productive each day without the whole carousel spinning out of control?

Like this.

Everybody has a job, an assignment, a role to play, responsibilities, large or small. Everybody has a place to sleep and to relax. Everybody has at least one designated social circle, like his/her Home Game. Residents are also divided into tribes, more manageable groups of ten or twelve people for recreational and educational activities.

Wake up for everyone is no later than eight; for many, if they are cooking breakfast or performing one of a dozen other chores, it is much earlier. So you attend to your toilet, shower and dress, and appear for a healthy breakfast. Did you know that dope fiends rarely eat breakfast? Did you know that addicts wouldn't know a vegetable if they fell in a garden of zucchini? Did you know that addicts don't know how to fuck? Or do many of the myriad things that so many of us take for granted every day? So saying that you begin the day with a healthy breakfast may seem obvious to you, but it's a huge deal for some others. A healthy breakfast is a revolution in behavior for a drunk or a drug addict.

The in-house daycare has been up and running since early morning. A few of the mothers are already working with the volunteer nurse. Other mothers will replace them after lunch and take their turn taking care of everyone's babies and toddlers until late afternoon.

After breakfast you attend a Morning Concept. Better yet, you conduct a Morning Concept. Everyone attends; everyone in time will lead. A Concept is simply a short meeting to consider one great idea and thus set the tone for the day. Ten minutes at the most. Someone writes the Concept on the blackboard or flip chart and reads it out.

"Be not ashamed of mistakes and thus make them crimes." Confucius.

"By appreciation, we make excellence in others our own property." Voltaire.

There's the idea. What do you think? Excellent. Thanks for the discussion, everybody. Let's get to work.

Before everyone sets off in twelve different directions at once, the necessary bane of all human organizations briefly appears—Announcements. In the army, these are known as DRO's, Daily Routine Orders.

"We're pleased to announce that having done a terrific job for the past six months, Shelley is moving on from her secretarial work at the executive offices with Carol. As of this morning, and at her own request, by the way—so don't ever be afraid to ask for that better job you've been eyeing— Shelley is joining Archie as his Second in Command on the Supply Crew. Let's wish her luck. We know you're going to be terrific, Shelley.

"Bev and Marvin will be at Windermere School at eleven talking to three senior classes. Now, for those of you who have never been on a school speaking engagement, what are you waiting for, a hand-painted invitation? If you're a righteous dope fiend or alcoholic, you've got a story to tell. Don't dramatize your sordid little tale and, above all, don't claim Bonnie & Clyde status. But if you speak simply and directly from the heart, who knows, you might just save one kid from heading down the wrong path. That's worth an hour of your time, isn't it?

"Speaking of the executive offices, Luis Molina is jumping up and down today. He wrote a grant application to a private charitable foundation last April, and what do you know, he just got word late yesterday that X-Kalay is being given $12,500 to keep us moving forward in our outreach program with Native women in the provincial court system. Way to go, Luis!

"In terms of fun and games, the Salish and Cree tribes, which together number about thirty of our best, are really revved today because they are off to the Queen Elizabeth Theatre tonight to see the great Ray Charles in concert. This is thanks, as always, to Hugh Pickett, Vancouver's famous impresario, who has been giving us free tickets to the symphony and the ballet and pop concerts since the beginning of time, I think.

"Finally, Bob and his kitchen crew have the Y pool exclusively to themselves this evening, so have a great time, folks, and a special thanks to Bill's excellent work the past two months dialoguing with several other community resources. Nobody in this life accomplishes anything entirely on his own, and X-Kalay depends on our connections to a heck of a lot of other people out there. Remember, gang: There are no solo swimmers in this river.

"Hey, have a great day, everybody."

Concepts and Announcement over, everybody heads to work.

The Shell gas station, the beauty parlor, the pizza restaurant, and B.C. Pen, the specialty advertising company, all have to be opened for business. Cooks and cleaners have to cook and clean. Accountants and office staff are busy with all the corporate paperwork. Receptionists are answering telephones or greeting callers at the front door. There are visiting social workers and parole and probation officers to be accommodated. Brett may not be able to start his morning shift at the gas station because he must first spend an hour with his parole supervisor. Anne is meeting over coffee with two workers from Catholic Youth Services about a boy they are thinking might best be placed in X-Kalay.

Some of the executive team is meeting off premises with Members of the Provincial Legislature or a Member of Parliament or City Councilors from Vancouver, Winnipeg, Burnaby, Richmond, or Abbotsford. Inevitably, one of the predictable three items is on the agenda: money or bodies or simply a further explanation of what we are doing. Governments are by their very nature conservative, no matter which flag they may be hoisting in a given season. Politicians, once in office, are cautious and they don't want to offend a single potential voter for the next election. Better to do little or nothing; we'll lose fewer votes that way. The status quo is always the strongest position. The bureaucracy is a big, big wheel that turns ever so slowly. What exactly is it that you folks are doing over there? It sounds exciting, but I'm not sure I understand it, and I'm not sure the community welcomes it.

Most of the people doing the jobs just described have never before worked a day in their lives. They've been hustling, hooking, dealing, and stealing. But interviewing social workers or cleaning windshields or discussing program ideas with government deputy ministers? You've got to be kidding. It is impossible to overestimate the sense of accomplishment that these kinds of days bring to people in recovery. Every little act of getting something done in the real world is part of the personal bricks and mortar that builds that mystery called self-esteem. Love is wonderful. Affection is sweet and hugs are nice. Take the three of them and add a buck fifty and you can't get yourself a good cup of coffee. It's all about the *doing*. Accomplishment is the only remedy.

Lunch is served. Work continues through the afternoon. Some of our younger resident clients, wanting to complete their matriculation, are at public school, a risky enough venture as any parent knows. There are more drugs in the halls of your average Canadian school than down on Skid Road. Other resident students are on site, studying at The Clubhouse. Volunteer teachers are pitching in.

Two interviews for potential new resident clients must be conducted.

One is a long time street junkie known to many X-Kalay people over the years. Our people are skeptical about a guy whose whole character has been defined by his chosen and fiercely defended image as a serious bad ass. Nevertheless they know too well where they have come from themselves. The interview is grueling for everyone. After three hours, they take a chance on the guy and admit him to the program.

The other prospect is the twenty-year-old daughter of a wealthy Kelowna family. She is spoiled, utterly self-involved, and, frankly, not very bright. To complicate matters, her parents, particularly her father, are high status meddlers. These are the Masters of the Universe, the people who control everything in their sight. It is with considerable difficulty that we manage to keep the father out of his daughter's interview for the first hour and a half. Just when we feel we're starting to get somewhere with the girl, dad bursts into the room. He is a persuasive fellow and he has convinced one of our people that he really does need to be in there with his daughter. We ask him to please sit quietly while we continue.

About twenty minutes later, we are focusing on the incident that has brought these two to our doorstep. The girl was stopped two weeks ago at a small Canada-USA border crossing with about $100,000 in illegal drugs in the car. We are on a bit of a roll, making fun of her as a big time Ma Barker. We're trying to bust past her temporary coping mechanism, her self-image as a scary criminal. She is finally starting to show some tiny signs of her own humanity, of the possibility that she is really a frightened child in way over her lovely coiffed head, when helpful dad joins in. "Christ, you didn't even make a good deal! A hundred grand! Are you kidding me?"

We throw them both out, as politely as possible, of course. No one goes out of his way to alienate the very rich. Later that night, several of our people on the way home from the Ray Charles concert, almost drive over the loving father. The man stumbled blind drunk out of a popular nightclub and stepped dangerously into the street. True story.

As the day winds down, people are drifting back into The Clubhouse, chatting, reading the paper, and, like any other family, swapping war stories about the interactions of the day. Dinner is served in the dining room. The pace is leisurely. What's the Swedish mantra? Eat less; chew more.

Games will begin at eight, about half the resident population participating on any given night. Game rooms are pre-set with chairs arranged in a circle. Everyone knows which room to attend. Most Sunday nights, there is a Stew, a special Game held in the Video Room. This Game has many senior staff and a Peanut Gallery, which is a bank of chairs for observers. The Stews are usually packed because they have the advance reputation of being high octane, always entertaining and full of raw emotion and often-startling insights. If you are not attending a Game on any given evening, you might be playing bridge or just taking advantage of some personal down time, reading, or playing the guitar.

Some will be part of the theatre group's production of the William Saroyan play, *Hello Out There*. There are only two characters, but many people are needed for costumes and set construction, lighting, and music. A friend of ours, Mallie, is a dynamic actress, director, and teacher from New York who runs a theatre school downtown. She is donating her time and energies to the occasion. She has a reputation for being tyrannical and very demanding with her paying students. At X-Kalay we find her to be tough for sure, but also the very soul of patience and support. She is a natural fit in our environment of tough love.

Some are working on the X-Kalay in-house newspaper. This is another labor of love at the Foundation. It is written, photographed, edited, laid out, and published entirely by X-Kalay resident clients. The paper is called *Out Front*. It is published monthly and it is the brainchild and baby of a friend of ours from San Francisco. No ordinary friend, Jack, worked for many years for the Hearst papers in America as an editor and layout specialist. In California, he helped Synanon get their newspaper up and running, and now that he has moved with his wife, Jan, to Vancouver, he is determined that we do the same. He has four X-Kalay residents working full-time at the paper and another ten or so pitching in weekends and evenings.

Think about that for a moment. These four burgeoning journalists are all recovering addicts and alcoholics. This kind of opportunity to study and learn and explore new and productive areas simply does not appear in your ordinary halfway house with five or ten residents. It can only happen in a therapeutic community model with its large population and its resources tapped into the larger community in which it functions. It was the great good fortune of X-Kalay to attract over the years many eager friends and helpers like Mallie and Jack, who seemed to find in X-Kalay a kind of creative energy and hopefulness that drew them in.

Forty years later, the *Out Front* newspaper is still being published, quarterly and in full color on high gloss stock, by the Behavioural Health Foundation in Manitoba.

If you are not involved in any of the activities already mentioned, including just plain resting, you might be part of a small team planning an upcoming party or celebration, or perhaps a special presentation for next Saturday's Open House.

Saturday Night Open House was a fixture of The X-Kalay Foundation from our second year on. At first, we held these evenings on borrowed premises, like the local Neighborhood House. Once we had acquired and built our Clubhouse on West 7th Avenue, visitors flocked to the food, entertainment, and often-provocative conversation available every Saturday night. If a guest became a regular, we were not surprised when he or she made the next move and asked to be a live-in part of the family.

Many of the best and most famous singers and musicians in town donated their time and talents to the Saturday Night Open House over the years. Resident greeters and guides were assigned each week, conducting tours of the facility, answering questions about the Foundation, and explaining from their own living experience how the program really worked.

Sundays were a day of rest. Recreational activities were on the low-key schedule and people were out and about in the city, playing ball games, going to the movies or simply walking on the beach. But they were rarely alone. The buddy system, just like in summer camp, is always at play in any mindful residential program. Alone, especially alone on the street, an addict could drown. With two or more people on hand, someone has your back.

The central theme of the therapeutic model is engagement. Keep people busy, active, involved, and thinking. X-Kalay was not a place for sitting on the sofa and daydreaming about how to continue your life as a shipwreck.

So many social services and government programs demonstrate by their very structure their complete lack of understanding of their own client base. Nine to five? There's an immediate giveaway. If you run an office that purports to treat addicts or alcoholics and that office keeps bankers hours, then perhaps you should switch to finance. Stop pretending you are in the people business. Stop wasting public funds that could go to programs that work. The worst part of the day for addicts is the evening; the worst days are the weekends. Why are evenings and weekends the highest risk periods? Simple. Structure, discipline, and schedules are all loosened. It's party time. Bring on the dancing bears. Only those of you with solid personal structure and self-discipline can survive and thrive. If the only home you have is junk city or the beer parlor, if your family and friends are self-destructive losers and lowlifes, how are you supposed to rise above the fray? The beauty of the X-Kalay model is that it is on its toes twenty-nine hours a day, twelve days a week.

The Game was the shining star of the X-Kalay program. But to focus entirely on that one element, as central as it was, is to miss the complexity of the environment and how it worked its wonders on individual resident clients. People at X-Kalay were energized, they were up and running and they were constantly challenged to perform. You never really know what will penetrate the addict haze of self-deception. Talk is great, it's essential. But it is only one avenue, one possible way out of the mire. Give more; do more. Increase the odds for something meaningful and healing to strike home.

Two sides of the coin were operating day and night. On the one hand, someone was forever putting his arm around your shoulder and praising you for a job well done. Or simply noticing you with a, "Hi. How's it going?" On the other hand, the moment you did something stupid, the second you reverted to your old dope fiend habits and stepped in the poo, you were being called on the carpet. You were being confronted with the truth about your behavior and being challenged to change.

The environment is the key.

It is impossible to do real rehab work on Skid Road or in prisons. We discovered that truth by experience. We may be the only non-profit society in history who gave money *back* to the Government of Canada. We had won a contract to run a program within the walls of Matsqui Penitentiary. After six months of hard work, the reality could not be avoided. This is impossible. The prison environment, which dictates a negative, punitive, gang-centered life of its own, precludes any sane, reasonable, progressive behavior. We tried. It's over. Here's your money back.

Clean is clean. Dirty is dirty.

Skid Roads and prisons are unholy messes. Almost nothing about them is human or humane or helpful to the human spirit. There are a handful of saints who work in these dreary settings. They are amazing, unique souls and you can count them on the fingers of one hand. They are better men and women than me. God bless them. For the rest of us, for those of us not built of such holy stuff, I say create a living, working community that holds as primary values health and sanity and helping others. Now you have a decent chance at building decent lives.

However, since I wrote the first draft of this book, I have been wonderfully surprised by a new development that has forced me to rethink my original belief that good rehab work cannot occur within prison walls.

In the summer of 2009, I received an email from a total stranger. "Hi David. You don't know me, but I know you. I have been following your career with great interest for many years now. My name is Don Moody and I am the warden of the Nanaimo Correctional Institution. Since 2007, we have been operating a "therapeutic community" modeled some-what after your X-Kalay work right here in the prison. We are the only prison in Canada to have such a program. Guthrie House is a unit, completely separate from the main popula-tion. We have twenty-eight clean and sober inmates. Would you consider visiting with us and sharing your experiences?"

I did exactly that within a matter of weeks. I spent two

days interacting with the inmates and staff and with France Tellier, the progressive and courageous Executive Director of the local John Howard Society.

I was astonished and deeply moved by what these brave souls have accomplished. I never thought I would see twenty-eight clean and sober inmates in a prison. Every prison in Canada is filled to the gills with drugs and alcohol and other contraband. The illegal traffic of drugs inside prison walls is the norm, not the exception. But here were a group of inmates staying clean and sober, each working hard to understand himself and support one another. Part of the secret of this success is that Guthrie House is a unit completely separated from the main prison population. But a culture is much more powerful than a frost fence. The greatest challenge every day in this case is the will to personal and social change. Great credit must be given to each of those men who braves this program and to the warden, Don Moody, who has quietly persisted in his faith that this kind of program is worth creating and building. At each step along the road he has had to politic and argue with and cajole the powers that be and then carefully document his successes. May others in the system pick up on Don's pioneering work. We might then have more men and women returning to the community with a better chance of success.

Guthrie House learned from X-Kalay and similar programs. The key is getting people involved on all levels. Get people *into* a new way of living, of doing, of interacting, of seeing. Get busy. Get quiet. Get silly. Get sad. Addictions are about stasis and decay. Addictions are about being asleep on your feet. Addictions are death on a stick. Effective treatment programs really are about cleaning up. Wake up, stand up, shout, play, hit the ball, run the workshop, fix the car, change the diaper, make the meal, live! Geoff Cue, my friend and mentor at the Company of Young Canadians, taught me many things. One of the first and most lasting lessons was this: *Do* something with people. It almost doesn't matter what the something is. Just *do* something. Play handball, go to a movie, get a milkshake, paddle a canoe, build a doghouse, or stage a rally. Whatever the activity, you and the other person are there together and talk will occur. Communication, if you listen closely, will happen. Ideas may be exchanged. Friendships and alliances will be formed.

One of the best, most effective phrases in working with people is "Let's." Let us, you and me, we, the two or six or ten of us do something together. Let's set our sights on a common goal, a mission, and head out in that direction.

Give addicts clean needles or substitute drugs or places to shoot up? Get serious.

I would rather see you work for one day in an X-Kalay, a Behavioural Health Foundation, Portage, Turning Point, Welcome Home, The Last Door, Innervisions, or Pacifica program. All of these enterprises and many more like them are dedicated to engagement and doing real things in the real world. None of them is about your drug of choice. All of them produce clean and sober citizens. The suffering and shame of the addict life is ended and human dignity is reclaimed.

When you head off to bed that night, you will be tired and you may just have a small smile on your face. Something has happened today. You did something.

17 the cook and a few cats

We were well into the eighth or ninth hour of a Trip when André spoke up. A Trip was the X-Kalay in-house version of a marathon group therapy that we had first experienced with Dr. Lee Pulos in our second rented house in July of 1967. Fifteen people gather in a large and comfortable room. The group is committed to staying in this room for the next twenty-four hours. Food is available and bathrooms are up the hallway. The theory is that after eight hours or so all customary social guards, defenses, and bridges over the moat are dropped. The masks are thrown off and real people emerge. Of course, this is much more than an idle theory. I have been in dozens of these Trips and I can attest to experiencing and witnessing some amazing transformations.

Imagine a face that has been essentially gray and immobile for months, a face to which you've grown painfully accustomed. Imagine that face changing before your eyes to something alive, pink with color, expressive, and human. I've seen exactly this many times.

André had come into our program in 1972 and, in only a few months, he became our number one cook. And a helluva first-rate chef he was. I'm not sure we ever ate so well at X-Kalay as we did during his tenure. He was funny and charming with his patented Québécois accent. He was also a complete and total stranger. We all felt in a vague sort of way that we liked him; we just didn't know who he was.

Now here was André in this Trip volunteering a piece of his own story. "So, one day we realized that my girlfriend had ratted on our gang."

"You had a gang?"

"You had a girlfriend?"

"What you think, I am a gay?"

"Forget your sexual preferences. What's this shit about a 'gang'?"

"Sure I was part of a criminal organization in Montreal, what you think?"

"A criminal organization. Very impressive! Everyone's fucking overwhelmed. What's the point, André?"

"Well, so we found out that Chantelle had been giving the coppers regular information about us, you know, what we were doing, and where, and how much, like dat."

"Chantelle! Wow! This gets better by the minute. I never met a Chantelle."

"But I had no choice really. I took Chantelle out for a ride, I told her we was just going to a ride, to the Laurentians, not far, you know. And when we get there, I tie her up."

"You tied her up? Like where, Nanook? In your secret cabin in the woods?"

"I have no cabin. Where you think I have a cabin? I tie her upside down from da tree."

"Upside down?"

"Yah, sure, she was hanging from her ankles from da tree."

"Don't tell us. Then you tickled her to death? You made her listen to your Andy Williams collection?"

"No, I don't like Andy Williams. I don't have dis guy."

"Great, you love Perry Como and Elvis! What are you doing with your alleged girlfriend tied upside down by her ankles to a tree in the scenic fucking Laurentians"?

"Well, then I get my lynx."

"Excuse me?"

"Your minks?"

"My lynx, my pet lynx."

"Of course, I knew that. I knew what he said. Everybody's got a pet lynx. You don't, Bev?"

'You have a pet lynx, André?"

"Had."

"Who you often schlep along for drives in the mountains? For what, just for nostalgia, so Elmer the Lynx won't forget where he really comes from after all those months in your apartment right der, off da Rue Sainte-Catherine?"

"Look, I don't care what you people think about anything, you know. I had a lynx and he was very dangerous. I mean he had very sharp claws and he was dangerous."

"OK, hotshot. We've got you and your girlfriend and your crazy cat up in the mountains. Now what?"

"You don't understand. She ratted on us! I had to deal with her."

"Deal?"

"Yes. She is hanging and I sig the lynx on her."

"What?"

"The lynx he starts scratching her and she's screaming and bleeding quite a bit, but, you know, we're up in the Laurentians, right, so who can hear her?

"Who, exactly?"

"Or is that whom? Whom can hear her."

"André, what the fuck is this? We're supposed to believe that you punished your blabbermouth girlfriend because she ratted on you and your very scary Frog versions of Al Capone and Bugsy Segal by throwing your vicious mountain lion at her while she's dangling from a Canadian Red Pine by her ankles? Is that what we're supposed to buy here?"

A largely academic discussion about the size of the cat's claws followed. After so many hours of this stuff, people can get pretty bizarre and inventive and detached. The women in the room, for example, were teetering dangerously between laughing their heads off and weeping in horror. After about an hour of this episode, I had to step in and do something unusual for a Game or a Trip. "André, I've got a problem."

"Sure, Dave."

"See, I'm listening to your lynx story with great interest and the truth is it presents a dilemma, a real dilemma."

"Yes?"

"Yes, indeed. The thing is here are the choices. Either you are telling the truth, I mean this is a completely true story, in which case you are a psychotic lunatic and I can't have you living in our house with women and children here. Or... or you've made this whole thing up, in which case you are a psychotic lunatic and I can't have you living in our house with women and children here. You see my problem?"

I asked André the Chef to leave our program at once. He was, as usual, very pleasant and compliant. Especially for a career criminal and one who turns wild animals loose on his best friends. Everyone was furious at me. They put me on the hot seat and yelled at me for about an hour. This echoed the very first day I had thrown Delphi the dope fiend out when we knew that she was high. Typically, corporate decisions were not executed in the middle of a therapeutic exercise. But, I was not only a therapist, I was the Executive Director and responsible for every aspect of Foundation life. There was never any question in my mind that I made the right decision.

On another occasion, several people came up to my office to tell me that they had just admitted a new member to the program. Why were they telling me this? We admitted new resident clients every day. "We found this in his luggage."

"What is this, a bullet?"

"Yes, Dave, it's a bullet."

"You mean like from an actual gun?"

"Looks like it, Dave."

"Restage the Interview. Bring him in. I'll be down in a moment."

What I found facing me when I sat down in the Interview Room was a big, handsome man in his early thirties. Blond hair and the coldest, most blank blue eyes I have ever seen. It was clear to me at once that we were in the presence of either a complete "nobody" or a total whacko. Whatever the case, it wasn't good. "Hi Roger. My name's David. I'm sorry to tell you that there's been a mistake made this afternoon. I know that the gang interviewed you and admitted you to the program a while ago. But it is obvious to me that this is not going to be the kind of program where you will thrive. This just isn't a good fit. I'm sorry about that, but I'm afraid we won't be able to take you in."

Like André the chef, Roger was polite and utterly indifferent to this news.

Sometimes, you just have to trust your gut.

. . .

Marvin Bergstrom ran our Salt Spring Island Hotel for almost two years. He was tall and redheaded and he seemed to spend all his spare time playing his guitar and singing in his perfect impression of Gordon Lightfoot. Marvin was a Scandinavian, a first generation Canadian who grew up in rural Saskatchewan, the oldest son of immigrants who scraped out a living on a small farm.

There are some guys who are just plain bad. There are some psychos and sociopaths who will never abandon their basic "me alone" approach to life. In the winter of 2012, a serial killer who had been convicted of several gruesome murders and claimed that he was responsible for quite a few more, was sent by Corrections Canada from a maximum security lockdown, where he rightly belonged, to a medium security prison in the valley just east of Vancouver. He was even given a cellmate—whom he promptly strangled to death. The killer's comment? "Hey, I'm a serial killer. That's what I do." An official enquiry quickly absolved the Corrections people of all responsibility for this dreadful incident. I would not. I think the fools who ignored the simple facts in front of them and put the man who died in direct harm's way should be sued, censured, and fired. You have to ask yourself who is the crazy person in this sordid tale.

I remember once running a workshop in Drumheller Penitentiary in Alberta that was filmed for a later showing by the CBC (Canadian Broadcasting Corporation). The three-hour encounter group was edited down to twenty-seven minutes and fifty seconds for airing, and it proved to be so popular (we are just ghouls, aren't we?) that they showed it twice in one week. One of the highlights for me was an inmate in his thirties who simply said, "Look, I'm not going to give up my identity for anybody or anything. This is who I am, and whether it gets me in prison or not doesn't matter. I like this identity." You can't beat honesty. You gotta love a guy who knows who he is.

Then, in contrast to the last two stories, there are guys who are basically good souls, but, through some weakness of character or the strength of the local tides, they drift into The Life. With this kind of man or woman, it isn't so much an active choosing of crummy behavior and lousy friends as it is *not* choosing the better alternatives when they're often sitting right in front of you.

Marvin was this kind of guy. By the time he was in his mid-twenties, Marvin was a heroin addict and a petty thief and the official world of cops and robbers had a file on him an inch thick. I could well imagine him being difficult, or even violent under some circumstances. Yet, in the several years that I knew and worked with him, I experienced only a kind and gracious guy with a very clear and practical savvy about him. He enjoyed nothing more than sitting out on the deck of the hotel, watching the sunset and talking about our people business. Everyone seemed to fascinate him.

What I remember most vividly about Marvin was his story about how he happened to come to X-Kalay in the first place. "I was doing federal time at Matsqui. I'd met some of the X-Kalay people on one of their visits to the joint, and I realized that I could probably get a three-day pass if I said I wanted to see X-Kalay for myself and check it out as a possible parole plan. Sure enough, that worked, even though, of course, I had no such good intentions about anything. I just wanted to get out of stir for a few days. I didn't really know what the Foundation was. I just figured it for another half-wit house. My idea was that I'd be sitting around all day on a couch, smoking cigarettes and plotting ways to get downtown and be crazy.

"Of course, that's not what happened. I arrived on a Saturday about noon and the very first thing that happened was somebody, I think it was Archie, gave me a tool belt and a hammer and a bag of nails and said, "Hey, Marvin, we're building all these rooms for the Clubhouse and we need your help."

So before I know it, I'm pounding nails in this Gyproc and I'm sweating and I'm talking to the guy next to me. Later, I was given nice fresh towels for a shower and we had a terrific dinner downstairs in the main dining room. That night was the Open House and someone gave a really interesting talk about the idea of, "Am I my brother's keeper?" Then, this great group got up and did a fantastic music set on the main stage. They were a professional jazz combo. They were donating their time. The whole thing just blew me away. On Sunday, I got into a big touch football game and got real competitive and a little banged up, but in a good way, you know, and I laughed my head off. That night Brett let me use his guitar and I did a kind of sing-along with several people in the lounge. One of whom was Bev, who I kind of had my eye on from day one."

No surprise. Bev and Marvin had been an item for about a year and a half when he was telling me this story.

"When they sent me back to Matsqui on Monday, my head was spinning. I was not really sure what had just happened. All I knew was that I liked it, whatever it was. Seemed to me this was the first chance I'd seen in a hell of a long time to get off the high wire act and stay off. I applied for a parole to the Foundation. I got it, and I've been here ever since."

There are two important lessons from Marvin's story.

The first is about motivation. I've written elsewhere in this book about the fallacy of motivation. Marvin is a perfect illustration of a man who falls into good behavior and practice through the worst possible impulse. Marvin came through our doors so he could get out of prison for three days, score some heroin and lug it back with him into the joint. We never worried ourselves for a minute about what brought a man or woman to our door. The salient point was that he or she got there. The environment and the program would do the rest. This is a significant consideration when it comes to the endlessly useless debate about mandatory treatment. There are those who truly do not understand the mechanics of addictions and recovery, who will argue, "It's not going to work until the person really wants it." At its most simplistic level, there is some small truth in this assertion. But, when the process is examined in all its complexities, one thing becomes clear. Put someone in the right setting and chances are that the *person's wants begin to change.*

It is a rare child who, being fed cookies, will suddenly declare, "I'm finished with cookies." So you plan to give addicts their drug of choice or substitute drugs and then expect them to choose abstinence? You plan to do all this in a colorless, antiseptic hospital setting and expect them to suddenly embrace life in all its vibrancy? Give your head a shake.

The other lesson from Marvin's story has to do with engagement.

I've spoken before in this book about learning from my friend Geoff Cue the power of the phrase "Let's…" Let's go for a walk; let's have a swim, a coffee, a game of pool, a chat. Let us, you and me, do something together. Sounds simple, doesn't it? You'd be amazed how many social workers, clergy, and others have never put this quiet, little tool to work. There are two simple parts to the magic of "Let's." The first is "Let," which is a verb, an action word. So immediately, you're up and about, no longer just talking, but *doing* something. The second is "us," as in "let us." The moment you say, "Let's," you are creating a new organism, a living, breathing animal called "we." We are a new group and we are bound together in action.

What Marvin Bergstrom found on that Saturday afternoon when he first came to The X-Kalay Foundation on a three-day pass for all the wrong reasons was the opposite of idleness. Archie said to him, "Let's build these rooms together." He found involvement and companionship. By the end of his visit, he had begun to get a glimpse of that ultimate gift, *purpose*. Joining forces with other like-minded people, people who have shared many of the same degradations and miseries of addiction and incarceration, can be a powerful force for good. Intention is everything. Purpose is the prize.

Keep in mind that X-Kalay never presented itself as a medical model. This was not a place where omniscient doctors declared you sick and where only they, the doctors, held the keys (pills, drug substitutes, professional therapy) to recovery. X-Kalay was a therapeutic community, a living definition of self-help. When we gave public talks about our work, people would inevitably ask, "What about psychologists?"

We'd always answer, "Oh, we help them too."

In the X-Kalay model, addictions are about two things. They are continuing acts of stupidity, lousy choices. And they are a spiritual sickness.

We have wandered from our homes and our truths. We are lost and aching with loneliness. We have a sickness of the heart. Believing that life has rejected us, we began to reject life. The beauty of the approach found in recovery centers like X-Kalay is that *you are the cure*. Salvation lies within you. The powerful memory of home is still living within you. Find it again. Reactivate it. Bring yourself home. All the way home.

The new choices you make on the road to building afresh your own dignity may start with a hammer and nails and some Gyproc.

Marvin Bergstrom was ambushed by a tool belt.

. . .

Guy Prairie had been in X-Kalay for two years when I ran into him one morning on the street. I was driving to work and he was walking briskly away from the Clubhouse.

Guy looked like a jockey. Small, wiry, intense, terribly funny and, for a righteous dope fiend, he was blessed with a core streak of real human decency. He was never going to be a star at anything in particular, but we had no expectations that everyone in the program would turn the world upside down. Guy was just one of those slow and steady guys who did good work for himself and for the corporation.

Now, here he was hot footing it up the street alone at nine in the morning. Alone? What happened to our buddy system? I stopped the car. "Hey Guy, what's going on?"

He was wound about as tight as he could get. He ranted and raved about various people who had been doing him wrong. This person didn't like him. That fellow didn't understand him. This girl couldn't see his point of view. "Anyways, that's it, Dave. I'm going downtown to score. I've had it. I've done my best, but that's the end. I can't take this anymore."

I was heartsick. Two years of work walking up the street. "OK that's fine, pal. You do whatever you think is right."

"Damn straight."

"But before you go, could I ask you just one question? One question, Guy, that's all."

"Yah, what?"

"How much do you weigh?"

"Fuck!"

"No, really. Just tell me how much you weigh."

"Are you fucking nuts, Dave?"

"How much?"

"One forty-five."

"You weigh 145 pounds?"

"Give or take. So, what's your fucking point?"

"No, I don't really have a point. It's just that I can't figure something out."

"Oh, man."

"See, I've got this picture in my mind of a scale, you know like a weigh scale you'd use in a store for veggies or something, and on the one hand there's you, Guy Prairie. You weigh 145 pounds you're telling me, and you've got a heart and skin and two arms, two legs, two eyes, two balls and many teeth and, I believe, at least I've been assuming all along, you've got a brain."

"Funny, Dave."

"So, now after two years of really hard work, good work, not just for you but for a lot of people, for everyone you've come in contact with since the day you first walked in the door, all the people you've helped and influenced just by your example, and all the people who helped you, after all that, you're going to go downtown and score some heroin."

"Right!"

"So, I'm looking at this scale, and on the one side, there's you, all 145 pounds of you, but now on the other side is this little bundle of silver paper all squished up from a cigarette package and inside that silver paper is this white, inert powder. It's basically a dead thing, this powder, this smack. And what does it weigh? A tenth of a gram? Tops.

"So, this little tenth of a gram of inert powder is going to beat you on this scale. You're 145, the powder is a fraction of a gram, and you're going to lose. That's what I'm trying to figure out, Guy. Tell you honestly, I just don't get it."

I walked away, got back into my car, drove around the back of our building, parked and went into the Clubhouse. First, I sat in the car for a minute and tried not to lose it. I felt sick. To see this fellow walk away from all the investment that he had made in his own recovery was so discouraging. And what about all the effort and thought that so many others in X-Kalay had made on his behalf?

This wasn't a new experience by any means. People left the program regularly long before they were ready. Some flourished, others fell by the wayside. On more than one occasion, I was called to the city morgue to identify the body of someone who had overdosed on heroin. When officials or the press or people at conferences asked about success rates, we always talked about the 25 percent. Half the people we ever met at X-Kalay stayed a day or a week or a month at the most and left. They weren't in our Win column. Half of those who did stay hung in there for many months and really absorbed some important ideas and new ways of working their life scripts. They were The Possibles. It was possible that, although they didn't stay long enough to really break old habits and try on new strategies, they might just have picked up enough new gambits to live different kinds of lives. The other half who stayed, we put confidently in the Success column. These folks stayed a year or two and worked the program. They emerged clean and sober and, by and large, stayed that way for the rest of their lives.

For people working in this field there are a number of regular and predictable challenging opposites at play. Over the years, I learned to stop seeing these emotional tugs-of-war as negatives. In time, I began calling them "creative tensions." The struggle itself became a signal for deep soundings and major choices. For me personally, there was always the tension between emotional investment and a self-protecting professional detachment. Like most people, I don't welcome loss. To see someone we had worked with fail, felt too often like a personal failure. To visit the morgue or learn of someone's death was sometimes devastating.

Now, what about Guy Prairie? By the time, I got around to the front reception area that morning, there was Guy sitting in the chair waiting for an Interview. He started the program again that afternoon from the beginning and stayed another year.

I ran into him on the street many years later. He never went back to jail and never used heroin again. "I have a beer sometimes, Dave, but that's it."

For a man who had spent too many years strung out on smack or wasting away in jail, having a beer sometimes was a sturdy measure of success.

18 dancing in the dark

The X-Kalay Foundation Manitoba Inc. went through two name changes over the years, first calling itself the St. Norbert Foundation, which recognized the surrounding community near the University of Manitoba in which it is housed. When the township of St. Norbert wanted that name for its own charitable activities, X-Kalay Manitoba became BHF, the Behavioural Health Foundation.

It is next to impossible for a righteous dope fiend in less than a month of treatment to learn much of anything that will stick to the ribs and stay. Today, BHF asks of new clients a commitment to a minimum stay of ninety days. Welcome Home, in Surrey, B.C. is looking for six months. Some programs in the Vancouver area ask for commitments of as long as a year. The carefully tracked follow-ups of these programs demonstrate clearly that the longer a client stays in or is involved with a program, the greater the success. Many private clinics offer twenty-eight- and forty-two-day programs, but even these centers encourage all clients to stay in their extended programs, (minimum but highly structured weekly or even daily involvements) and to stay very much in contact as long as the client feels the want or need. As we heard a thousand times at X-Kalay, "You've taken most of your life to screw up this badly; don't expect to be Jane Citizen tomorrow morning. Your recovery will take time and work. And it will take other people."

After the first year or so of running this fascinating business, we began to notice a predictable pattern of behavior. Here it is:

The first hump typically arrived about three weeks after someone joined the organization and became a resident client. This phenomenon is described very specifically in chapter fifteen, the fabulous flying brothers m. As in all therapy, everyone wants to get better. Everyone wants to confess. Everyone wants to get strong and healthy.

And at the same time, no one wants to change. No one really wants to give up his or her favorite shticks. After all, these maneuvers may be poison, but they are *my* poison, buster! Back the fuck off!

So people come into the therapeutic community. They wring their hands and they cry. They admit their inadequacies and loneliness. Their fears are put on the rug for all to see.

But *getting* married and *being* married are two very different things. The first is dramatic, ceremonial, ritualized. The second is free fall. Figure it out as you go. Question, compromise, disagree, kiss and make up. Or not.

The new resident is going through the motions, operating on ether, doing what he is told. He is trying to get along and not get in the goo. Enough already with cleaning the shitters. Who wants to do this for life? Suddenly he wakes up one morning and realizes that nobody is kidding. This is for real. These people really are working at understanding themselves and rebuilding their core foundations. Man, this is straight goods! What a threatening realization! As always, there are only two traditional responses to threat—fight or flight. These are the well-known reactions of children, raccoons, and addicts.

If a new house member didn't split in the dead of night after three weeks, we figured we'd weathered the first storm. If he stayed and fought with us, we smiled and applauded his courage. If she suddenly sought out more responsibility or spoke up a little more often in games or seminars, we knew she had now truly dived into the stream.

The second hump is all about quiet. It's a period that lasts three to five months. More involvement, more work, more revelation. Again, think of a marriage or a business partnership. The client becomes part of the furniture. We are familiar with one another. Slowly, steadily, we begin to see the stuff of which you are made. A good moment here, a miscue there. But, in time, a reasonable composite emerges. We begin to know with some certainty how dependable you are and what are your real strengths and your scariest weaknesses.

The trick at this point is not to take anyone for granted. I've grown accustomed to your face, it almost makes the day begin, sure, but that doesn't mean that now I can totally fathom your deepest nature. The individual and the group around him can be lulled into complacency. Continued support and further prodding are the order of the day here.

Danger! Danger! Six month hump on the horizon! Dive!

Periscopes up! Not everybody in treatment enters this particular tunnel. Not everyone survives the first six months in a therapeutic community. It is wall-to-wall tough love and both the tough and the love are demanding. When someone does make it to this stage the signs are all there and it's not always a pretty sight. The resident client has now enjoyed six months of eating good food three or more times a day. This is very different from his former dope fiend life, into which a vegetable, for example, never wandered. He is sleeping a normal eight. That's a first in many years. He has friends. That is, he has friends who are not sharing their needles and bottles and crack pipes. He has support and an enormous powerful structure around him providing buoyancy. Football, tennis, bridge, poker, music, dancing, books, newspapers, cameras. A life. Maybe a relationship. Sex. Yikes!

I must be better now. I must be cured. Time to conquer the world, show everyone my mastery.

Do you know a real, diagnosable manic-depressive? I do. When this character isn't sleeping all day, gaining weight, watching Oprah, and diagramming his suicide on napkins, he's reordering the periodic table, writing an astrology column for the local paper, and lecturing university graduates on hot careers in a cold, cold economy. The manic in the manic-depressive personality is a whirlwind of vanity and ambition. He has been sent from the heavens to save the world from its multiple failings. And this is a reasonable description of the six-month hump in addiction recovery. The addict, very much and understandably feeling his oats, has now decided that it is time to fly. There's a great job opening at the Native Health Worker's Society. A children's group needs more counselors.

Real estate is cooking and I can get a license in five weeks. See, this flyer tells me so. For the Type A, macho personality—and there are as many of these pilots in recovery as there are on Wall Street—everything is, of course, accelerated. Warp speed is their cruise control default setting. For these birds, the six-month hump may very well appear after a few weeks. Pretty soon, they not only want to run the program, they are planning to open a ranch for addicts in Montana and a seminary for deep thinkers in Tibet. Stand back!

These may all be good omens, and very bad. The good is that this outward looking and enthusiasm and planning speak to a new level of health and stability. Some dues have been paid and the addict is pointed in the right direction. But what the addict is not accounting for is that this wonderful new position has come about in a tightly structured, nurturing, and corrective environment. It has come about *because* of that environment. Now, more than ever, the real challenge for the recovering addict is to be still. Don't move. You are not nearly ready. Patience. Stay the course. Build on the healthy construct you have only just begun.

There are those among you who have thankfully never had to wrestle the addiction monster to the ground. You might think that six months or a year or two years is an awfully long time to get better. It isn't. Not even close. It takes a lifetime to screw up and another lifetime or two to change.

Do addicts have to be in the therapeutic community for two years or three or forever?

Many don't. Most can profitably move into a transition house after three months and go back to work or school. These people will check into the main program at least once a day for another few months so that the main treatment themes are maintained and strengthened.

Some do need to stay in the therapeutic setting for a very long time. This person living and working in an X-Kalay or a Delancey Street feels secure and can function often at a very high level for herself and others around her. Some will choose to stay in this milieu and make it their life's work. Why not? They are the experts. Who better to counsel those who are just beginning their journey?

Others will move on and back into the larger community when the time is right. When is that? I would say for many people at least a year. If the program is well run and it doesn't cost you or your family or the public health care system a fortune, then a year is a damn good investment. If your favorite addict is at home with you after a short treatment program, watch for these humps, these danger moments. Just like speed bumps in a relationship, they can be overcome. But that takes thought and intelligence and, more than anything, *the willingness* to overcome difficult moments.

The beauty of recovery programs like the Behavioural Health Foundation in Manitoba is that the door is always open. You need a refresher, a second or third run to truly *get* the idea? Come on in, brother and share your story with the client who is still working on Round One. Two years ago, I met a fellow at BHF in Winnipeg named Lyle. It's hard to miss him. He's an Aboriginal, towering about six feet four inches tall, 300 plus pounds and he favors bright red shirts. He immediately told me that this was his fifth kick at the cat. I couldn't believe it. But, guess what? A year later, he graduated from the program and Jean Doucha hired him to be an intake counselor and he's doing great. A long and winding road, indeed.

. . .

And speaking of humps, maybe we should spend a few moments talking about sex.

During my years with X-Kalay, I must have given a public speech of one kind or another at least once a week. One of the favorite questions from audiences was inevitably broached with a little delicacy.

"You have men and women there…"

"Yes?"

"Well, I mean, what do you do?

"Do?"

"Yes. What do you do about sex?"

"We fuck. What do you do?"

The reality of running a program with upwards of 125 people in residence is, of course, much more complicated. It is especially complex when most of those people are in a very real and fundamental sense coming back to life. The sex habits of drunks and dope fiends can be described in short words, like none, zero, zilch, de nada, and forget it. But when the addict's best friend and favorite toy—booze, heroin, coke—is thrown overboard, juices start to flow again and old friends will mysteriously, and sometimes troublingly, reappear. You cannot run a program like X-Kalay without a clear social interaction policy and vigilant enforcement. Our policy was simple enough. No sexual romances, intercourse, mutual pleasuring, or whatever clever combinations of carnal contact may suggest themselves for the first six months in the program. The exchange of precious bodily fluids was just not on the agenda until you were somewhat on your feet again and exhibiting behavior that closely resembled that of a reasonable human being.

Pairings, nevertheless, were inevitable. In X-Kalay every man and woman knew that his or her sexual and romantic interests would come under serious group scrutiny. Remember that everyone was in The Game at least three times a week, and that The Game was a no holds barred exposure. Pity the poor slob who wasn't very skilled in the arts of romance or sexual satisfaction. The truth is that most recovering alcoholics and addicts are not going to win awards in these areas. Intimacy is very different from nakedness and what's a fellow or gal to do without his chemical to hide behind? Sexuality is a core issue for all people, regardless of other social, intellectual, or financial adequacies. It is especially challenging for people who are so full of disquiet in their souls that they would choose to slowly destroy themselves with poisons. Workshops and the occasional private consultation did appear from time to time on how sex actually works.

X-Kalay was certainly a child of its times. Homosexuality was simply not accepted during our heyday in the sixties and seventies. I am pleased to say that many of us have grown up. The X-Kalay of today, Manitoba's Behavioural Health Foundation, posits clearly in its mission statement that it in no way discriminates against gays and lesbians in their care, nor does any other self-respecting institution of which I'm aware.

I was once hired in later years to be a therapist for a group of gay and lesbian addicts who had returned from treatment programs to their civilian lives. It only took a few sessions for the inevitable big question to emerge.

"How old were you when you first started abusing substances?"

Almost every woman in the group answered eleven or twelve. Almost every man said between twelve and fourteen. For many people in the group, this was some kind of light bulb moment. "Oh, my god, I never made that connection before. I started my drug abuse/drinking at puberty. I am gay/lesbian. Puberty was a nightmare for me. Along with my sexuality came self-hatred, self-doubt, and the beginning of my long slide into craziness."

At X-Kalay, like everywhere in life, sex was a constant presence. Sexual jokes and innuendos bounced around the community walls night and day. Romances blossomed, disintegrated, and were replaced by new liaisons. Many couples were, in time, married while in X-Kalay; at least half a dozen children were born from these unions. As American playwright, Arthur Miller, told us so clearly in *Death of a Salesman*, "Attention must be paid."

19 the whole family

The family is the seat of all love and all hate. It is the beginning and the end of all sorrows and happiness.

Addictions are the loneliest of personal journeys. Yet, they do not happen in isolation. There is a gestalt, an etching of foreground and background. Addictions occur in context—the family, the 'hood, the community, the religious belief system or absence thereof, the country and its political stances.

Many recovery programs will not allow new clients to have any contact at all with their families for the first week or three weeks or sixty or ninety days. Get clear. Stand on your own feet. Stop the chronic manipulations. Stop hustling mom and dad and uncle Harry and sister Sue for more money and more sympathy. Free yourself for a while of all the old family judgments, critiques, and blind alley advice.

Many recovery programs have very active family adjunct components. A recovery center for which I currently do therapy and counseling work once a week have clients' families on site most weekends in workshops and groups in addition to just visiting. If the goal for the addict or alcoholic is to return clean and sober to some semblance of a healthy lifestyle, then keeping the family informed, aware, and intact is part of that goal. In some rare instances, the family constellation is so tragically toxic that the best thing that can happen is that everyone moves on. Kenny Rogers was right. You gotta know when to hold 'em, know when to fold 'em.

Let's look at some of the dynamics of addictions and the family. Like addictions themselves, these highways and byways are myriad, complex, and often utterly confusing. But we might open this Pandora's box just a little and examine two important elements in the family-addict dance: the roles and functions that addictions can play in the addict's relationship with his or her family, and the ways that family can unwittingly nurse the addict further into his or her mess.

The personalities described in this chapter are constructs modeled on many real people with whom I've worked over the years.

Val is a well-credentialed academic in her early forties. For years now she has had two constants—she drinks and she has a series of boyfriend/partners that last a year or so. She is a drunk and a serial monogamist. She is also elegant and terribly smart. And, although drunk most nights, she has never missed a day's work because of her addictions, until now when she has wisely taken a medical leave to address her deepening problems.

Until recently, Val has had a completely codependent relationship with her mother. Their enmeshment is a kind of relentless strangulation.

As Val's father left the picture soon after she was born,

Val has been raised entirely by her mother. Val's mother has chosen never to date and never to bring another man into her own life. She has made it abundantly clear that her life's central purpose is Val, Val, and more Val. At the same time, she has been critical of almost everything in Val's life, starting with every article of clothing that Val has chosen for herself since she was a child.

This is not to make a case for Val's mother being the villain in this melodrama. Glenn's mother is very much at the heart of the next story as well, but in both cases, these are strong, very capable women trying in their own ways to make sense of challenging and baffling circumstances. In both cases, the addict client is not making things easier for anyone. No one in these scenarios is to blame. This is not about blame. This is about learning to see what is before us and choosing strategies that will have better payoffs for all, strategies that, by the way, leave the substance of choice in the dust.

What purposes do Val's alcoholism and Val's serial dating serve in the constant central power struggle between her and her mother?

The drinking is as always a way to kill the pain, numb the heart, and avoid facing the music. The music in this case, as in most others, is…I'm exhausted by the love/hate arm wrestling with my mom and dad, but I don't know how to change it or end it and, after all, it's what I know so, miserable though it makes me, it is the mess in which I am most comfortable. In short, I don't want to grow up. Adulthood means "the fear of flying." Adulthood entails letting go of all my petty or deep grievances and being fully responsible for my own life choices now that I'm of voting, shaving, and childbearing age.

The drinking has another deeper intent. And this one is true for almost every alcoholic or addict I've ever met.

The drinking/doping/smoking/shooting up is MY SECRET.

It is an enormous FUCK YOU to mom and dad and the church and the school and my square friends and anybody else I can add to the list of people who have been complicit in life handing me such bad cards. It's a huge, "Leave me alone already."

Anyone who has survived parenthood will recall the terrible twos, that enchanting period when our kids know basically one word and the word is, "No!" This may be maddening, but it is part of the natural process of differentiation. Look, I am me, I am no longer merely a reflection of those tall people, I am uniquely me and I can say and do and be what I want.

The addict or alcoholic is still struggling with a process that most others got through and over years ago. The addict's way to find separation is to have a dirty secret called heroin or gin or cocaine. This addict life may be ugly and strange to you, but it's mine, so there.

Glenn is twenty-one and he has already made his mark in the world of classical music. He is also good looking, warm, kind, considerate, and terribly bright. Everyone at the recovery center loves this kid. What's not to like?

And, oh yes, before we forget, he is a blackout drunk. In his last incident, he woke up in the bathroom of a community center and he has no idea how he got there. He comes from a well-to-do family and he is usually dressed in the latest styles. On the day he comes out of this latest alcoholic coma, he's leaning on a filthy sink, and he looks like he just fell off the back of a potato truck.

How can this be?

It turns out that Glenn's alcoholism is in some basic ways identical to Val's. There's that huge FUCK YOU element, there's that need to be ME-and-not-you at any ridiculous cost. We learn, as the conversations with Glenn and his family continue over a period of weeks, that half a dozen of the boys that Glenn went to an expensive private school with have similar or even more desperate experiences. The commonality here is the rule of outrageously high expectations. Each of these youngsters has been under the gun from an early age to BE WONDERFUL, BE FABULOUS, EXCEL AT EVERYTHING. Have their parents ever heard of down time? Has it not occurred to them that silly time or doing nothing is part of life? Sometimes nothing is the best thing we can do and the best thing we can let our children do. For Glenn, drinking is one of the few ways he's figured out how to *Stop the World, I Want to Get Off.* Unfortunately, his drinking is not only stupid, wasteful, and unworthy of such a basically decent kid, it's also mortally dangerous.

The plot thickens. For both Val and Glenn, drinking swiftly goes beyond the back-off-leave-me-be mechanism. Just to make the party really interesting, they learn as they progress in their madness that drinking can also become their leverage, their bargaining chip. I call this maneuver the Fuck Up Tango—Tough guy–victim, tough guy–victim, tough guy–victim. And the band plays on. Within the family melodrama, the alcoholic is able to use his or her drinking in a thousand tiny ways to intimidate, hustle, cajole, blackmail, and even kidnap the family's attentions or fortunes at will. Can't steal the family spotlight by becoming mayor or an architect or an oncologist? No problem, bunkie. There's always my addiction waiting in the wings to seize center stage. Doctors, nurses, shrinks, social workers, police, the courts, probation, all the good second bananas are lined up with their scripts in hand, anxious to add to the frivolities. See, isn't my addiction just about the best show in town?

And what about Val's parade of dedicated true loves? What role do they serve in this play? Each is exactly like the other—cute, sexy, drunk, and compliant. Val holds all the power in these relationships. It is only now in her recovery work that she recognizes that she and her lovers haven't shared one real moment of intimacy. Nakedness, of course, by the barrel, and lots of laughs and fist fights and disruptions and drama. But never can she remember a quiet moment of honesty, of sadness perhaps, or tenderness, or even fearlessly spoken anger. She has never allowed herself to be vulnerable. How could she? If the floodgates of her inner torment were ever opened, the tears might never stop.

Her boyfriends are both a diversion (from getting down to the business of the real work and commitment in an adult relationship) and a card in the deck in the war with mother. Of course, Val's mother detests all these men. Of course, Val gets to fight with mother over each of her lousy annual choices. Of course, Val is able to pawn these men as vaudeville sideshows even with her mother—because as long as they're fighting over this inconsequential nonsense, they never have to confront their suffocating emotional entanglements. Val and her mother need never abandon their parent/child positions and finally come to know each other as adults.

At a very profound level, Val's boys are also an aching attempt by Val to solve her mother's loneliness and her own sense of isolation, to find the rightful place in both their lives for the man in the house. The ghost of papa prattles and floats through their lives, dragging his chains and searching for a moment of peace.

Glenn too has a very deep, buried motivation that drives him to his periodic episodes of self-destruction. He is grieving for his childhood.

He is a kind of Peter Pan; he never wants to grow up. Childhood has been so sweet. I have been so taken care of why would I want to shoulder any responsibilities on my own? Growing up sucks. After considerable work in recovery, Glenn finally shows some real emotional connection to his own dilemma. Until this moment, he has been clever and adept, but never quite present. Now, his eyes fill with tears as he admits that he recalls clearly at the age of nine being overwhelmed by a sense of sadness that his childhood had an expiry date.

Val's mother, like many a parent or spouse or sibling of many an addict or alcoholic, furthers and enables the continuing disaster by bailing out and rescuing her daughter over and over again. She pays bills that Val could easily pay herself. She follows Val to bars and restaurants and shames her and lectures her. She expects constant attention from her daughter to herself and to her own demanding and aging mother.

Glenn's father has his own demons. He has lost work because of his own dance with the bottle. (Does Glenn want to please his dad by imitating him?) Glenn's kid brother has phobias, anxieties, and eating disorders. Glenn's mother dominates the entire family landscape. She admits that she over-manages and micro-manages the family; after considerable work, she begins to let go her vice grip. She acknowledges how very tired she is from holding on so tightly to the reins. Someone notices that when the family drives away after a weekend visit, the defeated father sits in the back seat, the mother and younger brother in the front. Mother and son are joined at the hip. If you see them sitting on a bench talking, you would think they were a young couple in love. At moments, they look to be one person. He doesn't want to grow up and she doesn't want him to grow up. She wants always her handsome, talented, adoring baby boy. Fabulous—they have a common cause!

It takes at least two to tango, sometimes three or even six or twenty-four and what one learns in treatment is that everyone plays his and her part in both the disaster and the reclamation. No one is to blame and no one is blamed. The addict/alcoholic is a key player in a dreadful social dance involving many unique personalities. Whether or not the parents, spouses, siblings, or children participate to any degree in the recovery process is entirely up to them. In the stories mentioned in this chapter, the families became actively engaged in the communication work necessary to clear the tracks and start afresh. These clients are alive and well, clean and sober, and doing fine, thank you very much.

We would always hope that friends and family support and encourage and participate in an addict's recovery. We would hope that friends and families learn not to enable or propel addict behavior in any fashion and to recognize danger signs as they may inevitably appear. But for the addict, there is a tough and unavoidable reality. Whether or not you have the backing of your friends and family, it is you who has the problem and it is you who must dive into the work of recovery.

An old adage instructs us that he who serves two masters will have to lie to one of them. The addict may bow to one master called cocaine or scotch and, if she does, she must then do everything in her power to appease the demands of that demon. What choice can she allow herself with regard to her other master, say her husband or career or father? She must create an intricate maze of deceptions, each tiny fib about where she is going, what she did last night, whom she is seeing adding to her new character as a full-blown liar. She senses at the very deepest level that with each new fabrication, she has cemented further highways and alleys of separation between herself and the very people she most yearns to embrace. Sooner or later, in those rare, quiet moments of reflection, the addict finds herself asking, "Is this what I meant to become—a daughter or wife known by her lies?"

In traversing the shores and shoals of addictions, one learns to cheat, steal, and present 101 fictional faces to the world. All of that is dreadful and demeaning, but nothing is as gruesome as the hideous ways addicts treat themselves. Here is a quick peek into how the addict faces each day alone in his or her misery. I call this The Symphony of Self-Defeat or How I Talk Trash to Myself:

I have no boundaries.

I can't stop, start, go, leave, love, piss, or get off the can.

I won't allow myself to succeed, fail, improve, or live honestly.

I have no self-worth, self-esteem, or self-nurturing.

My waking thoughts are dominated by The Grievance Committee. They are the official symposium of my intractable victimhood. He said, she said. What good is this or that? Why can't I get a break? Fuck it, fuck it, and fuck it!

It is said in recovery work that the head doesn't really hear until the heart starts to listen. Nothing changes until your gut is involved, until that recess of deep feelings, those wellsprings of hate and love are sounded, explored, and put to the test.

Having knowledgeable, loving, and consistent friends and family with the courage to join in the process is always a good thing.

20 I want my kids

Every day for one solid year, Liz Alfred told us that she wanted her kids back. She never missed a day.

Liz was a middle-aged Native woman from Alert Bay. She was tall and slim and looked like everybody's favorite aunt or librarian. I'm not sure how many kids Liz had given birth to over the years, but when I met her in 1970, she had five children who were wards of the court. They were in foster care with white families in Alert Bay. Liz was a drunk. She came to us from Skid Road in Vancouver and she was a real mess. She cleaned up and went to work with us, quickly becoming a beloved part of our growing family. She was a terribly sad person with a generous heart and a huge laugh. It is quite appropriate to say that Liz was sweet. Almost from the moment she arrived, her prayer poured forth. "I want my kids. I want my kids."

Our reaction was simple and direct. "Stay sober for one year, Liz, and we'll make sure you get your kids back."

Perhaps this seems harsh to you. We once had a researcher

from the Provincial Drug Directorate spend three weeks with us, counting noses and delving into our collective methods and subconscious. His conclusions read something like this:

"X-Kalay is the most serious and best run program in the province. Everyone involved is clean and sober and everyone's complete focus is that all resident clients remain clean and sober. In a hundred different ways, night and day, management and residents—who are indistinguishable from one another—work tirelessly at this common goal. On the walls of any of their many facilities, you will find a constantly changing signboard called CLEAN MAN DAYS. Each day one person in X-Kalay remains clean and sober is counted as a Clean Man Day. To this writing, X-Kalay proudly boasts hundreds of thousands of Clean Man Days. I can't recommend them highly enough."

In spite of this salutary report, the Chair of the Provincial Drug Directorate refused our request for much-needed funding. When the researcher who wrote the report asked if they had read his evaluation, the Chair responded, "Yes, of course, I read your paper and that's all well and good, but I don't like them." The researcher quit on the spot. This cautionary tale emphasizes once again that everything is political and everything is personal.

So Liz wanted her kids back and we demanded a year of sobriety. She was serious and so were we. At the end of that year, Liz was still sober, so we went to work. Our first call to the social workers in Alert Bay brought this conversation:

"If Mrs. Alfred leaves X-Kalay, we will consider reuniting her with her children."

"Leaves X-Kalay?"

"Yes. We're not going to have children living with drug addicts and the like."

"Well, we already have many children living here at X-Kalay, where, by the way, everyone is clean and sober."

"Be that as it may, she can have her children if she moves."

"Perhaps you don't understand that the sole reason that she is sober, and has been sober for over a year now, is that she lives at X-Kalay."

"She could find a place nearby."

"That's right. She could find a place nearby and she'd be drunk in a week."

They weren't buying it. They had their paradigm and we had ours. How were we to know that, in a decade or two, everyone would be lugging around a paradigm in his backpack? We turned for help to our favorite lawyer, Tom Berger. Thomas R. Berger was an MP, and MLA in the provincial legislature, and the leader of the provincial New Democratic Party. Berger was appointed to the Supreme Court of British Columbia in 1971, shortly after this incident occurred. He is a member of the Order of British Columbia and the Order of Canada. He is probably best known for his work as commissioner of the Mackenzie Valley Pipeline Authority and for his later work on The Nunavut Project.

A year before the Liz story, Tom had represented us in a court challenge against the City of Burnaby. There was a marvelous property in North Burnaby that we knew was perfectly suited to our residential and educational purposes. The property, a half city block square, included an enormous Tudor mansion, gardens, and a low-rise school building. Earl Allard and I flew to Halifax and negotiated a deal to buy the site, known as Seton Academy, from the owners, a religious order known as The Sisters of Charity. We then secured the same kind of generous financing from Central Mortgage and Housing that had allowed us to open our Clubhouse on West 7th Avenue. Our excitement was soon dashed by the sudden appearance of a neighborhood petition demanding that X-Kalay not be allowed to move in. The same old dynamic was at play. Native Indians, addicts, prostitutes. Lordie, lordie! How are we good citizens meant to survive? We quickly mounted our own counter-petition, easily outstripping the Not in My Neighborhood poll by about 5,000 signatures to 300. We pinned up hundreds of posters in the area showing two of our children, one blond and one Native Indian sitting in a bathtub together. Then we hit the streets. Dozens of our people knocked on doors and engaged our potential new neighbors in conversation. The result was that so many of the people who had originally signed the first petition with very little real information were now signing our counter-petition.

Nevertheless, Burnaby City Council, facing a raucous crowd, managed to pull that classic political stunt, which allows a body politic off the hook; they created a stalemate, voting neither for nor against our right to buy a piece of property like anyone else. The result was that we couldn't proceed with the purchase of Seton Academy.

Lurking in the background was a powerful politician. Ron Basford was the sitting Member of Parliament for the district and a man with considerable personal and social power. Basford had been approached by the Not in My Neighborhood forces in North Burnaby who were dead set against X-Kalay. What is truly unfortunate is that Basford made up his mind without once visiting our program or investigating what we were about or what successes we may have achieved. He didn't, as far as we were ever to learn, even look at the need for a service like X-Kalay in his riding. He simply responded to the first people who made a noise in his direction and then used his considerable influence to stop us in our tracks.

Mr. Basford, who has since passed away, was well liked and well respected by very many people. There are parks and other civic monuments named in his memory. No doubt he made his worthy contributions. Nevertheless, it is difficult for me not to be deeply disappointed by his actions in this matter.

Tom Berger refused to let the situation just die. He took the City of Burnaby to court. The gist of the case was that Seton Academy was in an area zoned single family. Berger hauled out cases and arguments going back to ancient Greece, arguing that families were not necessarily, by definition, consanguineous. A family could comprise people with common goals, values, or ideals, if not necessarily shared bloodlines. Aiding Tom at the time was a young lawyer named Don Rosenbloom, who would go on in later years to develop a deserved reputation as a great defender of civil rights.

The judge hearing our case was not only popping pills openly in court, but in one instance, noticing a particularly nervous witness in the box, he offered her a tranquillizer. A few months after finding against us and in favor of the City of Burnaby, the judge stepped out onto his well-manicured Shaughnessy lawn and put a bullet in his head. We all felt it was a shame the good judge hadn't come to us with his prescription medication addiction and overwhelming depression; we might have helped him.

Soon thereafter, the Seton mansion and school building were torn down and a massive high-rise was built for seniors. There is no doubt that this was and is a good social use for this property, but the question remains, in what way was this use any closer to single family zoning than the X-Kalay project?

The Seton Academy-City of Burnaby case was our first opportunity to work with Tom Berger. Getting Liz Alfred's children back to her became our second. I phoned Tom and gave him a quick briefing of the Liz Alfred situation. I'll never forget his very precise instructions. "David, you call that social worker and ask her to remind you about the day and time for the court hearing in Liz's case. When she tells you, just say that you wanted to check so you could advise your counsel. The next thing that will happen is she will ask you who your counsel is. When you tell her it's Tom Berger, she may drop the phone."

And like a script, almost word for word, that is exactly what happened. When I told her that our counsel was Tom, I thought I heard her gasp.

A few days later, Tom, Liz, and I boarded a Beaver floatplane and took the short and spectacular flight to Alert Bay, swooping down to a landing pontoons pointing up in exact imitation of a Canada goose.

The court proceeding couldn't have lasted more than five minutes.

The flight back included five of Liz Alfred's children, Stanley, Janet, Lance, Sandra, and Dot.

For a while, Lance, Sandra, and Janet stayed in our house with my wife and son when they weren't with Liz, engaged in X-Kalay activities or just basking in each other's company. Stanley was a gifted artist and a wonderful young man, who was tragically struck down and killed crossing a street many years later. Lance, Sandra, and Dot all did fine over the years. Sandra and I remained friends over the intervening forty years and we still email, talk on the phone, and have the occasional coffee.

Early in this century, following the most exhaustive and costly criminal investigation in living memory, a pig farmer named Robert Picton was charged with multiple counts of murder. It is alleged that he brought street prostitutes from Vancouver's infamous Skid Road to his farm, shared their favors with any number of regular guests, and then killed the prostitutes. Although none of them have ever been charged, several small-time local politicos were widely rumored to be fixtures on the party list. The orgies are said to have been fuelled by steady supplies of booze and drugs. It is further alleged that Picton disposed of the women's bodies by adding what little was left of them to the compacted pig remains that he sold to a local reduction plant.

Janet Henry, Liz Alfred's daughter, disappeared just before this story came to light. She has never been located, her body has never been found. No DNA of hers has been verified at the crime scene site. Nevertheless, it is now believed, widely enough to be taken as a fact, that Janet was one of Robert Picton's victims. A memorial service for her has been held recently in Vancouver.

I was reminded with unfortunate regularity that X-Kalay

was not a game or an amusing diversion. It was a matter of life and death. Here is another tragic example:

In the spring of 1969, shortly after we had acquired our beautiful red brick mansion on West 16th Avenue, I was brought suddenly awake by the phone ringing. It was five in the morning. The R.C.M.P. had a body in the local funeral hall in Hope, B.C. They believed that this was a fellow I knew named Robin. Could I drive out and confirm this identification?

I picked up Robin's wife, Louise, at the X-Kalay house on West 7th Avenue. Robin and Louise and their infant son were natives from the Fraser Valley, not far from Vancouver. They were not alcoholics or users. They were simply reserve Indians who were "lost" in the city. We were happy to have them in the program. Robin's younger brother, Jack, had also moved in and he hopped in my car that morning to join Louise and me on the ninety-minute drive to Hope. I learned from Louise that Robin, who was only twenty-four, had decided the day before to visit his father. He drove his little Vespa scooter. We learned later that the scooter's taillight had burned out. Coming round a turn in the road, a car came up behind Robin, and, not seeing him at all, knocked Robin off the bike and onto the gravel at the side of the road.

The funeral parlor was being used by the R.C.M.P. as a temporary morgue. When we pulled up alongside this small wood-frame building, I told Louise and Jack to stay in the car. I didn't want either of them seeing a dead body unless it was absolutely necessary. What silliness. They were reserve Indians who had probably seen many more dead than I. But my internal den mother was never too far from the surface.

Maybe this wasn't Robin. How could it be? I had just talked with him the day before. What if this? What if that? *The Constant Gardner* in charge of other people's lives.

There was a body lying on a table. It didn't look like Robin to me. It didn't look like much of anybody at first. His face had been scraped almost beyond recognition. Slowly, I realized that this form was Robin. I put my hand on his chest. It felt like a rock. My reaction may have seemed strange, but it was perfectly in keeping with my pattern for many years. My first response to almost any kind of stress or unhappiness was always anger. It wasn't until I was in my forties that I learned how to go to some other more legitimate or appropriate emotion under pressure.

I started pounding my closed fist on Robin's chest. "What are you doing? What the hell is the matter with you? How could you be so fucking stupid?"

The police have seen it all; they were absolutely unfazed.

When asked about aging, Paul Newman liked to quote Bette Davis who once said, "Old age ain't for sissies." She was right, and she might have added that the people business and rehabilitation work with addicts and alcoholics ain't for sissies either.

You can shed the occasional tear, but laughter is what will allow you try again another day.

Today, Manitoba's Behavioural Health Foundation is home to many complete families—mom, dad, and the kids all move in and all work at living the clean and sober lifestyle. In one short recent visit, I met half a dozen young men and women who were resident clients at the Foundation on their own. Each of them was waiting to be reunited with his or her children. Forty years after Liz Alfred finally got her kids back, these haunting dysfunctions continue to plague our communities at industrial strength. Forty years later, the same question remains: Do we, who like to pride ourselves as captains of an enlightened democratic society, have the courage to face these challenges and work at real solutions?

Liz Alfred moved on into old age clean and sober, grateful for her blessings and at relative peace with life. Let's give more people the chance to experience that kind of fulfillment.

21 riverrun, past Eve and Adam's

"...riverrun, past Eve and Adam's, from
swerve of shore to bend of bay,..."

JAMES JOYCE, *Finnegans Wake*

One afternoon in 1975, I noticed a potential new resident walking tentatively through the front door. My first thought was, "Oh, brother, there's another two years of work." My next thought was, "Isn't that a lovely way to think?" I realized then and there that I had a serious problem. Instead of welcoming some lost soul into the land of the living, I was seeing a burden and a chore. This is not good. What is happening to me?

Some years earlier I had acquired a great teacher. His name was Dave Pellin. Like me, he was a Winnipeg Jew with no particular formal training in psychology or social work. Nevertheless, operating out of a small storefront on West 4th Avenue, Dave became the guru and savior for thousands of disaffected and drug-addled kids during the hippie era. He ran this small operation he called, The Activator Unit. Inside, there were couches and chairs and an always-available coffee pot. An aura of peacefulness was evident the moment you walked in the door. Dave was basically a teacher and he presented a grand irony in his teaching style. On the one hand, what he preached through his "activator philosophy" was reasonableness and calm. "Be cool. Stay coolie, cool, boy." On the other hand, he taught these goals of tranquility with all the passion and fervor of a tent revivalist. I attended many of his lectures about human behavior and personality and they were always a revelation. He had found fresh ways of looking at who we are and what we do, and these original models of his were readily understandable.

One day he astonished me with a prediction, a bit of prescience that came true sure enough about five years down the road. "You know, David, we are all thankful for what you are doing with X-Kalay. But you must know that you won't be able to do it much longer."

"Excuse me?"

"Your interests are just too broad. Don't get me wrong. What you're doing is great. But the focus—Indian ex-convicts, drug addicts—is just not going to hold your attention for the next thirty years or so. You love the arts, singing and music and theatre, painting, athletics. Government and politics fascinate you. Even engineering and science. You're just one of those guys who is captivated by almost everything in life. That's a blessing. And a real curse."

Dave Pellin was right. What had been a joy for many years was now becoming an albatross. To the same degree as I had loved my work, I was now beginning to hate it. Yes, hate it. The fervor and excitement that had carried me through the past eight and a half years had gone. I would show up at the office during the day and go through the motions. Dedicated people like Archie would talk to me about some urgent concern, and they could tell that my answers and decisions were barely responsive. I could see the disappointment and the confusion in their eyes. Instead of pulling myself up and embracing the moment, I would only resent their need for attention even more. I was a classic case of burnout. After years of living in a flame, burning with an uncommon intensity and attending to every minor detail of the work round the clock, now I was walking through the day and serving nobody at the level that was necessary. I urgently needed to move on. It took me one and a half years from that moment to extricate myself from work I could no longer do.

We had begun with nothing. In our first four years, we had leapfrogged from three guys and $130 on the table to an organization with over 200 people in residences in Vancouver, Winnipeg, and Salt Spring Island. We owned and operated half a dozen businesses that employed fifty men and women at any given time. Most importantly, we were saving lives. Desperately lonely, self-destructive people were moving through our program and coming back to life. Their vital signs were returning in every way and they were becoming full-fledged members of their communities.

We had no government funding for the first five years of operation and that, as it turned out, was a blessing. The bigger we became, the more money we needed and the more money we needed, the more often we would have to go to government with hat in hand. Down that sorry road came the intricacies and detritus of politics and demands from mandarins who hadn't the first notion of how programs like this worked.

I had some real areas of strength and some real blind spots. Tact and diplomacy were never my long suits and the results showed in our usually fractious relationship with governments. Perhaps, more importantly, I hadn't done a very good job at creating a succession in British Columbia, and, by the time I was ready to retire, there was really no one in place to take over. Between that sorry situation and the constant struggle for money and support, the Board and I were faced with the inevitable.

In the summer of 1976, we closed down all Vancouver and Salt Spring Island operations, sold off the society's assets and donated any remains to various charities.

However, the Winnipeg chapter of X-Kalay continued to grow in every way. Today, more than forty years later, that organization, the Behavioural Health Foundation, is a fixture on the local scene and a steady resource for hundreds of people annually. The program has shifted slightly in tone and style, but the basics still hold. The organization is much more thoroughly integrated into the Manitoba communities that it serves and it does great work, widely acknowledged by courts and schools and hospitals, among others. The Foundation has worked hard to receive worldwide accreditation from a number of international bodies and the funding sources are solid. Moreover, the present Foundation does an infinitely better job than we *ever* did at getting recovering addicts and alcoholics into high school and university programs and pointing them up the highway to independent jobs and homes.

On a personal level, I will confess that I am enormously proud of the work that we all did. One of my rabbi friends has told me, "You know, David, it is written that if you save one soul, you save the world."

A few years ago, my son said, "Hey, Dad, I heard you lose it on the air the other day."

I was about to close an afternoon of my talk radio show. We were discussing the Vancouver urban nightmare known as the Downtown East Side, a zone peopled by drug addicts, dealers, mentally challenged, and the homeless. We had time for just one more call. "Let's go to Vancouver. Hello Hamish."

Hamish came on the air via his cell phone and voiced his agreement with me about the Downtown East Side and the terrible waste of millions of dollars in social programs that seemed to be accomplishing nothing but more misery. After a few moments, I realized that I knew this voice. "Oh, is this the Hamish that I know?"

"Yes, of course, David."

"Oh, I'm sorry that I didn't recognize you at once, Hamish, but tell the listeners why we know each other."

"Sure. When I met you I was a nineteen-year-old heroin addict."

"And now, thirty years later?"

"I have my Masters in Science and I have a great life."

"That's fantastic, Hamish."

"David, it's real simple. If I hadn't met you when I did, I would be dead now."

That's the place where I got choked up enough for my son to say a few days later, "Hey, Dad, I heard you lose it."

So, the fact that we did any of this in the first place and the fact that it continues in the Winnipeg facility and in other programs that have been influenced by our model, those facts continue to amaze me.

But there is more.

In the years since X-Kalay, I have worked as a broadcaster, an actor, and a writer. I have traveled extensively and seen much of the world. I have met hundreds and hundreds of wonderful and fascinating people. I've interviewed on radio and television prime ministers, premiers, sports stars, musicians, singers, actors, movie stars, doctors, scientists, and undersea explorers. It's been exciting and a blessing. But the truth is nothing can compare to the sheer intensity, fun, and reward of those first ten years of my working life. I feel exactly like what some of my friends have described as the residue of serving in World War II. Yes, it was miserable and barbaric. Yes, the home gardens of peace and delight with their families are better in every way. Yet nothing can replace that sense of camaraderie and mission. And accomplishment.

In this regard, I feel I have been two and three times blessed.

F. Scott Fitzgerald famously said, "There are no second acts in American life." That may have been true for Jay Gatsby, but Fitzgerald never met the brave souls who have tackled rehab and claimed second lives.

What lives within me to this day is the palpable sense of the people with whom I worked—Shirley, James, Richard, Carol, Maureen, Charlie, Bob, Archie, Brett, Paul , Earl, Liz, and hundreds of other extraordinary men and women. Not everyone made it. Some fell by the wayside; some crashed spectacularly. It took me a long time not to take every loss as a personal failure. All you can do is your best. The rest is up to the gods. Some changed their lives in tiny ways, ameliorating bits and pieces of behavior and bad habits that had been getting them into the soup for too many years. Some were superstars. They made turnarounds that seemed at first and even second glance impossible.

Regardless of where they went in their journeys, each of these living breathing souls was funny and dynamic and unforgettable. Surviving on their instincts, many were brilliant natural psychologists and therapists. I used to say that many of our resident clients could walk into a hotel ballroom with two hundred people and within minutes single out the genuine people you could safely trust and point the finger at the fakers and phonies. The X-Kalay radar was extraordinary. Only recently over dinner, a friend asked who trained these people to run the Games and Stews and psychodramas. I said that I did, but had to quickly add that the training was by osmosis. You played, you learned. You participated and then you led. And we were in constant teaching mode. Games were studied and analyzed. Techniques that were spontaneous were deconstructed and reconstructed.

The X-Kalay resident clients, the people I've described in these pages, were my heroes. Over and over again, they demonstrated remarkable courage. Think about the disruption you experience if you decide to remodel your kitchen or second bathroom. The whole family is on edge; your toys have been moved. Where's that big white bath towel? The dissonance threatens to bring down the house. Now put yourself for just a moment in the old beat up shoes of a heroin addict. *Everything* must change. Giving up the drug is only the first tiny step. Now you have to give up your friends, this wonderful circle of losers who have been aiding and abetting your slow death every day. You've shared jokes and needles and getaways and jail cells with these comrades in hell. Now, you have to reach out to the alien straight world and make new friends. You have to change your most personal and intimate habits of hygiene and nutrition. You have to rediscover the joys of playing at sports or listening to or making music. The journey from user to health and citizenship is frightening and perilous.

Every day that I witnessed these journeys being lived out in full color I knew I was seeing small miracles.

. . .

In August 2009, I received completely out of the blue an email that said, "Hi David. You may not remember me, but in 1976 I served you breakfast at X-Kalay, Manitoba. My name is Jean Doucha and now I am the Executive Director of the Behavioural Health Foundation, which is X-Kalay renamed. We often speak about you here. You are sort of a legend as the founder of the Foundation, but nobody here has ever met you and I never thought I would connect with you, However, recently I read an article you wrote about addictions for the National Post. I Googled you and there you were. Do you ever come to Winnipeg? I would love to see you, and it would be great to hear about the history of X-Kalay from the one person who really knows it first-hand."

I phoned Jean Doucha almost immediately. I learned that she had come to X-Kalay from Minnesota, a bit of a drug user, but mostly a drinker. She told me that her husband had been a heroin addict and that they have been clean and sober over thirty-four years. They have two children and several grandchildren. Jean's daughter works with her at the Foundation and her son, Del, is a marvelously talented composer, singer, recording artist, and performer.

The next thing I knew I was on a plane for Winnipeg to visit the program I had begun but not seen in thirty years.

So there I am, in the late summer of 2009, in St. Norbert, an old French settlement on the outskirts of Winnipeg, just a skip up Pembina Highway from the University of Manitoba. Almost a century ago this site was an orphanage, then for many years it was an Oblate seminary. In 1971, the X-Kalay Foundation Manitoba Inc. moved into the great four-story stone structure that still dominates the landscape. These are the spacious grounds of what was once called X-Kalay—The Unknown Path—now the Behavioural Health Foundation. Where did the hockey rink come from? Oh, it's a gift of the local community. We played touch football every autumn— sun, rain, or early snow. The rink should have been obvious. Plus there is the adult education building and the new house for the dozen young girls and the three Aboriginal centers, not to mention the trio of sweat lodges, each being prepared for the afternoon rituals. It's astonishing. This site is still standing forty-three years later. Not only has it survived, but it has flourished and grown. How is this possible? A little program that everyone and his cat said would never, ever work. The sunburnt grass underfoot, the rustling aspens, and the ever-present Red River snaking round the hundred-acre property bring back a flood of memories.

I can't believe I am here. This is the property that I signed off on in 1971 when the Oblate Fathers gave it to us for a dollar a year. "You are doing God's work." Five years later, I walked away from this mission and, in the intervening years, Jean and the folks who ran the program before her, bought the site outright for about half a million dollars. Today, you'd have to team up with a very good real estate agent to find a 650 square foot condo in Vancouver for that price.

As we cross the yard, a boy does a sort of double take, a looking-back-to-see. It's not that we know or recognize each other. Only that he has some need to connect. Maybe I recognize that need because I feel exactly the same way at this moment. I stop and turn. I stick out my hand.

"Hi. I'm David."

"I'm James." He is eighteen years old. When I inquire, he tells me proudly that he's been in the center's residential program for two months.

"And what do you think?" I ask him.

"Oh, I love it!" His broad, keen smile lights up the gray morning.

"Really? You love it! Why, James?"

"I feel safe here."

There are whispers of anger and despair not far from the surface. The reflex to quit at any moment hovers nearby. But his smile holds back at least for the moment the ever-present threat of eruption. To me, he is beautiful. His goodness and his desire to triumph over the old familiar evils are right there, up front.

We shake hands and part, he heading on toward the big main house and me turning back to my guide, Jean Doucha, who has been waiting patiently. I try to speak, but find myself choking back tears instead. Over forty years ago I dropped a pebble in a pond, and now the ripples of that almost accidental act have brought this young man, James, face to face with the possibility of his very best self, his truest destiny. He was not yet born when I set out on this unknown path that would lead to the X-Kalay Foundation. At the time I was only a few years older than he is now. I fell into a purpose that I didn't even know existed.

I am staggered by this brief encounter.

Jean needs no explanation for my reaction. She's been here for ages and she knows the territory. She began as a client and now she is the wizard at the top of the heap. This is as it should be. Jean and all the others have taken this notion and built on it and nurtured it and today there are 136 people on any given day who are living here clean and sober. They boast over one million clean living days and counting. Want to get in, straighten up, and fly right? There is a six-month waiting list. People are graduating from the program, getting their high school completions and University degrees, and moving into transition houses up the street or on to their own independent lives. They stay in touch. Occasionally, if they are faltering, they come back. Sometimes they come back to be counselors or program managers.

According to its website (www.bhf.ca), the Foundation offers "long-term residential programming for men, women, teens and families experiencing a variety of addiction problems and co-occurring mental health concerns." Only fifty minutes away by car in the town of Selkirk, Manitoba, the Young Boys Program with sixteen youths and the program for adult alcoholic women is thriving on a 300-acre lot in a forest.

Jean herself is the calm center in a mighty social storm that is wracking our communities. It's a weather front called addictions. In response, some people are providing free needles, crack pipe kits, and places to shoot up—not Jean. She's leading people to the clean waters of good health and self-respect and self-reliance. Day in and day out, Jean and her staff are churning out clean and sober citizens. They work from a place of profound compassion, tempered by street-smart realism. The dopers and drinkers with whom they work want some powder or bottle or smoke to simplify their daily challenges. These are their silver bullet solutions to life's challenges. Some community leaders look for an equally ready answer to a complex problem. But those of us who have worked or continue to work in abstinence-based prevention and recovery programs know that there are no quick fixes, no simple magical potions. We believe in the work and honesty and consistency that declare loud and clear, "We love you. We're just not too crazy about what you're doing at the moment. We know you can do better; you *are* better. You can get healthy and strong. We will work with you. Please give yourself a chance."

Jean asked me to give a speech to a large invited audience of residents, staff, the Board of Directors, and invited guests. I delivered that speech, The History of X-Kalay, on the evening of Friday, August 28, 2009 in the big main room on the ground floor of the main facility in St. Norbert. I blathered on for an hour and forty minutes. I was funny and I was in tears. The audience laughed and they were in tears. When I was finished, over a hundred people, residents and staff, formed a line to come up and shake my hand. Nobody shook my hand. There were only more tears and a lot of hugging.

I sent a video copy of the speech to my old friend and X-Kalay colleague, Luis Molina, who at that time was living and working in Geneva, Switzerland. Luis had such an enormous influence of the Foundation's beginnings and it was Luis who discovered the St. Norbert facility and closed the deal to acquire it. He watched the video and emailed back, "You probably saved a few lives that night."

Jean next invited me to return for several days in November and again the following January to conduct a few workshops for both resident clients and staff. After thirty years, I have been invited back to the future. If you want to make God laugh, tell him your plans.

· · ·

Today, the Torah of public policy is the illusive Four Pillars. This is a notion visited upon the world by a former mayor of Vancouver, Philip Owen, who served from 1993 to 2002. Mr. Owen is a bright and decent and charming fellow. He was, measured against any of the customary standards, a pretty good mayor. One day, late in his last term, Mayor Owen asked me to meet him for breakfast. He had a few questions about drug addictions. We spent the better part of two hours together in the coffee shop of the hotel across the street from city hall. I poured out much of what you have been reading in this book, the two-hour version, and Mayor Philip Owen, armed with a pen and a tablet of lined paper, took notes. He agreed enthusiastically with my understanding of the mechanics of addictions and my recommendations for sound public policy with regards to treatment. He had a cousin or a nephew whose behavior fit to an alarming degree all my descriptions of the typical addict modus operandi.

Shortly after that meeting, Mayor Owen produced a document which a) made him famous and much admired, b) was embraced by practically everyone in official circles as the way to go, and c) was in complete opposition to everything we had agreed upon over our bacon and eggs. Politicians can be like that.

The so-called Four Pillars are harm reduction, enforcement, prevention, and treatment. The unfortunate truth is that, from the first day this new mythology surfaced, we have had only one pillar and three matchsticks. Most of the time, money and energy have been invested in what is popularly called harm reduction—free needles, free crack pipes, free heroin, free methadone, and 'safe' places to shoot or smoke up. As of this writing, we are giving 320 heroin addicts free heroin on a three year trial. (What will we learn from that? Dope fiends shoot dope?) And every hour, in the name of some convoluted misunderstanding of the word compassion, we are giving free booze to some chronic alcoholics. Just recently, the local health authority announced that, having proudly given out more than 93,000 free crack pipe kits, they would like to have some more tax money to continue this visionary work.

There are many people, myself included, who believe that

"harm production" is but the opening volley in a long-term strategy whose ultimate goal is the legalization of practically everything. These days medical marijuana is all the rage. I know of one fifty-year-old entrepreneur whose main income for years has been small residential construction projects. This good fellow is now feverishly preparing to run a chain of medical marijuana storefront shops. He anxiously awaits government approvals, bank loans, and the Porsche he has ordered when all his other pipe dreams come true.

Very little money has been spent on prevention programs and, shockingly, the proponents of "harm seduction" actively lobby *against* treatment. They argue that treatment doesn't work. I don't know how they explain away the millions of people who have become clean and sober after attending Alcoholics Anonymous and Narcotics Anonymous meetings. How do these naysayers rationalize Cocaine Anonymous, Overeaters Anonymous, Emotions Anonymous, and Gamblers Anonymous and the millions of people who willingly attend and benefit from those meetings? I don't know how they explain the hundreds of thousands who have left their drug of choice behind after spending weeks or months in treatment centers. How quick these clever proselytizers are to utterly dismiss people who don't fit conveniently into little orthodoxies.

Harm reduction is now woven and imbedded clearly into government plans and strategies across the land. Universities teach harm reduction philosophies and methodologies and applaud themselves for being progressive and in the know.

If I ever learn that, because of these efforts, one single identifiable human being moves from being a using addict or alcoholic to treatment or recovery, then I too will rise from my seat and cheer, "Bravo!" Alas, I have yet to hear of this happening in the real known world.

Harm reduction is palliative. It masks by excuses and apologies. It strives to ease symptoms without ever approaching the affliction.

There is not a single impulse in my instinctive soul that would hand a drunk a clean shot glass and think that I was helping. It would never occur to me for a second to do such a thing. Nor would I consider giving a dope fiend a needle or a fixing kit or a comfortable place to continue being an addict. If you knew that your daughter was self-mutilating, would you sharpen and disinfect her razors?

Let's look at the mechanics of addiction.

What does an addict want? An addict wants MORE. More what? Not more tickets to the hockey game or the opera, not more bridal showers, bicycle trips, insurance policies, medical texts, cultural exchanges, remodeled basements, flight instructions, or nieces and nephews. Addicts want more drugs. Plain and simple. Addicts want more drugs. Drunks drink. Dope fiends shoot dope. Addicts want drugs. Unwilling and unable to cope with the complexities of daily life, the alcoholic bottles all his concerns into a single container; the heroin addict encapsulates all his flagging energies into a small gram of inert white powder.

So we can give these sorry enslaved souls drugs and substitute drugs and replacement drugs and 'safe' places to take their drugs. We can give them clean needles and clean crack pipe kits and condoms. And we may indeed save a life or two from overdose or disease and that certainly is better

than doing nothing. But we have no right to be surprised—
knowing what we do about addicts, that all they want is
MORE—when we discover that they are still shooting up
in the back alley an hour or two after we have given them
our help. And this, as any cop on the beat will tell you, is
exactly what the addict is doing.

Treatment, when it is properly and seriously framed and
delivered, works. I choose to believe that we must work from
a foundation of hope. We start with the central expectation
that everyone is salvageable. All addicts, until proven otherwise, are capable of living without their self-inflicted poison
of choice. All children have the right and the power to never
venture down the ugly roads of addictions. All children have
the right to be healthy of mind, body, and spirit. This is not
something I read in a magazine or culled from one of the
Great Books or saw in a moving picture show. I lived it. I ate
it, slept it, and breathed it twenty-nine hours a day, twelve
days a week for many years. I have witnessed the suffering
move on and I continue these days to work in a much smaller
way to support abstinence based prevention and recovery.

On September 30, 2012, several of us organized the first
ever Recovery Day Rally and March held in Canada. The
event took place in downtown Vancouver. Vancouver Mayor
Gregor Robertson signed a proclamation officially recognizing
September 30th as Recovery Day. Over 1,500 people participated. Twenty recovery agencies manned tables and booths.
People sang and danced and gave short speeches expressing
their gratitude for their clean and sober lives. After two and a
half hours, we recorded in attendance 1,753 years of sobriety!

Other cities, hearing what we were doing, joined in the

celebration. Watch for this to soon be an annual national event in Canada.

I've reached a point in my life when I think an addict manifesto or an addict bill of rights is called for. And this is what it would say:

> For addicts and alcoholics, treatment should be a right, a part of the universal health care statutes, not a second-cousin option at the bottom of a long list of horrors like "safe" injection sites, free crack pipe kits, free booze for chronic drunks, and free narcotics for heroin addicts.

I don't want to give broken-hearted people the very things that limit them. Let's set our sights higher. Let us aim always for hope and dignity.

As doctors have the Hippocratic Oath, in which they promise, among other things to do no harm, addiction workers should swear on a stack of whatever they choose to believe in that their first communication with a client will always be, "Come on, buddy, let's get you out of this mess."

The X-Kalay Foundation Society was one of many examples of the therapeutic community model that you can still find worldwide. Portage, begun in Eastern Canada in 1970, is one such. In British Columbia alone, there are Pacifica, Turning Point, The Last Door, Together We Can, Innervisions, Baldy Hughes, Westminster House, Welcome Home, The Orchard, and Edgewood, among many others. Each of these programs—many non-profit, some for-profit—works in its own unique way. Many take in clients who require medications for co-occurring mental problems. Some clients are on a methadone schedule. But all of these institutions aim for abstinence and their track records are impressive and they are all getting better at tracking and documenting their successes. Furthermore, there are many dozens of similar programs scattered across the country, coast to coast. In America, Daytop and Phoenix House are still going strong. Just north of Venice, Italy is the community of San Patrignano, which is a much studied and inspiring demonstration of the power of hard work and honesty in action. X-Kalay was the first in Canada. Now, under its new name, The Behavioural Health Foundation, it continues to be one of the leaders.

Many of these programs are based on or use extensively the Twelve Steps of Alcoholics Anonymous. Today, twelve-step programs modeled after and sanctioned by A.A. include Narcotics Anonymous, Emotions Anonymous, Gamblers Anonymous, and Overeaters Anonymous, among others. No presidents, no hierarchies, no money; just twelve steps and twelve traditions and like-minded people meeting for ninety minutes in church basements and community halls around the world. Every day of the week, several times a day, in communities far and wide, someone is celebrating one year or eight years or twenty-four years of sobriety. Millions and millions of human beings have jettisoned their poisons of choice and reclaimed their dignity thanks to these programs.

More power, blessings, and thanks to all those good and frightened souls who have stepped courageously past their fears and into the light of sobriety and citizenship. More power, blessings, and thanks to those who continue the work.

In 1967, David Berner created the X-Kalay Foundation, Canada's first residential treatment centre for addicts, alcoholics, and others. The program continues today in Manitoba as the Behavioural Health Foundation. David is also a broadcaster, actor, and writer. He has hosted radio and television public affairs programs in Vancouver, Edmonton, and Ottawa. David has acted in over fifty films and played major roles on stages across Canada from Vancouver, B.C. to St. John's, Newfoundland, and as far afield as Venice, Italy. He has been a *Vancouver Province* newspaper columnist and written for many magazines and online journals. Today, David runs therapy groups with addicts and alcoholics at the Orchard Recovery Centre on Bowen Island, B.C., consults with other recovery and prevention programs, and is the Executive Director of the Drug Prevention Network of Canada. He lives in Vancouver.

www.davidberner.com

CPSIA information can be obtained at www.ICGtesting.com
Printed in the USA
LVOW120309060613

337152LV00002B/18/P